Reptiles, Amphibians, and Invertebrates

An Identification and Care Guide

Patricia P. Bartlett, Billy Griswold, DVM, and R.D. Bartlett

Dedication

To Karin, for her endless encouragement, support, and understanding. To the educators who have guided my development as a person and as a professional, and to those who, regardless of age, look upon reptiles and amphibians with the fascination and enthusiasm of a child.   B.G.

Cover Photos

All cover photos were taken by R. D. Bartlett and Patricia Bartlett.

Photo Credits

Billy Griswold: pages 14, 22, 26, 27, 28, 29, 31, 32, 34, 35, 40, 41, 42, 43, 44, 45, 46, 47, 51, 52, 56, 63, 64, 66, 72, 73, 85, 89, 91, 93, 96, 99, 104, 114, 117, 127, 152, 169, 173, 181, 199, 201, 217, 223, 225, 226, 232, 233, 251

All other photos were taken by R. D. Bartlett and Patricia Bartlett.

Acknowledgments

Chris Bednarski, Jan Benn, Karin Burns, Scott Cushnir, Terry Dunham, Todd Gearhart, Jim Harding, Joe Hiduke, Chuck Hurt, Rob MacInnes, Lisa Manfredi, Mike Manfredi, Paul Moler, Mike Stuhlman, Courtney Watkins, and Kenny Wray are due our thanks for allowing us to photograph their reptiles, amphibians, or invertebrates, and for providing photographs, or for offering thoughts on the species to be covered. Frank Indiviglio's input greatly enhanced the value of this work.

About the Authors

Patricia Bartlett is the author of 25 books on Florida history and natural history. She writes regularly for national magazines on pet shop management and reptile and amphibian husbandry.

R. D. Bartlett, a herpetologist, has authored numerous articles and books on reptile and amphibian field identification and husbandry. He travels and lectures extensively and guides tours to the Amazon. In 1978, he began the Reptile Breeding and Research Institute, a private facility. Since RBRI's inception, more than 150 species have been bred, some for the first time in the United States under captive conditions.

Billy Griswold is a veterinarian practicing small animal and herpetological medicine in Tempe, Arizona. He is an active member of the Association of Reptilian and Amphibian Veterinarians. His photographs and writings have appeared in several books and periodicals.

All inquiries should be addressed to:
Barron's Educational Series, Inc.
250 Wireless Boulevard
Hauppauge, NY 11788
http://www.barronseduc.com

International Standard Book Number: 0-7641-1650-9

Library of Congress Catalog Card Number: 00-067614

Library of Congress Cataloging-in-Publication Data
Bartlett, Patricia Pope, 1949–
    Reptiles, amphibians, and invertebrates : an identification and care guide / Patricia P. Bartlett, R.D. Bartlett, and Billy Griswold.
        p. cm.
    Includes bibliographical references (p.).
    ISBN 0-7641-1650-9
    1. Reptiles as pets. 2. Amphibians as pets.
3. Invertebrates as pets. I. Bartlett, Richard D., 1938–
II. Griswold, Billy. III. Title.

SF459.R4 B37 2001
639.3'9—dc21   00-067614

Printed in Hong Kong
9 8 7 6 5 4 3 2 1

Contents

Introduction

Immense strides have been made recently in the husbandry of reptiles, amphibians, and invertebrates, but there are times when something as simple as an accurate identification can be problematic. There are no rules regarding the naming of obscure terrarium animals, and indeed, some are so poorly known that they have never been given common names. Therefore, the common names under which the herps and insects are sold vary by supplier, sometimes accidentally, sometimes intentionally. Other factors in the common names game relate to the area of the world from which a given species originates in the pet trade, the color phase of the specimen, or even the whim of the importer supplier. Perhaps most confusing, if a given species does not sell well under one name, it will subsequently be offered by one or more different names, and the names will continue to change until one triggers the desired sales effect. Of course, if a dealer or hobbyist does not have an accurate identification, the regimen of husbandry provided can be incorrect.

With that in mind, we have provided in these pages a pictorial identification and the basic husbandry of more than 300 species and subspecies of reptiles, amphibians, and invertebrates currently available in the pet markets of the world. There is an ever-burgeoning number of excellent care books and it is to these that we refer you for detailed information on care, diet, caging, and breeding for the species contained in this book. Most of these books are readily available from your wholesaler or pet shop.

Caging

The proper caging of reptiles, amphibians, and invertebrates can be confusing both to dealers and hobbyists.
- The vast majority of these creatures are persistently territorial.
- Males, especially during the breeding season, are very territorial.
- Because they are disoriented by capture, as well as by the addition and removal of cagemates, large numbers of male and female reptiles and amphibians are housed together by importers, often without showing signs of overt physical aggression.
- Despite the lack of physical aggression in such circumstances, communal caging can be stressful and quickly debilitating to reptiles and amphibians. This is particularly true of adult specimens, and for chameleons, anoles, basilisks, water dragons, and some other agamids.

- Aggression and dominance are often more quickly established in cages containing only two or three specimens than in cages containing a dozen or more. This *does not mean* that the situation is more serious in the sparsely populated cage—only that it is more overtly visible. Similarly, movement to a larger cage may result in aggression among formerly peaceable (but stressed) animals. Such animals may establish territories when given enough space.
- Many species establish territories and dominance through body color, pattern intensity, and body language. These cues are as stressful and debilitating to a subordinate specimen as physical aggression.
- In emergency situations, cages with many hiding areas and visual barriers may be able to temporarily house a greater number of specimens than normal.
- Stressed specimens can show either diminished or enhanced colors, often remain along the sides or in the corners of their cages, may attempt to shy away from approaching cagemates, may (if of an eye-lidded species) keep their eyes closed for extended durations, and are often very nervous. Stress can be reduced by the addition of hiding places and visual barriers.

Solution: Do not overbuy. Have terraria available in suitable numbers and properly set up for those species purchased. Purchase only those specimens and species. Do not house males together. Stress can be caused by any number of factors. Such factors include, but are not limited to, improper caging, crowding, cage humidity that is either too high or too low, an untenable load of endoparasites, or improper diet. Stress is quite probably the single greatest potentially debilitating problem to be faced by any keeper of reptiles or amphibians. Stress can prevent proper feeding by subordinate specimens, may contribute to the development of respiratory and other ailments, may allow a potentially lethal proliferation of endoparasites, or may cause other health risks.

Suggestions for Pet Stores and Hobbyists

Do not purchase reptiles, amphibians, or invertebrates on impulse. Learn the natural history of the species in which you are interested before purchase. Set up the caging before purchase. Do not be lulled into complacency by unnatural caging setups at wholesalers. Remember that an 8-inch-long baby green basilisk can attain more than 30 inches in length when adult, and a 10-inch-long baby great green iguana may exceed 6 feet in length when fully grown. Can you provide adequate caging for these? The time to determine this is before purchase.

Provide vertically oriented caging for arboreal species and horizontally oriented caging for terrestrial forms. Semiaquatic species should be provided with easily cleaned swimming facilities. Despite the fact that they are often more spectacularly colored than the females, trying to house more than a single male of a given species in a single cage is not suggested; with some species it is an absolute impossibility! Reproductively active males of most species are especially quarrel-some. Even with species such as anoles—lizards that are routinely housed in large numbers in small quarters—communally housing males in numbers can be stressful and should be avoided. In some cases (such as with male veiled chameleons), even if housed in separate cages it may be necessary to prevent them from seeing each other.

Although it may be possible to keep juvenile specimens of some species com-munally, as adulthood is attained it may become necessary to separate the animals. Territoriality and dominance will be established more quickly by your specimens when they are provided with a suitable cage. Research, purchase wisely, and be prepared to handle any problems immediately.

Part I
Reptiles

Snakes

For years, the synonym for herpetoculture among hobbyists might as well have been "snakekeeper." Snakes are the most popular of all reptiles and amphibians, and we know more about their husbandry and breeding than any other group. In this book, just two families are included, the Boidae, the pythons and boas, and Colubridae, the huge family of snakes that includes rat snakes, kingsnakes, water snakes, garter snakes, the racers, and indigo snakes. Members of these families inhabit aquatic, arboreal, terrestrial, and subterrestrial niches in boreal to temperate to tropical regions. Although all the snakes in this book are nonvenomous, there are members within the Colubridae that possess enlarged teeth in the rear of the upper jaw. A few of these (notably the boomslangs, African twig snakes, and the Asian keelbacks) are capable of delivering bites fatal to human beings. Many snakes of both families are powerful constrictors.

Snakes are remarkably adaptive as a group, and a snake or two can be found in almost any microhabitat. The sand boas are adapted to xeric conditions; keeled green snakes to the humid southeastern states, boas to the neotropics, and the West African burrowing python to moist, forested situations. Human trash, like discarded roofing tins or mattresses, provide quality housing sites for rat snakes and garter snakes (at least from their viewpoint).

Hobbyists seem willing to "try" almost any kind of nonvenomous snake as a pet, but there are a few considerations that must be thought through before the purchase or acquisition. Does the snake, generally speaking, do well in captivity? Even if a snake does eat well in captivity, can you find the food for it? If the food is readily available, will it bother you to feed thawed, once-frozen mice, rats or bunnies? Does the snake stay a reasonable size?

If you can answer these qustions readily and there are no legal restrictions in your area against the snake you want to keep as a pet, go ahead. You're going to enjoy keeping your snake.

Common Boa Constrictor

Trade Name(s):
Colombian Boa,
Boa Constrictor,
Colombian
Red-tailed
Boa, Central
American Boa,
Emperor's Boa,
Hog Island Boa,
Honduras Boa.

Family & Scientific Name:
Boidae; *Boa constrictor imperator.*

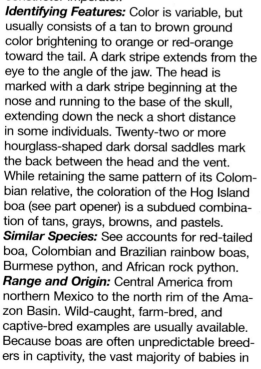

Identifying Features: Color is variable, but usually consists of a tan to brown ground color brightening to orange or red-orange toward the tail. A dark stripe extends from the eye to the angle of the jaw. The head is marked with a dark stripe beginning at the nose and running to the base of the skull, extending down the neck a short distance in some individuals. Twenty-two or more hourglass-shaped dark dorsal saddles mark the back between the head and the vent. While retaining the same pattern of its Colombian relative, the coloration of the Hog Island boa (see part opener) is a subdued combination of tans, grays, browns, and pastels.

Similar Species: See accounts for red-tailed boa, Colombian and Brazilian rainbow boas, Burmese python, and African rock python.

Range and Origin: Central America from northern Mexico to the north rim of the Amazon Basin. Wild-caught, farm-bred, and captive-bred examples are usually available. Because boas are often unpredictable breeders in captivity, the vast majority of babies in

the pet trade are bred on farms in Honduras and Colombia.

Adult Size: 6–12 feet. Hog Island boas tend to be smaller than mainland boas.

Life Span: 20+ years.

Terrarium Size: Young boas quickly outgrow aquariums and similar enclosures. Housing for adults should be a *minimum* of $2 \times 2 \times 4$ feet.

Terrarium Type: Humid, rain forest, or plain cage with a bowl large enough for soaking.

Social Structure: Solitary; boas are best housed together only for breeding.

Diet: Includes mice, rats, chicks, and rabbits.

Potential Problems: Low ambient humidity often leads to shedding problems (dysecdysis) and retained spectacles (eye-caps). Wild-caught boas are especially prone to tick and mite infestations as well as internal parasites. All boas and pythons are susceptible to Boid Inclusion Body Disease (IBD), a virus that can cause respiratory, digestive, and neurologic problems in affected animals. Common boas can grow to be large and dangerous animals; before purchasing one, be sure that you can commit to its proper care throughout its life.

References:
Wagner, Doug. *Boas.* Hauppauge, NY: Barron's Educational Series, Inc., 1996.

Red-tailed Boa

Trade Name(s):
Guyana Red-tail, Suriname Red-tail, Peruvian Red-tail, South American Boa, Amazon Basin Boa.

Family & Scientific Name:
Boidae; *Boa constrictor constrictor.*

Identifying Features: Distinguished by gray, brown, or pinkish background with darker (red-brown to maroon or red) hourglass-shaped dorsal saddles. The tail is more brilliantly colored than that of the common boa. This boa has a dark stripe beginning behind the eye and gradually widening as it progresses toward the angle of the jaw.

Similar Species: See accounts for common boa, Colombian and Brazilian rainbow boas, Burmese python, and African rock python.

Range & Origin: Central and northern South America east of the Andes Mountains. Wild-caught, farm-bred, and captive-bred animals are all available. Export from many of the countries of origin is limited (or prohibited), so captive-born animals are relatively more common.

Adult Size: 6–12 feet.
Life Span: 20+ years.
Terrarium Size: Housing for adults should be a *minimum* of 2 × 2 × 4 feet.
Terrarium Type: Humid forest, rain forest, or plain cage with a bowl large enough for soaking. Some boas enjoy the opportunity to climb and use securely attached, non-resinous branches placed in the cage.

Social Structure: Solitary. Boas should be housed together only for breeding.

Diet: Includes mice, rats, chicks, and rabbits.

Potential Problems: Like the common boa, red-tails can have problems shedding if adequate humidity is not provided. Inclusion Body Disease can affect all boas and pythons (see account for common boa). Plan ahead for the large adult size of these snakes; zoos and other institutions are overwhelmed with offers of pet snakes that have grown too large for their owners to handle.

References:
Wagner, Doug. *Boas.* Hauppauge, NY: Barron's Educational Series, Inc., 1996.

Amazonian Tree Boa

Trade Name(s): Garden Tree Boa, Tree Boa.
Family & Scientific Name: Boidae; *Corallus hortulanus (=enydris).*
Identifying Features: These boas are extremely variable. It is a slender snake with a relatively large head and prehensile tail. It may be gray, tan, olive, yellow, orange, or orange-red with or without dorsal bands or rhombs that contrast to the background color. (Darker specimens have light dorsal markings and lighter specimens have dark dorsal markings.) Some examples may be nearly unicolored; those that are uniformly red or red-orange are most coveted.

Similar Species: See accounts for emerald tree boa and Solomon Island tree boa.
Range & Origin: Found throughout much of tropical South America. Amazonian tree boas are most commonly available as imported wild specimens. Captive-bred babies are available in limited numbers.
Adult Size: 3–5 feet.
Life Span: 12–20 years.
Terrarium Size: Height is most important for this arboreal (tree-dwelling) snake. A minimum of a 20-gallon, long aquarium turned on one end, or a similarly shaped terrarium, is best.

Terrarium Type: Rain forest terrarium with plenty of perching and climbing areas. High ambient humidity and good ventilation are very important.
Social Structure: Solitary. Males can be especially aggressive toward each other during the breeding season.
Diet: Young animals may prefer lizards over warm-blooded prey, but adults consume chicks, mice, and small rats. Prefer to drink droplets from water misted onto body or from elevated water dish with roiled surface; some will not drink still water.
Potential Problems: Difficulty shedding is commonly encountered if ambient humidity is too low. Poor ventilation combined with high humidity can lead to respiratory problems. All boas and pythons are susceptible to Inclusion Body Disease (see account for common boa). Not known for a placid disposition, the Amazonian tree boa can deliver a painful bite and prove difficult to tame. Mites, ticks, and intestinal parasites are common in wild-caught animals.
References:
Wagner, Doug. *Boas.* Hauppauge, NY: Barron's Educational Series, Inc., 1996.

Emerald Tree Boa

Trade Name(s): Green Tree Boa.
Family & Scientific Name: Boidae; *Corallus caninus.*
Identifying Features: Newborns are brick red or yellow, a juvenile coloration that is lost after the first few sheds. Dorsal col-

oration of adults is a deep emerald green; yellow below may extend onto the lips and face. Variable white dorsal bars may be connected by a thin white dorsal stripe.
Similar Species: See account for Amazonian tree boa.
Range & Origin: Tropical South America. Captive-bred juveniles are becoming more common each year; imported animals are available as well.
Adult Size: 6–7 feet.
Life Span: 12–20 years.
Terrarium Size: This climbing snake requires a cage at least 4 feet high as an adult. A small "footprint" is acceptable, as the emerald tree boa spends little time on the ground. Turn a large aquarium on its short side to make a suitable terrarium.
Terrarium Type: Well-ventilated rain forest terrarium with plenty of sturdy, non-resinous branches for climbing. The diameter of perches should be roughly equal to the diameter of the snake at midbody.

Social Structure: These solitary snakes are best housed individually except when breeding.
Diet: Includes chicks, mice, and rats. Avoid large prey, as emerald tree boas are prone to regurgitation of large meals.

Potential Problems: These boas drink water droplets misted onto their body or from an elevated water dish with roiled surface. Low humidity leads to shedding problems; mist the cage lightly on a daily basis. High humidity with poor ventilation can lead to respiratory ailments. Inclusion Body Disease may affect this species along with other boas and pythons (see account for common boa). Regurgitation seems to be a common problem in this species. Possible causes include inappropriate cage temperatures, stress, parasitism, and oversized meals. Ticks, mites, and internal parasites are common in wild-caught animals. Like the Amazonian tree boa, the emerald is not known for its pleasant disposition.

References:

Bartlett, R. D., and Patricia Bartlett. *Snakes.* Hauppauge, NY: Barron's Educational Series, Inc., 1998.

Wagner, Doug. *Boas.* Hauppauge, NY: Barron's Educational Series, Inc., 1996.

Solomon Island Tree Boa

Trade Name(s): Pacific Tree Boa, Bibron's Tree Boa, Round-snouted Boa.

Family & Scientific Name: Boidae; *Candoia bibroni australis.*

Identifying Features: This is a long, slender snake with an angular head

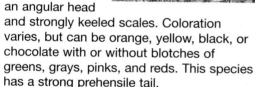

and strongly keeled scales. Coloration varies, but can be orange, yellow, black, or chocolate with or without blotches of greens, grays, pinks, and reds. This species has a strong prehensile tail.

Similar Species: See accounts for Amazonian tree boa and Solomon Island ground boa.

Range & Origin: Solomon Islands. Most specimens are currently imported, although captive breeding is increasing.

Adult Size: 2–5 feet.

Life Span: 10–15 years likely.

Terrarium Size: 20-gallon, long aquarium or larger for a single adult. A vertical orienta-

tion is appreciated by this species, although they spend a fair amount of time on the ground.

Terrarium Type: Humid forest or jungle. A large water bowl is essential for humidity and to allow soaking.

Social Structure: Solitary.

Diet: Juveniles appreciate tree frogs and lizards, but may be enticed to pink mice if they are scented with preferred prey. Many adults readily accept rodents of appropriate size.

Potential Problems: Low humidity can lead to shedding problems. Wild-caught animals may harbor intestinal parasites, as well as ticks and mites. Poor ventilation can predispose this species to respiratory problems.

References:

Wagner, Doug. *Boas.* Hauppauge, NY: Barron's Educational Series, Inc., 1996.

Solomon Island Ground Boa

Trade Name(s): Halmahera Ground Boa, Pacific Ground Boa, Isabel Ground Boa, Viper Boa.

Family & Scientific Name: Boidae; *Candoia carinata paulsoni*.

Identifying Features: Background highly variable from white to red, pink, orange, gold, gray, silver, brown, or black; some specimens may show a combination of colors. A characteristic zigzag stripe extends from the neck to the tail. Ground boas have flat, triangular heads, keeled scales, and a strongly prehensile tail.

Similar Species: See account for Solomon Island tree boa.

Range & Origin: Solomon Islands in the south Pacific. Most specimens are imported, although captive breeding is increasing.

Adult Size: 3–4 feet.

Life Span: Likely in excess of 10–12 years.

Terrarium Size: A 20-gallon, long aquarium or larger is recommended for this snake.

Terrarium Type: Humid forest with a large water vessel suitable for soaking.

Social Structure: Solitary.

Diet: Mice and rats; juveniles, especially neonates, often prefer lizards or treefrogs.

Potential Problems: Low humidity and lack of a soaking bowl can lead to shedding problems and retained spectacles (eye-caps). High humidity and poor ventilation can contribute to the formation of respiratory illness. Wild-caught animals may harbor internal and external parasites. Boas of all species may be infected with Inclusion Body Disease (see account for common boa). Recent imports may be aggressive and bite freely.

References:
Wagner, Doug. *Boas.* Hauppauge, NY: Barron's Educational Series, Inc., 1996.

Kenyan Sand Boa

Trade Name(s): Loveridge's Sand Boa, Kenyan Boa.
Family & Scientific Name: Boidae; *Eryx colubrinus loveridgei.*
Identifying Features: The brown to olive background is marked dorsally and laterally with irregular patches of white, buff, yellow, or orange. Albino and anerythristic color mutations are available. This stocky species has a dorso-ventrally flattened head designed for burrowing and scales that become progressively more keeled as they approach the tail.
Similar Species: See account for rough-scaled sand boa.
Range & Origin: Found in the deserts and savannahs of Kenya and Tanzania. Very few animals are imported at this time; availability is due to captive breeding.
Adult Size: Females may reach two feet in length; males are slightly built and consider-ably shorter when fully grown.
Life Span: In excess of 15 years.
Terrarium Size: A 20-gallon, long aquarium or similarly sized terrarium is ideal.
Terrarium Type: Desert or savannah with a 3–5-inch layer of sand to allow for burrowing. A small water bowl should be provided.
Social Structure: Solitary.
Diet: Mice and small rats. The occasional newborn prefers lizards.
Potential Problems: Stress-induced anorexia may occur if these snakes are not provided with an opportunity to burrow or a suitable hide box. All boas and pythons are susceptible to Inclusion Body Disease (see account for common boa).
References:
Wagner, Doug. *Boas.* Hauppauge, NY: Barron's Educational Series, Inc., 1996.

Rough-scaled Sand Boa

Trade Name(s):
Short-tailed
Sand Boa,
Keeled Sand
Boa.

Family & Scientific Name:
Boidae; *Eryx
(=Gongylophis)
conicus* ssp.

***Identifying
Features:*** This
boa has a tan,
buff, gray, or
yellowish
ground color marked with three rows of
large dark spots, one on each side, and a
broad row down the back. The spots may
fuse into bars or irregular stripes. As the
common name implies, the scales are
keeled, especially toward the tail. The
head is flat with an enlarged rostral (nose)
scale.

Similar Species: See account for Kenyan
sand boa.

Range & Origin: Common to the savannahs
of Pakistan, India, and Sri Lanka. Specimens are primarily captive-born due to
restricted exportation from India and
Pakistan.

Adult Size:
Approximately 2
feet for females;
significantly less
for males.

Life Span: More
than 12 years.

Terrarium Size:
A 20-gallon, long
aquarium or
larger terrarium
is ideal.

Terrarium Type:
While less-gifted
burrowers than
the Kenyan sand boa, rough-scaled sand
boas appreciate a savannah/desert setup
with plenty of sand for burrowing.

Social Structure: Solitary.

Diet: Rodents of appropriate size are
accepted.

Potential Problems: Potential host for
Inclusion Body Disease (see account for
common boa).

References:

Wagner, Doug. *Boas*. Hauppauge, NY:
  Barron's Educational Series, Inc., 1996.
Bartlett, R. D., and Patricia Bartlett. *Snakes*.
  Hauppauge, NY: Barron's Educational
  Series, Inc., 1998.

Colombian Rainbow Boa

Trade Name(s): Same.

Family & Scientific Name: Boidae; *Epicrates cenchria maurus.*

Identifying Features: Russet to brown with indistinct dorsal ocelli (spots) and lateral spots bordered above by

light crescents. Neonates are more brightly colored than adults, which usually appear to be unicolored. Smooth, iridescent scales.

Similar Species: See account for Brazilian rainbow boa.

Range & Origin: Costa Rica, Colombia, and border regions of adjacent countries. Most animals seen in the pet trade are born in captivity. Imported irregularly and in extremely limited quantities.

Adult Size: 5–8 feet.

Life Span: More than 12 years.

Terrarium Size: A 20-gallon, long aquarium will last only a few years as housing for this species. Adults may require 75-gallon aquariums or larger custom terraria.

Terrarium Type: Humid forest or woodland.

Social Structure: Solitary.

Diet: Rats, mice, and chicks.

Potential Problems: High humidity combined with cool temperatures can lead to respiratory problems. This snake can grow to a large adult size and is known for a nippy temperament; carefully consider these facts *before* purchasing a rainbow boa. Inclusion Body Disease may affect this species (see account for common boa).

References:

Bartlett, R. D., and Patricia Bartlett. *Snakes.* Hauppauge, NY: Barron's Educational Series, Inc., 1998.

Wagner, Doug. *Boas.* Hauppauge, NY: Barron's Educational Series, Inc., 1996.

Brazilian Rainbow Boa

Trade Name(s): Same.

Family & Scientific Name: Boidae; *Epicrates cenchria cenchria*

Identifying Features: These have a rich orange to orange-brown ground color marked with large dorsal ocelli outlined in dark brown or black. Lateral spots are bordered above by black-edged crescents of pink or buff. Scales are smooth and iridescent. Neonates tend to be less richly colored than adults.

Similar Species: See account for Colombian rainbow boa.

Range & Origin: Tropical Brazil and parts of adjacent countries. Available specimens are almost exclusively captive-born.

Adult Size: 5–8 feet.

Life Span: More than 12 years.

Terrarium Size: A 20-gallon, long aquarium to start. Adults require a 75-gallon aquarium or large terrarium.

Terrarium Type: Humid forest or rain forest.

Social Structure: Solitary.

Diet: Eats mice, rats, and chicks.

Potential Problems: Respiratory problems are seen when high humidity is combined with cool temperatures. Inclusion Body Disease can be a silent killer of this and other species of boas and pythons (see account for common boa). Rainbow boas grow to be large and potentially irritable adults; carefully consider your purchase.

References:

Wagner, Doug. *Boas*. Hauppauge, NY: Barron's Educational Series, Inc., 1996.

Bartlett, R. D., and Patricia Bartlett. *Snakes*. Hauppauge, NY: Barron's Educational Series, Inc., 1998.

Desert Rosy Boa

Trade Name(s): Same. These snakes may also be named for the locality of the breeding stock.

Family & Scientific Name: Boidae; *Lichanura trivirgata gracia.*

Identifying Features: A stocky snake with a small head and a heavy, though not blunt, tail. Prominent, even-edged stripes of rose, reddish brown, or tan on a buff, gray, or bluish gray background.

Similar Species: See account for Mexican rosy boa.

Range & Origin: Occurs naturally in western Arizona and extreme southeastern California. The sale of wild specimens is prohibited; therefore captive-bred animals are the rule.

Adult Size: 2–3 feet.

Life Span: More than 15 years.

Terrarium Size: A 20-gallon, long aquarium is adequate for all life stages.

Terrarium Type: Arid, rocky habitat. Be sure that rocks are placed in tank before the substrate is added to avoid injuries.

Social Structure: Solitary, but may be kept in pairs or trios year-round.

Diet: Eats rats and mice. In some cases, neonates may prefer lizards over rodents.

Potential Problems: High humidity is associated with respiratory problems in captivity. In addition, humidity may be a contributing factor in regurgitation syndrome described by keepers. In humid regions, provide a small bowl of water on every second or third day to keep cage humidity to a minimum.

References:

Bartlett, R. D., and Patricia Bartlett. *Snakes.* Hauppauge, NY: Barron's Educational Series, Inc., 1998.

Wagner, Doug. *Boas.* Hauppauge, NY: Barron's Educational Series, Inc., 1996.

Mexican Rosy Boa

Trade Name(s): Same. May be identified by the specific locality from which breeding stock originated.

Family & Scientific Name: Boidae; *Lichanura trivirgata trivirgata*.

Identifying Features: This is a stout-bod-

ied snake with a small head and a heavy tail. Three wide stripes of chocolate brown to black are found on a yellow, buff, beige, or light brown background.

Similar Species: See accounts for desert rosy boa.

Range & Origin: Northern Mexico and the adjacent portions of extreme southwestern Arizona. Wild populations are protected from commercialization; all specimens should be captive-bred.

Adult Size: 2–3 feet.

Life Span: More than 15 years.

Terrarium Size: A 20-gallon, long aquarium or similarly sized terrarium.

Terrarium Type: Dry, rocky habitat. Cage furnishings should be securely anchored to avoid crushing injuries.

Social Structure: Solitary, but may be kept in pairs or trios.

Diet: Eats mice and rats; neonates may prefer lizards in some instances.

Potential Problems: Excessive humidity is often associated with respiratory problems; it may also contribute to a regurgitation syndrome seen in captive rosy boas. In humid areas, keep cage humidity to a minimum by providing a small water bowl for 12–24 hours every 2–3 days. Feeding smaller prey may reduce regurgitation problems.

References:

Bartlett, R. D., and Patricia Bartlett. *Snakes.* Hauppauge, NY: Barron's Educational Series, Inc., 1998.

Wagner, Doug. *Boas.* Hauppauge, NY: Barron's Educational Series, Inc., 1996.

Reticulated Python

Trade Name(s): "Retic."

Family & Scientific Name: Boidae; *Python reticulatus.*

Identifying Features: This is a slender python with an intricate pattern consisting of yellow diamonds on the back and a busy

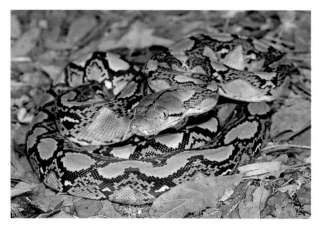

network of brown, black, cream, and even purplish markings on the flanks. Background color is gray, gray-green, olive, or brown; there is much geographic variation in coloration in this species. Albinos are now being bred in captivity.

Similar Species: The reticulated python is not easily confused with other species.

Range & Origin: Southeast Asia. Imported, captive-hatched, and captive-born specimens are available.

Adult Size: 18–22 feet; this species may be capable of attaining lengths in excess of 28 feet.

Life Span: 12+ years.

Terrarium Size: A room-sized enclosure is necessary to properly house adults.

Terrarium Type: Humid forest.

Social Structure: Solitary. Males may gravely injure each other during combat in the breeding season.

Diet: Eats mice and rats initially; large adults require prey as large as small pigs.

Potential Problems: This giant snake is not recommended as a pet for a variety of reasons. The beautiful baby "retics" found at pet stores and import houses rapidly grow into potentially deadly predators. Reticulated pythons are known for their unpredictability and volatile dispositions. Not only can adults deliver a painful bite, they are also very capable of killing an inexperienced handler. Respiratory disease, parasites, and Inclusion Body Disease are all seen in reticulated pythons. Large pythons may be illegal in some areas; check your local and state laws. Zoos and other institutions are overwhelmed with offers of pet snakes that have grown too large for their owners to handle.

References:
Bartlett, Patricia, and Ernie Wagner. *Pythons.* Hauppauge, NY: Barron's Educational Series, Inc., 1996.

Burmese Python

Trade Name(s): "Burm," Indian Python.

Family & Scientific Name: Boidae; *Python molurus bivittatus.*

Identifying Features: This large constrictor has a tan to brown background marked

with irregular dark-edged olive to brown dorsal and lateral blotches. A well-defined dark "spearpoint" marks the top of the head. Amelanistic albinos (inset) are colored in yellow, orange, and pearlescent white.

Similar Species: See account for African rock python.

Range & Origin: Burma, Indonesia, Malaysia. Captive-bred in great numbers; importation is limited primarily to unusual specimens.

Adult Size: 12–14 feet on average. May grow from a 16-inch hatchling to 8 feet in just 2 years.

Life Span: 12–20 years.

Terrarium Size: A minimum of 4 × 8-foot enclosure at least 4 feet tall is recommended for adults.

Terrarium Type: Grassland, woodland, or forest.

Social Structure: Solitary.

Diet: Eats mice, rats, rabbits, and chickens.

Potential Problems: This species is not recommended for the casual hobbyist.

This large and potentially dangerous snake rapidly grows from a cute hatchling into a large predator, capable of killing its owner. Zoos are overwhelmed with offers of Burmese pythons that have grown too large for their caretakers to handle. Acute and chronic respiratory problems are particularly common in this species, especially when temperature and humidity requirements are not met. Inclusion Body Disease is perhaps more common in Burmese pythons than in any other species. While most tame easily with frequent handling, babies are often "nippy."

References:

Bartlett, Patricia, and Ernie Wagner. *Pythons*. Hauppauge, NY: Barron's Educational Series, Inc., 1996.

African Rock Python

Trade Name(s): Rock Python.

Family & Scientific Name: Boidae; *Python sebae.*

Identifying Features: This is a large beige to tan python with dark-edged brown to olive blotches on the back and sides. Lacks the "spearpoint" head marking seen in Burmese pythons.

Similar Species: See account for Burmese python.

Range & Origin: Southern and Central Africa. Imported specimens and occasional captive-bred hatchlings are available.

Adult Size: 14–16 feet.

Life Span: 12+ years.

Terrarium Size: Full-grown adults require a cage with a floor space of 4 × 8 feet.

Terrarium Type: Grassland with stout branches for climbing.

Social Structure: Solitary.

Diet: Eats mice, rats, rabbits, and chickens.

Potential Problems: Not recommended for casual hobbyists due to its large adult size and unpredictable temperament. Adults are capable of killing and consuming humans. Rock pythons are susceptible to respiratory infections and Inclusion Body Disease.

References:
Bartlett, Patricia, and Ernie Wagner. *Pythons*. Hauppauge, NY: Barron's Educational Series, Inc., 1996.

Spotted Python

Trade Name(s): Children's Python, Eastern Children's Python, Small-blotched Python.

Family & Scientific Name: Boidae; *Antaresia (=Liasis) maculosa.*

Identifying Features: The yellow, olive, or brown ground color is marked with irregular brownish to reddish-brown dorsal and lateral blotches. The scales are smooth and somewhat iridescent.

Similar Species: See account for Children's python.

Range & Origin: Coastal Queensland and Northeastern New South Wales, Australia. Australian wildlife is strictly protected from exportation; all specimens should be of captive origin.

Adult Size: Approximately 3 feet.

Life Span: 12–15 years is expected.

Terrarium Size: A 30–50-gallon aquarium comfortably houses an adult pair.

Terrarium Type: Wild habitats include savannahs, forests, and rocky hillsides.

Social Structure: Solitary, but may be safely kept in pairs or trios.

Diet: Lizards (especially hatchlings), mice, and rats.

Potential Problems: These well-adapted captives pose few problems. Respiratory disease and Inclusion Body Disease can occur in all python species.

References:

Bartlett, R. D., and Patricia Bartlett. *Snakes.* Hauppauge, NY: Barron's Educational Series, Inc., 1998.

Green Tree Python

Trade Name(s): "Chondro," Chondropython, Green Python.

Family & Scientific Name: Boidae; *Morelia (=Chondropython) viridis.*

Identifying Features: Adults are dull to bright green with irregular small white

spots or a thin white line dorsally, and white to yellow ventral scales. Hatchlings are bright yellow or brick red, and rapidly undergo a change to adult coloration (a process known as ontogeny) after a few sheds of their skin. Green tree pythons are strong climbers with a prehensile tail.

Similar Species: See account for emerald tree boa.

Range & Origin: New Guinea and the Cape York Peninsula of northeastern Australia. Imported and captive-born specimens are available.

Adult Size: 4–6 feet.

Life Span: Likely in excess of 12 years.

Terrarium Size: Height is most important with this species. Turn a 20-gallon, long or larger aquarium on end to provide adequate space for climbing.

Terrarium Type: Humid forest. Misting snakes allows them to drink droplets of water that collect on their scales.

Social Structure: Solitary. Animals housed together, especially males paired during breeding season, may bite one another savagely.

Diet: Eats mice, rats, and chicks; hatchlings may have to be "tease-fed."

Potential Problems: Poor ventilation and high humidity can contribute to skin and respiratory problems. The security of high perches and suspended hide areas can minimize stress-related anorexia. This species often refuses to drink from a bowl of standing water and will become dehydrated if not misted regularly. Handle with care, as some "chondros" can be high-strung and irascible.

References:
Bartlett, R. D., and Patricia Bartlett. *Snakes.* Hauppauge, NY: Barron's Educational Series, Inc., 1998.

Jungle Carpet Python

Trade Name(s):
Carpet Snake, Atherton Carpet Python, Atherton Tableland Carpet Python, Rain Forest-phase Carpet Python.

Family & Scientific Name:
Boidae; *Morelia spilota cheynei.*

Identifying Features: This relatively small, slender python has a large head. The pale cream to bright yellow background is marked by black-edged dark dorsal blotches giving an overall banded appearance.

Similar Species: Hybrids between the jungle carpet and diamond pythons may be confused with the pure jungle carpet python.

Range & Origin: Occurs naturally along the watercourses draining the Atherton tablelands in a small part of eastern Queensland, Australia. Australia's strict regulation of commerce in its wildlife necessitates that all specimens available are captive-bred in origin.

Adult Size: To about 5½ feet.

Life Span: Likely in excess of 15 years.

Terrarium Size: Fares best in a 60-gallon aquarium or equivalent terrarium with excellent ventilation.

Terrarium Type: Rain forest or humid deciduous forest. Appreciates stout branches for climbing.

Social Structure: Solitary.

Diet: Mice, rats, and chicks of appropriate size.

Potential Problems: High humidity and cool conditions can lead to respiratory and/or skin infections. Always provide good ventilation for herps kept in high-humidity enclosures. Like other boas and pythons, jungle "carpets" are susceptible to Inclusion Body Disease. Parasites are not common in this exclusively captive-bred snake.

References:
Bartlett, Patricia, and Ernie Wagner. *Pythons*. Hauppauge, NY: Barron's Educational Series, Inc., 1997.

Children's Python

Trade Name(s): Same.

Family & Scientific Name: Boidae; *Antaresia childreni.*

Identifying Features: Small python dressed in purplish-brown to tan with irregular, poorly defined, small spots of dark reddish

brown on the back. These blotches form 4 rows, with the spots of the two dorsal rows frequently merging to form larger ovals. Hatchlings are more contrastingly colored than adults.

Similar Species: See account for spotted python.

Range & Origin: Occurs naturally in the northern portions of eastern Western Australia, the Northern Territory, and western Queensland, Australia. All specimens offered for sale should be of captive-bred origin.

Adult Size: This small python reaches an adult length of 3 to 4 feet.

Life Span: 15–20 years.

Terrarium Size: A 30-gallon, long aquarium is sufficient for a single adult.

Terrarium Type: Dry woodland, rocky aridland, or forest. A secure hide should be provided for this species, which often seeks shelter in termite mounds in the wild.

Social Structure: Solitary, may be safely kept in pairs year-round.

Diet: Mice and rats; hatchlings may prefer lizards.

Potential Problems: While not commonly infected, this species is susceptible to Inclusion Body Disease of boas and pythons.

References:

Bartlett, Patricia, and Ernie Wagner. *Pythons.* Hauppauge, NY: Barron's Educational Series, Inc., 1997.

Ball Python

Trade Name(s):
Royal Python.
Family & Scientific Name:
Boidae; *Python regius.*
Identifying Features: Small python with a reticular network of light-edged black markings on a tan to coppery-brown background.

shy species.
Social Structure: Solitary, but may be safely kept in pairs or small groups of one male and 2–3 females year-round.
Diet: Mice and rats predominantly; recently-imported adults may prefer gerbils or hamsters.

Often, a series of brown ovals is present within the black vertebral stripe. The ball python is now being bred in several "designer" colors and patterns including caramel, ghost, albino, "jungle," "clown," and axanthic (anerythristic).

Similar Species: See accounts for Burmese python and African rock python, the young of which may be confused for the ball python. Also see account for Borneo short-tailed python.

Range & Origin: Western Africa. Captive specimens may be wild-caught imports, "farm-raised" hatchlings, or captive-born.

Adult Size: To approximately 4 feet.

Life Span: In excess of 20 years, the record is 50+ years (Philadelphia Zoo).

Terrarium Size: A 20-gallon, long aquarium or equivalent terrarium is ideal for an adult.

Terrarium Type: Dry scrub or savannah. A secure hidebox should be provided for this

Potential Problems: The ball python is notorious for being an unreliable feeder. This problem is especially common in imported adult snakes. Ensure that the snake you purchase is captive-bred to minimize feeding difficulties. Rodent bites occur commonly in this species, primarily when a live rodent is left unsupervised in the cage of a snake that is reluctant to eat. **Never leave a live rodent unattended with any snake; a bite from uneaten prey can be deadly!** If it is absolutely necessary, try a pink mouse or newborn rat, neither of which can bite. Like other boas and pythons, ball pythons may contract Inclusion Body Disease.

References:
Bartlett, Patricia, and Ernie Wagner.
  Pythons. Hauppauge, NY: Barron's
  Educational Series, Inc., 1997.

Borneo Short-tailed Python

Trade Name(s): Blood Python, Borneo Blood (Python).

Family & Scientific Name: Boidae; *Python curtus breitensteini*.

Identifying Features: Brown to yellow-brown with an irregular pattern of light-edged chocolate to reddish-brown

enough for the snake to stretch out its entire length and wide enough to allow it to turn around comfortably. Custom terraria with a "squarish" footprint are better suited for short-tailed pythons than the traditional narrow aquariums.

markings. A dark stripe runs the length of the top of the head and a light strip beginning behind the eye runs to the angle of the jaw.

Similar Species: None.

Range & Origin: Coastal areas of the island of Borneo, Indonesia. Both imported and captive-born specimens are available

Adult Size: 5 feet or less; this species looks large due to its girth and heavy body.

Life Span: In excess of 12 years.

Terrarium Size: A terrarium larger than that used for slender snakes of similar length is suggested. The terrarium should be large

Terrarium Type: Humid forest.

Social Structure: Solitary.

Diet: Mice and rats.

Potential Problems: This species is especially susceptible to respiratory and skin infections. The high humidity required for proper husbandry must be carefully monitored, and good ventilation is a must. Conversely, a cage that is too dry can lead to difficulties shedding, poor appetite, and, potentially, respiratory problems as well.

References:

Bartlett, Patricia, and Ernie Wagner. *Pythons.* Hauppauge, NY: Barron's Educational Series, Inc., 1997.

Gray-banded Kingsnake

Trade Name(s): Gray-band, Gray-banded King, Alterna, Blair's Kingsnake, may also be identified by the geographic origin of breeding adults.
Family & Scientific Name: Colubridae; *Lampropeltis alterna.*

Adult Size: 3–4 feet.
Life Span: 20+ years.
Terrarium Size: A 20-gallon, long aquarium or larger for adults.
Terrarium Type: Rocky hillside or canyon. Be sure all rocks are securely anchored to avoid crushing injuries.

Identifying Features: A very variable snake; the two phases of gray-banded kingsnake were at one time believed to be separate species. Both phases have a background of blue gray to charcoal and differ in their dorsal markings. The *"blairi"* or *"Blair's"* phase has black-bordered red saddles of variable width dorsally. In the *"alterna"* phase, the red is greatly reduced or absent, creating an essentially black-banded gray snake. Between primary bands are smaller bands or a series of dots forming broken bands— the "alternates" that lead to the phase's common name.

Similar Species: See accounts for Mexican kingsnake and Ruthven's kingsnake.

Range & Origin: Found in Trans-Pecos, Texas, and a small portion of adjacent New Mexico. This species is bred in great numbers in captivity; wild-caught animals are rarely offered for sale.

Social Structure: Solitary. Kingsnakes are known to eat other snakes in the wild.

Diet: Mice and rats. Hatchlings often steadfastly refuse pink mice and require lizards or lizard-scented mice.

Potential Problems: Difficulty in getting hatchlings to feed is perhaps the most notable husbandry problem for gray-banded kingsnakes. Most reputable breeders sell only well-started hatchlings. Reluctant feeders are often offered at lower prices and without a guarantee.

References:

Bartlett, R. D., and Patricia Bartlett. *Snakes.* Hauppauge, NY: Barron's Educational Series, Inc., 1998.

Markel, Ronald G., and R. D. Bartlett. *Kingsnakes and Milk Snakes.* Hauppauge, NY: Barron's Educational Series, Inc., 1995.

Mexican Kingsnake

Trade Name(s):
San Luis Potosi Kingsnake, Potosi King, Mex-Mex, Variable Kingsnake, Thayer's Kingsnake, Thayeri, Nuevo Leon Kingsnake, Durango Mountain Kingsnake.

Family & Scientific Name: Colubridae; *Lampropeltis mexicana.*

Identifying Features: The variable kingsnake is just that—variable. At one time divided into three subspecies, the Mexican kingsnake is now recognized as a single species with great variation in color throughout its range. The three subspecies are now considered color phases of the same snake. The San Luis Potosi or *"mexicana"* phase is gray or gray-green to charcoal with a series of large, squarish, black-edged red dorsal blotches. The first blotch is usually in the shape of a Y with the forks pointing toward the head. The Durango Mountain or *"greeri"* phase is light gray to buff with white-bordered black saddles that may or may not have a red center. The head is marked with black, and the neck blotch is elongated and has a convex margin toward the head (instead of a Y). The variable or *"thayeri"* phase is the most variable of the three former subspecies. It may be colored similarly to the above phases, banded in red, black, and white (much like a scarlet kingsnake), or solid black. Some individuals have pearl gray or cream background colors. Still others have dorsal bands that are so restricted that they appear as crossbars rather than bands.

Similar Species: See accounts for gray-banded kingsnake and Ruthven's kingsnake.

Range & Origin: Mountains and adjacent deserts of eastern central Mexico. Mexico prohibits exportation of its native reptiles; all specimens should therefore be of captive lineage.

Adult Size: 3 feet, rarely more.

Life Span: 15–20 years.

Terrarium Size: A 20-gallon, long or larger aquarium or similarly sized terrarium.

Terrarium Type: Rocky aridlands. Secure all rocks to avoid injury to your snake.

Social Structure: Solitary. Kingsnakes are known to eat other snakes.

Diet: Mice and rats. Hatchlings may prefer lizards.

Potential Problems: Difficulty feeding hatchlings is probably the biggest problem with this species. The best breeders sell only hatchlings that are guaranteed to be feeding on mice.

References:
Markel, Ronald G., and R. D. Bartlett. *Kingsnakes and Milk Snakes.* Hauppauge, NY: Barron's Educational Series, Inc., 1995.

Arizona Mountain Kingsnake

Trade Name(s):
Arizona Mountain King, Sonoran Mountain Kingsnake, Pyro, Pyromelana.

Family & Scientific Name:
Colubridae; *Lampropeltis pyromelana* ssp.

Identifying Features: A slender tricolored kingsnake

banded in red, black, and white. Red may be present in distinct bands, or reduced to lateral triangles when neighboring black bands meet mid-dorsally.

Similar Species: See account for Ruthven's kingsnake.

Range & Origin: Found at higher elevations in several mountain ranges in Arizona, southwestern New Mexico, Utah, Nevada, and northern Mexico. Arizona prohibits commercialization of native wildlife; all specimens offered for sale should be captive-born.

Adult Size:
2–4 feet.

Life Span: In excess of 15 years.

Terrarium Size:
A 20-gallon, long aquarium or similarly sized terrarium is adequate for adults.

Terrarium Type:
Rocky woodland or coniferous forest.

Social Structure: Solitary. Known to eat other snakes.

Diet: Mice, rats, and lizards. Young are especially fond of lizard prey.

Potential Problems: Hatchlings may be problematic feeders, although most captive lineages readily accept nestling mice.

References:
Markel, Ronald G., and R. D. Bartlett. *Kingsnakes and Milk Snakes.* Hauppauge, NY: Barron's Educational Series, Inc., 1995.

Eastern Kingsnake

Trade Name(s): Eastern King, Chain King, Chain Kingsnake.

Family & Scientific Name: Colubridae; *Lampropeltis getula getula.*

Identifying Features: A large, heavy-bodied colubrid with white,

cream, or yellow crossbands on a dark chocolate to black background. On the sides, the crossbands divide to form upside-down Y shapes at each end. Adjacent Y's are linked at the ventrolateral margin to form the chainlike pattern for which this snake is named.

Similar Species: See accounts for Florida kingsnake, blotched kingsnake, and California kingsnake.

Range & Origin: Found along the eastern coastal plain from the New Jersey pine barrens to northern Florida and west to the Apalachians and southeastern Alabama. Both captive-bred and wild-caught specimens are available with regularity.

Adult Size: 4–6 feet.

Life Span: 15–20 years.

Terrarium Size: A 20-gallon, long aquarium or larger enclosure is recommended.

Terrarium Type: Humid forest.

Social Structure: Solitary. Kingsnakes are famous for eating other snakes.

Diet: Mice, rats, lizards, frogs, and snakes.

Potential Problems: Some hatchlings can be difficult to entice to feed on pink mice, often requiring scenting with a lizard or another snake. Wrapping thawed, frozen pinkies in small pieces of freshly shed snakeskin may help. Kingsnakes kept in poorly ventilated cages with high humidity are extremely susceptible to pustular dermatitis, a skin infection commonly known as "blister disease" or "skin rot." Internal parasites are very common in kingsnakes collected from the wild.

References:

Bartlett, R. D., and Patricia Bartlett. *Snakes.* Hauppauge, NY: Barron's Educational Series, Inc., 1998.

Markel, Ronald G., and R. D. Bartlett. *Kingsnakes and Milk Snakes.* Hauppauge, NY: Barron's Educational Series, Inc., 1995.

Florida Kingsnake

Trade Name(s): Florida King, South Florida King(snake), Brook's King(snake), Brooksi.

Family & Scientific Name: Colubridae; *Lampropeltis getula floridana.*

Identifying Features: The scales of adult

Florida kingsnakes are best described as two-toned, with a light spot in each mahogany to chocolate-brown scale. Indistinct light crossbands are often obscured by the overall "speckled" appearance. The lip scales are barred in yellow and black. Hatchlings are more contrastingly colored and lack the light spot on each scale, a trait that develops with each successive shed. Many of the snakes sold as Florida kingsnakes are, in fact, intergrades between the true Florida kingsnake of south Florida and the eastern kingsnake that occurs to the north. The wide zone of intergradation forms a belt across much of peninsular Florida. These intergrades tend to be darker in overall coloration with more distinct cross-banding and degenerate lateral "chain" markings.

Similar Species: See accounts for Eastern kingsnake, blotched kingsnake, and desert kingsnake.

Range & Origin: Found in the oolitic limestone and sawgrass prairies of south Florida. Captive-bred and wild-caught specimens are routinely offered for sale.

Adult Size: 4–5 feet.

Life Span: 15–20 years.

Terrarium Size: A 20-gallon, long aquarium or similarly sized terrarium is recommended.

Terrarium Type: Moist prairie or woodland.

Social Structure: Solitary. Kingsnakes readily kill and eat other snakes.

Diet: Mice, rats, lizards, and frogs.

Potential Problems: Only the rare hatchling refuses nestling mice as its first meal. Internal parasites are especially common in wild-caught kingsnakes. Chronically damp quarters can rapidly lead to the development of blister disease.

References:

Markel, Ronald G., and R. D. Bartlett. *Kingsnakes and Milk Snakes.* Hauppauge, NY: Barron's Educational Series, Inc., 1995.

Bartlett, R. D., and Patricia Bartlett. *Snakes.* Hauppauge, NY: Barron's Educational Series, Inc., 1998.

Blotched Kingsnake

Trade Name(s):
Apalachicola Kingsnake, Apalachicola Lowlands Kingsnake, goini, Goin's Kingsnake.

Family & Scientific Name:
Colubridae; *Lampropeltis getula* ssp. (=*"goini"*).

Adult Size: To nearly 6 feet, most are 3–5 feet in length.

Life Span: 15–20 years.

Terrarium Size: A 20-gallon, long aquarium or similarly sized terrarium will do nicely for a single adult.

Terrarium Type: Humid woodland or pineland.

Identifying Features: A highly variable snake which may be blotched, banded, striped, or patternless. Background coloration is brown to mahogany with lighter markings. The most brightly-colored specimens may appear to be light snakes with thin dark stripes. Often, the darker background becomes speckled with light markings as the snake ages, producing an indistinct "washed-out" pattern.

Similar Species: See accounts for Florida kingsnake, desert kingsnake, and California kingsnake.

Range & Origin: Occurs in the Florida panhandle between the Apalachicola and Chipola Rivers. Due to the secretive nature of this species, few animals are collected from the wild.

Social Structure: Solitary. Kingsnakes are notorious snake-eaters.

Diet: Mice, rats, lizards, and frogs.

Potential Problems: Kingsnakes are particularly susceptible to blister disease if kept under excessively moist conditions. Provide adequate ventilation and an area that is completely dry to minimize the risk of skin infections.

References:

Markel, Ronald G., and R. D. Bartlett. *Kingsnakes and Milk Snakes.* Hauppauge, NY: Barron's Educational Series, Inc., 1995.

Bartlett, R. D., and Patricia Bartlett. *Snakes.* Hauppauge, NY: Barron's Educational Series, Inc., 1998.

Desert Kingsnake

Trade Name(s):
Sonoran
(Desert)
Kingsnake,
Desert
Grasslands
Kingsnake,
Splendida.
Family & Scientific Name:
Colubridae;
*Lampropeltis
getula splendida.*
**Identifying
Features:** A

Adult Size: To 4
feet.
Life Span:
15–20 years.
Terrarium Size:
A 20-gallon, long
aquarium or terrarium of similar
volume.
Terrarium Type:
Desert or arid
grassland.
Social Structure: Solitary.
Kingsnakes can

black to brown kingsnake with sides speckled in white, cream, or yellow. The dark back
is crossed at regular intervals by a series of
thin crossbars that link the speckled sides.
The overall appearance is that of a yellow-speckled snake with black ovals on its back.
Similar Species: See accounts for eastern
kingsnake, Florida kingsnake, and California
kingsnake.
Range & Origin: Found in desert and grass-lands from southern Texas west to south-eastern Arizona. Both wild-caught and
captive-born specimens are routinely
available.

and will eat other snakes.
Diet: Mice, rats, lizards, and frogs.
Potential Problems: While they are found in
dry habitats, kingsnakes often seek out
areas of high humidity, such as cattle tanks
and desert washes. Failure to provide a hide
area with adequate humidity can lead to difficulties shedding. Wild-caught kingsnakes
often harbor internal parasites.
References:
Markel, Ronald G., and R. D. Bartlett.
Kingsnakes and Milk Snakes. Hauppauge,
NY: Barron's Educational Series, Inc.,
1995.

California Kingsnake

Trade Name(s):
Cal King.
Family & Scientific Name:
Colubridae;
*Lampropeltis
getula californiae.*
**Identifying
Features:** Black
to brown with a
pattern of light
white, cream, or
yellow stripes,
bands, or an

aberrant combination of the two. Numerous
color and pattern "phases" are perpetuated
by captive breeding. The coveted "desert
phase" is dark black with pure white
bands.
Similar Species: See accounts for eastern
kingsnake and desert kingsnake.
Range & Origin: Baja Mexico, most of the
state of California, and parts of Oregon,
Nevada, Utah, and Arizona. This subspecies
is bred in huge numbers each year; a few
wild-caught animals are seen as well.
Adult Size: 3–4 feet, rarely larger.
Life Span: 15–20 years.

Terrarium Size:
A 20-gallon, long
aquarium or terrarium of similar
volume.
Terrarium Type:
Desert, arid
grassland, or
rocky hillside.
Social Structure: Solitary.
Kingsnakes are
confirmed
snake-eaters.
Diet: Mice, rats,
lizards, and frogs.
Potential Problems: Excessive humidity
may lead to pustular dermatitis (blister disease); inadequate humidity can cause difficulty shedding and retention of old
spectacles (eye-caps).

References:

Bartlett, R. D., and Patricia Bartlett. *Snakes.*
  Hauppauge, NY: Barron's Educational
  Series, Inc., 1998.
Markel, Ronald G., and R. D. Bartlett.
  Kingsnakes and Milk Snakes. Hauppauge,
  NY: Barron's Educational Series, Inc.,
  1995.

California Kingsnake, Albino

Trade Name(s): Albino Cal King, Lavender Cal King, Lavender Albino Cal King, Ruby-eye Albino Cal King.

Family & Scientific Name: Colubridae; *Lampropeltis getula californiae.*

Identifying Features: Albinos are opalescent white to pink with white, cream, or yellow markings and red eyes. Lavender "albinos" (inset) are ghostly purplish-gray with light stripes, bands, or a combination of both. The eyes are typically a deep, ruby red.

Similar Species: Albino California kingsnakes are not easily confused with other snakes.

Range & Origin: Baja Mexico, California, and adjacent Oregon, Nevada, Utah, and Arizona. While the founder stock of these captive strains were found in the wild, nearly all albinos are captive-bred.

Adult Size: 3–4 feet.

Life Span: 15–20 years.

Terrarium Size: 20-gallon, long aquarium or similar terrarium.

Terrarium Type: Desert, arid grassland, or rocky hillside.

Social Structure: Solitary. Kingsnakes are confirmed snake-eaters.

Diet: Mice and rats.

Potential Problems: There are few problems associated with this well-adapted snake.

References:

Markel, Ronald G., and R. D. Bartlett. *Kingsnakes and Milk Snakes.* Hauppauge, NY: Barron's Educational Series, Inc., 1995.

Bartlett, R. D., and Patricia Bartlett. *Snakes.* Hauppauge, NY: Barron's Educational Series, Inc., 1998.

Prairie Kingsnake

Trade Name(s): Prairie King.

Family & Scientific Name: Colubridae; *Lampropeltis calligaster calligaster.*

Identifying Features: A heavy-bodied kingsnake with light tan to dark olive ground color marked

with dorsal blotches of reddish-brown to chocolate. Lateral dots or blotches are evident slightly below and between dorsal blotches. A striped phase, consisting of two dark stripes running down the back just lateral to the spine, is also bred in fair numbers. Albinos (inset) are yellow to yellow-orange with peach to red-orange markings; they may be blotched or striped.

Similar Species: See accounts for corn snake, and great plains rat snake.

Range & Origin: Indiana to Nebraska and southward along the Mississippi valley to eastern Texas and western Louisiana. Both captive-bred and wild-caught specimens are available.

Adult Size: To 3½ feet.

Life Span: 15+ years.

Terrarium Size: A 20-gallon, long aquarium or similarly sized terrarium.

Terrarium Type: Field, prairie, or woodland.

Social Structure: Solitary; prairie kingsnakes are known to eat other snakes.

Diet: Mice, rats, lizards, and frogs.

Potential Problems: Excessive humidity may lead to skin infections. Hatchlings are small; if they are reluctant to feed on pink mice, try small lizards.

References:
Markel, Ronald G., and R. D. Bartlett. *Kingsnakes and Milk Snakes.* Hauppauge, NY: Barron's Educational Series, Inc., 1995.

Scarlet Kingsnake

Trade Name(s):
Scarlet King.
Family & Scientific Name:
Colubridae;
Lampropeltis triangulum elapsoides.
Identifying Features: A small, slender kingsnake (technically a milk snake) that is banded in brilliant red, yellow or white, and black. Both the red and yellow scales lack red tipping. The pointy nose is red.

Similar Species: See accounts for Arizona mountain kingsnake, red milk snake, Pueblan milk snake, Mexican milk snake, and Sinaloan milk snake.

Range & Origin: A snake of the well-drained pinelands of the southeastern Coastal plains from southern Virginia to extreme southeastern Mississippi.

Adult Size: Rarely exceeds 18–22 inches.
Life Span: 15+ years.
Terrarium Size: A 10-gallon aquarium or small terrarium is ideal for this small snake.

Terrarium Type: Sandy pine forest.
Social Structure: Solitary. The scarlet kingsnake will kill and eat other snakes.
Diet: Lizards and small mice.

Potential Problems: This small kingsnake can be difficult to feed. Hatchlings are truly tiny and frequently refuse mice entirely, preferring small skinks and other lizards. Scarlet kingsnakes are extraordinary escape artists; cages must have tight-fitting lids and be free of even tiny gaps.

References:
Markel, Ronald G., and R. D. Bartlett. *Kingsnakes and Milk Snakes.* Hauppauge, NY: Barron's Educational Series, Inc., 1995.
Bartlett, R. D., and Patricia Bartlett. *Snakes.* Hauppauge, NY: Barron's Educational Series, Inc., 1998.

Honduran Milk Snake

Trade Name(s): Honduran, Honduran Milk, Tangerine, Tangerine Dream.

Family & Scientific Name: Colubridae; *Lampropeltis triangulum hondurensis.*

Identifying Features: A relatively large tri-

or bicolored milk snake. The tricolored form is banded in cream or yellow, black, and red; of the three colors, the red bands are the widest. A wide dark eyeband extends over the top of the head. In the tangerine phase, the yellow bands are replaced by bands of rich orange. In the most spectacular examples (so-called "tangerine dreams"), the orange and red bands are of nearly the same hue. Variable amounts of black tipping may be present on the red scales in both phases. In recent years, albino, axanthic ("anerythristic"), and hypomelanistic strains have been propagated in some numbers.

Similar Species: See accounts for Arizona mountain kingsnake, scarlet kingsnake, red milk snake, Pueblan milk snake, and

Sinaloan milk snake.

Range & Origin: Nicaragua and Honduras. This species is primarily captive-bred, although occasional imports do appear on stock lists.

Adult Size: To 4 feet.

Life Span: 15+ years.

Terrarium Size: A 20-gallon, long aquarium or similar terrarium.

Terrarium Type: Forest or woodland.

Social Structure: Solitary.

Diet: Mice and rats.

Potential Problems: Problems are rare in this well-adapted species. Wild-caught snakes may harbor internal and external parasites.

References:

Markel, Ronald G., and R. D. Bartlett. *Kingsnakes and Milk Snakes.* Hauppauge, NY: Barron's Educational Series, Inc., 1995.

Bartlett, R. D., and Patricia Bartlett. *Snakes.* Hauppauge, NY: Barron's Educational Series, Inc., 1998.

Red Milk Snake

Trade Name(s):
Red Milk.
Family & Scientific Name:
Colubridae;
Lampropeltis triangulum syspila.
Identifying Features: A white, beige, or light gray snake with black-bordered orange to red saddles. On the most spectacular examples, the saddles are wide enough to be considered crossbands.

Terrarium Size:
A 10-gallon or larger aquarium comfortably houses an average-sized adult.
Terrarium Type:
Forest or grassland.
Social Structure: Solitary, known snake-eaters.
Diet: Small mice, lizards.

Similar Species: See accounts for scarlet kingsnake, Pueblan milk snake, and Mexican milk snake.
Range & Origin: Found in a broad band from western Kentucky to eastern Oklahoma, north to Minnesota and south to Mississippi.
Adult Size: 2½–3 feet.
Life Span: 15+ years.

Potential Problems: The red milk snake is among the hardiest of the North American milk snakes. While hatchlings are small, most are willing and able to consume newborn mice.
References:
Markel, Ronald G., and R. D. Bartlett.
    Kingsnakes and Milk Snakes. Hauppauge, NY: Barron's Educational Series, Inc., 1995.

Pueblan Milk Snake

Trade Name(s): Pueblan, Pueblan Milk, Campbell's Milk Snake, Sockhead.

Family & Scientific Name: Colubridae; *Lampropeltis triangulum campbelli.*

Identifying Features: Now one of the most

commonly bred milk snakes, the Pueblan milk was unknown to herpetology less than 20 years ago. This pretty tricolor is adorned with bands of red, black, and white that are all approximately equal in width. The snout is black, and the first white band behind is usually quite broad; selective breeding may widen it even more, giving rise to the term, "sockhead." The "apricot" phase occurs when the white bands are replaced with pale orange.

Similar Species: See accounts for Arizona mountain kingsnake, Honduran milk snake, red milk snake, and Sinaloan milk snake.

Range & Origin: Native to Puebla, Morelos, and Oxaca, Mexico. Restrictions on the exportation of Mexican wildlife necessitates that all specimens are captive-bred.

Adult Size: To about 3 feet.

Life Span: 15–20 years.

Terrarium Size: A 20-gallon, long aquarium or similar terrarium comfortably houses a single adult.

Terrarium Type: Semiarid grassland, savannah.

Social Structure: Milk snakes are known to be snake eaters; house them individually except for breeding.

Diet: Eats mice and rats. Hatchlings usually feed readily on rodents.

Potential Problems: Few problems are associated with this species. Some specimens, like many of the tricolor milk snakes, may be flighty and nervous when handled.

References:

Bartlett, R. D., and Patricia Bartlett. *Snakes.* Hauppauge, NY: Barron's Educational Series, Inc., 1998.

Markel, Ronald G., and R. D. Bartlett. *Kingsnakes and Milk Snakes.* Hauppauge, NY: Barron's Educational Series, Inc., 1995.

Mexican Milk Snake

Trade Name(s): Mexican Milk, Annulata.

Family & Scientific Name: Colubridae; *Lampropeltis triangulum annulata.*

Identifying Features: The head and snout of this tricolored milk snake are predominantly

black; a wide yellow or cream band crosses the neck. The red bands are approximately the same width as the black-yellow-black triads between them. All bands are interrupted by black midventrally. This is a slender milk snake with a somewhat pointy snout and indistinct neck.

Similar Species: See accounts for Arizona mountain kingsnake, scarlet kingsnake, red milk snake, Sinaloan milk snake, and Ruthven's kingsnake.

Range & Origin: Southwestern Texas and parts of northern Mexico. Most specimens are captive-bred.

Adult Size: 24–30 inches.

Life Span: 12–16 years is likely.

Terrarium Size: A 10-gallon aquarium is sufficient for smaller adults. A 20-gallon, long aquarium, or similar terrarium, is adequate for all specimens.

Terrarium Type: Semiarid grassland, rocky hillside.

Social Structure: Solitary. Milk snakes are confirmed snake eaters.

Diet: Eats mice, predominantly.

Potential Problems: Even snakes from arid areas require an area of increased relative humidity to permit normal shedding. The small hatchlings may prefer lizards as a first meal.

References:

Bartlett, R. D., and Patricia Bartlett. *Snakes.* Hauppauge, NY: Barron's Educational Series, Inc., 1998.

Markel, Ronald G., and R. D. Bartlett. *Kingsnakes and Milk Snakes.* Hauppauge, NY: Barron's Educational Series, Inc., 1995.

Sinaloan Milk Snake

Trade Name(s): Sinaloan Milk, Sinaloan.

Family & Scientific Name: Colubridae; *Lampropeltis triangulum sinaloae.*

Identifying Features: The 10–16 red rings on this sub-species are very wide and com-

pletely encircle the body. The intervening white to cream bands are bordered on both sides by black. The nose and head are black with the exception of white nasal scales.

Similar Species: See accounts for Arizona mountain kingsnake, Honduran milk snake, Pueblan milk snake, Mexican milk snake, and Ruthven's kingsnake.

Range & Origin: Found in the lowlands of Sinaloa and adjacent Sonora and Chihuahua, Mexico. All legal specimens are currently of captive lineage.

Adult Size: 4 feet.

Life Span: 15–20 years.

Terrarium Size: A 20-gallon, long aquarium or similar terrarium.

Terrarium Type: Semiarid grassland, savannah.

Social Structure: Solitary. Milk snakes are known to eat other snakes.

Diet: Mice and small rats are readily accepted, even by most hatchlings.

Potential Problems: The large hatchlings pose little problem in feeding. Like other tricolors, Sinaloan milks can be nervous and flighty when handled.

References:

Bartlett, R. D., and Patricia Bartlett. *Snakes.* Hauppauge, NY: Barron's Educational Series, Inc., 1998.

Markel, Ronald G., and R. D. Bartlett. *Kingsnakes and Milk Snakes.* Hauppauge, NY: Barron's Educational Series, Inc., 1995.

Ruthven's Kingsnake

Trade Name(s): Ruthven's King, Ruthveni, Queretaro Kingsnake.

Family & Scientific Name: Colubridae; *Lampropeltis ruthveni.*

Identifying Features: A member of the *mexicana* kingsnake complex, Ruthven's kingsnake more closely resembles a tricolor milk snake than the other *mexicana*. Bands of red, white, and black bordered with barely visible outlines of lime green. The red and white blend to a shade of tan ventrally. The broad head is black with variable areas of red or tan. Albino specimens are now common in captivity; they are white, yellow and red.

Similar Species: See accounts for Arizona mountain kingsnake, Honduran milk snake, Mexican milk snake, and Sinaloan milk snake.

Range & Origin: From the states of Jalisco, Queretaro, and Michoacan on Mexico's central plateau. The vast majority of specimens offered for sale are captive-bred.

Adult Size: 2½–3 feet.

Life Span: 15–18 years is expected.

Terrarium Size: A 20-gallon, long aquarium or similar terrarium is recommended.

Terrarium Type: Rocky woodland.

Social Structure: Solitary. May eat other snakes.

Diet: Eats mice and small rats.

Potential Problems: Improper cage humidity can lead to shedding difficulties (dysecdysis), skin infections, and respiratory problems. The hatchlings of this species usually accept nestling mice readily.

References:
Markel, Ronald G., and R. D. Bartlett. *Kingsnakes and Milk Snakes: A Complete Pet Owner's Manual.* Hauppauge, NY: Barron's Educational Series, Inc., 1995.

Corn Snake, Normal and Amelanistic

Trade Name(s): Corn, Red Rat Snake, Red Rat, Okeetee Corn. There are also innumerable trade names applied to the various genetic mutations produced in captivity.

Family & Scientific Name: Colubridae; *Elaphe guttata guttata.*

Identifying Features: A normal or wild-type corn snake is truly beautiful. The head is adorned with a distinctive spear point or "fleur-de-lis" marking. Ground color varies from orangish to gray, depending upon the snake's origin. Black-edged dorsal saddles and lateral saddles are some shade of rust-orange to red. The belly is a checkerboard of black and white. The name "Okeetee" implies that the specimen described is of particularly brilliant coloration with wide black borders around the dorsal saddles. This name comes from the region of South Carolina associated with snakes of this appearance. Amelanistic, or "red albino" corn snakes (inset), lack black pigment and are red, pink, and orange on white.

Similar Species: See accounts for prairie kingsnake, and great plains rat snake.

Range & Origin: A snake of the eastern seaboard states from the New Jersey pine barrens to the tip of the Florida keys and as far west as Kentucky and eastern Louisiana. Corn snakes are captive-bred by the tens of thousands each year, but wild-caught specimens of this popular species are available as well.

Adult Size: 3–5 feet.

Life Span: Record longevity for the species is nearly 22 years.

Terrarium Size: While a 20-gallon, long aquarium provides adequate floor space, this species is also a powerful climber and appreciates the vertical dimensions of a 30-gallon or larger aquarium.

Terrarium Type: Woodland or forest, with opportunities for climbing.

Social Structure: Pairs or trios may be housed safely together year-round.

Diet: Eats mice and rats.

Potential Problems: Wild-caught snakes should be evaluated for parasites by a qualified veterinarian. Hatchlings from some lines prefer lizards over nestling mice.

References:

Bartlett, R. D., and Patricia Bartlett. *Corn Snakes and Other Rat Snakes.* Hauppauge, NY: Barron's Educational Series, Inc., 1996.

Bartlett, R. D., and Patricia Bartlett. *Snakes.* Hauppauge, NY: Barron's Educational Series, Inc., 1998.

Corn Snake, Anerythristic and Snow

Trade Name(s): Corn, Anerythristic, Aneryth, Axanthic, Black Albino, Melanistic, Snow Corn, Snow.

Family & Scientific Name: Colubridae; *Elaphe guttata guttata.*

Identifying Features: Similar in pattern to the normal corn snake described previously. The anerythristic and snow mutations round out the four basic color morphs found in the corn snake. Anerythristic snakes lack red pigment; they are gray-brown to silver in coloration. Some show a suffusion of yellow on the neck and face. Others lack this coloration and are often described as "Type B" or "muted" anerythristics. Snow corns (inset) are both amelanistic *and* anerythristic. They are pearlescent white with white, pink, or yellow markings. Some specimens (green-blotched snows) have a distinctive lime-green hue to the dorsal saddles.

Similar Species: See accounts for prairie kingsnake, and great plains rat snake, which may be confused with anerythristic corns; snow corns are quite distinctive and should not easily be confused with other species.

Range & Origin: Anerythristic snakes may be found in the wild. Nearly 20 percent of some populations in southwest Florida may bear this coloration. The chance of the snow mutation occurring in the wild is probably less than one in a million. Both are bred in large numbers each year; occasional wild-caught anerythristic snakes are offered for sale.

Adult Size: 3–5 feet.

Life Span: Up to 22 years.

Terrarium Size: As described for normal and amelanistic corn snakes.

Terrarium Type: Woodland.

Social Structure: May be housed safely in pairs or trios throughout the year.

Diet: Eats mice and rats.

Potential Problems: If any snake species can be described as "domesticated," it would be the corn snake. Problems are rare with proper care. Wild-caught specimens should be checked for parasites.

References:

Bartlett, R. D., and Patricia Bartlett. *Corn Snakes and Other Rat Snakes.* Hauppauge, NY: Barron's Educational Series, Inc., 1996.

Bartlett, R. D., and Patricia Bartlett. *Snakes.* Hauppauge, NY: Barron's Educational Series, Inc., 1998.

Great Plains Rat Snake

Trade Name(s): Great Plains Rat, Emory's Rat Snake, Emory's Rat.

Family & Scientific Name: Colubridae; *Elaphe guttata emoryi.*

Identifying Features: Overall pattern is similar to that of the closely related corn snake. The spearpoint marking is present on the head, as are the dorsal and lateral blotches. The coloration of the great plains rat snake, by comparison, is drab. Background coloration is tan to gray-brown; markings are a darker shade of gray-brown or chocolate. The belly of most specimens bears the checkerboard markings of the corn snake.

Similar Species: See accounts for prairie kingsnake, and corn snake.

Range & Origin: From Missouri and Arkansas to Colorado and New Mexico; north to Nebraska from northern Mexico. An isolated population exists on the Colorado/Utah border. Captive breeding is limited; most specimens are wild-caught or captive-hatched from wild mothers.

Adult Size: 3–5 feet.

Life Span: 15–20 years.

Terrarium Size: A 20-gallon, long to 30-gallon, tall aquarium is appreciated, especially by larger specimens.

Terrarium Type: Woodland or grassland/savannah.

Social Structure: Pairs or trios may be housed together safely.

Diet: Eats mice and rats.

Potential Problems: Wild-caught specimens frequently harbor intestinal parasites and should be evaluated by a veterinarian. Few problems are associated with this hardy species.

References:

Bartlett, R. D., and Patricia Bartlett. *Snakes.* Hauppauge, NY: Barron's Educational Series, Inc., 1998.

Bartlett, R. D., and Patricia Bartlett. *Corn Snakes and Other Rat Snakes.* Hauppauge, NY: Barron's Educational Series, Inc., 1996.

Black Rat Snake, Normal and Albino

Trade Name(s): Black Rat, (positive) Red Albino Black Rat Snake, (negative) White Albino Black Rat Snake.

Family & Scientific Name: Colubridae; *Elaphe obsoleta obsoleta.*

Identifying Features: Hatchlings are

not black at all, but gray with bold black dorsal saddles. Adults lose the juvenile pattern for the most part. In some areas, colored skin between the black scales allows remnants of pattern to be visible in adults. Black rats from the western parts of their range may be black-blotched brown snakes. The throat and chin are white, even in adults. Albinos (inset) are pink or red on white, pink, strawberry, or orange. Overall color depends upon the presence or absence of tyrosinase, an enzyme required for pigment production. Tyrosinase positive snakes are redder than their tyrosinase negative counterparts.

Similar Species: See account for black pine snake. Hatchlings may be confused with those of the yellow rat snake, everglades rat snake, Texas rat snake, and Baird's rat snake.

Range & Origin: Massachusetts and New Hampshire to the Carolinas, and west to central Nebraska and Oklahoma. This popular species is bred in captivity and collected from the wild with roughly equal frequency.

Adult Size: The largest examples may reach 7 feet. Most are 4–5 feet in length.

Life Span: 15–20 years.

Terrarium Size: A 30-gallon, tall or larger aquarium, or large terrarium, is recommended for these climbing snakes.

Terrarium Type: Woodland with plenty of opportunities for climbing.

Social Structure: May be housed safely together in pairs or trios all year. Group housing requires larger cages in most cases.

Diet: Eats mice and rats.

Potential Problems: This species seems more sensitive than others to high relative humidity, which can cause skin infections (pustular dermatitis or blister disease). Active and strong, black rat snakes that are held in small cages often develop rostral abrasions from rubbing their nose along cage walls and tops. Wild snakes frequently harbor internal parasites.

References:

Bartlett, R. D., and Patricia Bartlett. *Snakes.* Hauppauge, NY: Barron's Educational Series, Inc., 1998.

Bartlett, R. D., and Patricia Bartlett. *Corn Snakes and Other Rat Snakes.* Hauppauge, NY: Barron's Educational Series, Inc., 1996.

Everglades Rat Snake

Trade Name(s): Everglades Rat, Rossalleni.

Family & Scientific Name: Colubridae; *Elaphe obsoleta rossalleni.*

Identifying Features: Hatchlings bear a muted pattern of gray blotches on a gray background; the

overall coloration often has a pinkish or orangish wash. Adults bear four indistinct dorsal and lateral stripes on a warm orange to rust-colored background. The eyes and tongue are red.

Similar Species: This species is deeper orange than the yellow rat snake. Hatchlings are lighter than those of the black rat snake, yellow rat snake, Texas rat snake, and Baird's rat snake.

Range & Origin: Once found from Florida's Kissimmee prairie, south to the sawgrass-covered Everglades, habitat destruction has made this subspecies rare in the wild. Wild-caught examples are sometimes offered for sale, but are almost uniformly inferior in color to those bred in captivity. Most specimens are captive-bred.

Adult Size: 5–7 feet.

Life Span: 15–20 years.

Terrarium Size: These climbers appreciate the vertical space of 30-gallon and larger aquariums and terraria.

Terrarium Type: Prairie or woodland.

Social Structure: Pairs and trios may be housed safely together year-round.

Diet: Eats mice and rats.

Potential Problems: While found in moist habitats in the wild, Everglades rat snakes are typically found in trees and shrubs, where they remain relatively dry. Avoid too much humidity, which can lead to skin infections. Rostral abrasions are common in this species, especially when housed in cages that are too small.

References:

Bartlett, R. D., and Patricia Bartlett. *Corn Snakes and Other Rat Snakes.* Hauppauge, NY: Barron's Educational Series, Inc., 1996.

Bartlett, R. D., and Patricia Bartlett. *Snakes.* Hauppauge, NY: Barron's Educational Series, Inc., 1998.

Texas Rat Snake, Normal and Leucistic

Trade Name(s): Texas Rat, Lindheimer's Rat (snake), Leucistic Rat (snake), White Texas Rat (snake).

Family & Scientific Name: Colubridae; *Elaphe obsoleta lindheimeri.*

Identifying Features: This race of the common, or North American, rat snake maintains its juvenile pattern throughout its life. The black-blotched hatchlings rapidly grow to adults bearing dark blotches on a beige, brown, yellowish, or gray background. The head is typically unmarked gray or charcoal. Leucistic specimens are stark patternless white with blue or blue-gray eyes. Albinism has been bred into some leucistic lines, giving rise to the so-called "red-eyed white (leucistic) Texas rat snakes."

Similar Species: Adults are distinctive; hatchlings may be confused with those of the black rat snake, yellow rat snake, Everglades rat snake, and Baird's rat snake.

Range & Origin: Southern Louisiana to central Texas. Intergrades with the black rat snake in parts of Oklahoma. Most normal Texas rat snakes are wild-caught. Normal-appearing hatchlings that carry the gene for leucism are seen with some regularity. Leucistic specimens are captive-bred.

Adult Size: 5–7 feet.

Life Span: 15–20 years.

Terrarium Size: A 30-gallon aquarium or similarly sized terrarium is recommended.

Terrarium Type: Woodland. The Texas rat snake appreciates the opportunity to climb.

Social Structure: May be housed safely in pairs or trios all year.

Diet: Eats mice and rats.

Potential Problems: There are few harmless snakes that could be described as more irascible. Texas rat snakes are typically of poor disposition and eager to bite. Many of the leucistic specimens offered are bug-eyed or pop-eyed, likely the result of inbreeding. Such specimens are often sold for less than market price; prices that appear too good to be true probably are. Wild-caught specimens frequently harbor intestinal parasites. Rostral abrasions are common in this powerful and active subspecies.

References:

Bartlett, R. D., and Patricia Bartlett. *Corn Snakes and Other Rat Snakes.* Hauppauge, NY: Barron's Educational Series, Inc., 1996.

Bartlett, R. D., and Patricia Bartlett. *Snakes.* Hauppauge, NY: Barron's Educational Series, Inc., 1998.

Baird's Rat Snake

Trade Name(s):
Baird's Rat, Bairdi. Breeders may also differentiate between animals originating from Texas and Mexico.

Family & Scientific Name:
Colubridae; *Elaphe bairdi.*

Identifying Features:
Hatchlings are gray with numerous thin dorsal saddles and lateral blotches. Adults are typically pearlescent gray, orange-brown, or burnt orange. The interstitial skin (the skin between the scales) may be suffused with orange, red, or salmon. Two indistinct lateral stripes are present, as are two dorsal stripes, which are often connected by the faded juvenile pattern. Mexican specimens are generally more brightly colored than those from Texas and have unmarked gray heads.

Similar Species: See accounts for Everglades rat snake, and Texas rat snake. Hatchlings superficially resemble those of the black rat snake, yellow rat snake, Everglades rat snake, and Texas rat snake.

Range & Origin: Found in southwestern Texas and in disjunct portions of northeastern

Mexico. Wild Texas specimens are sometimes seen on price-lists, but the majority of Baird's rat snakes are captive-born.

Adult Size: This relatively slender species grows to 3–5 feet.

Life Span: 15–20 years.

Terrarium Size: A 20-gallon, long aquarium, or similar terrarium, comfortably houses a single adult.

Terrarium Type: Rocky desert.

Social Structure: May be housed safely in pairs or trios.

Diet: Eats mice and rats.

Potential Problems: Native to arid regions, this snake requires an area of higher humidity to promote normal shedding. Generally hardy and even-tempered.

References:
Bartlett, R. D., and Patricia Bartlett. *Corn Snakes and Other Rat Snakes.* Hauppauge, NY: Barron's Educational Series, Inc., 1996.

Bartlett, R. D., and Patricia Bartlett. *Snakes.* Hauppauge, NY: Barron's Educational Series, Inc., 1998.

Trans Pecos Rat Snake

Trade Name(s): Trans Pecos Rat, Subocularis, Suboc.

Family & Scientific Name: Colubridae; *Bogertophis* (= *Elaphe*) *subocularis*.

Identifying Features: This is a slender, big-headed, and bug-eyed rat-

snake. A row of small scales (suboculars) separates the eye from the lip scales. Ground coloration ranges from sandy buff to straw yellow, or yellow-orange. A pair of dark, broken, dorsolateral stripes and dark dorsal saddles combine to form a pattern of H-shaped markings. A ladder pattern may be present on the neck, where the stripes tend to be continuous in most specimens. The blonde phase is typically brighter yellow in overall color and has small, faded, diamond-shaped dorsal blotches.

Similar Species: This species only superficially resembles the yellow rat snake.

Range & Origin: Southwestern Texas, south central New Mexico, and northeastern Mexico. Captive-born specimens far outnumber those collected from the wild.

Adult Size: 3–5 feet.

Life Span: 15–20 years.

Terrarium Size: A 20-gallon, long or larger aquarium or terrarium serves as adequate housing for a single adult.

Terrarium Type: Desert.

Social Structure: Pairs and trios may be housed safely together all year.

Diet: Eats mice and rats.

Potential Problems: Even desert snakes require an area of increased humidity to promote normal shedding. Wild-caught specimens frequently harbor intestinal parasites. Large hatchlings rarely refuse nestling or fuzzy mice.

References:

Bartlett, R. D., and Patricia Bartlett. *Corn Snakes and Other Rat Snakes.* Hauppauge, NY: Barron's Educational Series, Inc., 1996.

Asian Stripe-tailed Rat Snake

Trade Name(s): Beauty Snake.
Family & Scientific Name: Colubridae; *Elaphe taeniura* ssp.
Identifying Features: The varying subspecies of this Asian rat snake vary in pattern and coloration. All are fairly slender with

elongated heads. A busy pattern of dark blotches and crossbars predominates anteriorly before giving way to dark stripes on the caudal half of the body. Background coloration varies from cream to greenish-yellow. Most subspecies have a dark line passing through the eye from the snout to the angle of the jaw.
Similar Species: While the subtle differences between subspecies can be confounding, this beautiful snake is not easily confused with other species.
Range & Origin: Taiwan, China, Burma, and Thailand. Wild-caught, imported animals are very common; captive breeding is increasing on an annual basis.
Adult Size: 5–7 feet.
Life Span: 12–15 years.
Terrarium Size: A 30-gallon or larger aquarium should be turned on end to provide a

tall enclosure. similarly sized and larger vertically oriented terraria also work well.
Terrarium Type: Tropical forest with plenty of stout, non-resinous climbing branches.
Social Structure: May be housed safely in pairs or trios.
Diet: Eats mice, rats, and chicks. Some hatchlings may prefer lizards or tree frogs.
Potential Problems: Most imported Asian rat snakes are literally infested with parasites, both internal and external. Recent imports are frequently dehydrated. Acclimation to captivity should always begin with a full veterinary examination. Many wild-caught specimens are ill-tempered and ready to bite. Selecting a captive-bred hatchling will help minimize problems.
References:

Bartlett, R. D., and Patricia Bartlett. *Corn Snakes and Other Rat Snakes.* Hauppauge, NY: Barron's Educational Series, Inc., 1996.

Bartlett, R. D., and Patricia Bartlett. *Snakes.* Hauppauge, NY: Barron's Educational Series, Inc., 1998.

Bullsnake

Trade Name(s): Same.

Family & Scientific Name: Colubridae; *Pituophis catenifer sayi.*

Identifying Features: This snake is heavy bodied and small headed with an enlarged, triangular, rostral scale.

Dorsal scales are keeled. Yellow, cream, or buff with large black, brown, or reddish-brown dorsal blotches and a busy pattern of smaller lateral blotches. Dorsal blotches are usually darker toward the head and tail. Several color mutations, including an amelanistic strain, are perpetuated in captivity. Capable of producing a loud and imposing hiss.

Similar Species: See accounts for Sonoran gopher snake, Pacific gopher snake, Southern Baja gopher snake, and northern pine snake.

Range & Origin: Ranges widely through the Great Plains states, south to northern Mexico and north to southern Canada. Captive-bred in large numbers, wild-caught bullsnakes also are offered commonly.

Adult Size: At 6–8 feet, bullsnakes are among North America's largest serpents.

Life Span: 15–20 years.

Terrarium Size: 55-gallon aquariums and large terraria are needed to house this large species.

Terrarium Type: Grassland or woodland.

Social Structure: Large enclosures may be used to house a pair or trio all year.

Diet: Eats mice and rats. The largest specimens are capable of consuming young rabbits.

Potential Problems: Wild-caught bullsnakes can be aggressive, but usually become calm with gentle handling. Wild specimens should have a fecal analysis to identify intestinal parasites. Larger wild-caught specimens may be reluctant to feed on domestic rodents.

References:

Bartlett, R. D., and Patricia Bartlett. *Snakes.* Hauppauge, NY: Barron's Educational Series, Inc., 1998.

Sonoran Gopher Snake

Trade Name(s): Sonoran Gopher.

Family & Scientific Name: Colubridae; *Pituophis catenifer affinis.*

Identifying Features: This is a thick-bodied snake with a small head, enlarged rostral scale, and

keeled dorsal scales. Ground color is cream to straw-yellow with brown to reddish-brown dorsal blotches that darken toward the tail. A busy pattern of small blotches marks the sides. Albino specimens are commonly bred and offered for sale. May hiss loudly when aroused.

Similar Species: See accounts for bullsnake, Pacific gopher snake, Southern Baja gopher snake, and northern pine snake. Both wild-caught and captive-bred individuals may be found.

Range & Origin: Southern Colorado, Arizona, New Mexico, western Texas and southward into Mexico.

Adult Size: 4–5 feet.

Life Span: 15–20 years.

Terrarium Size: A 20-gallon, long aquarium or terrarium is recommended.

Terrarium Type: Desert or semiarid grassland.

Social Structure: Pairs and trios may be housed safely together if provided with adequate space.

Diet: Eats mice and rats.

Potential Problems: Wild-caught snakes may harbor intestinal parasites. Recent captives are often defensive and bite willingly. Most tame easily with gentle handling.

References:

Bartlett, R. D., and Patricia Bartlett. *Snakes.* Hauppauge, NY: Barron's Educational Series, Inc., 1998.

Pacific Gopher Snake

Trade Name(s): Pacific Gopher.
Family & Scientific Name: Colubridae; *Pituophis catenifer catenifer.*
Identifying Features: This snake is solidly built with a small head, enlarged rostral scale, and keeled dorsal scales.

This variable race is straw-yellow to buff with a pattern of dark dorsal blotches or dark longitudinal stripes. Dorsal blotches are small and numerous. Albinos of both patterns have been found and are bred in captivity. May hiss loudly when disturbed.
Similar Species: See accounts for bullsnake, Sonoran gopher snake, and Southern Baja gopher snake.
Range & Origin: Native to much of western Oregon and California. Captive-bred animals predominate, but occasional wild-caught specimens are also offered.
Adult Size: 4–5 feet.
Life Span: 15–20 years.
Terrarium Size: A 20-gallon, long aquarium or similar terrarium is recommended.
Terrarium Type: Scrub or grassland.
Social Structure: Adult pairs and trios may be housed safely together all year.
Diet: Eats mice and rats.
Potential Problems: Wild-caught specimens should be evaluated for internal and external parasites. Recent captives may be nervous or aggressive, but tame readily with gentle handling.
References:
Bartlett, R. D., and Patricia Bartlett. *Snakes.* Hauppauge, NY: Barron's Educational Series, Inc., 1998.

Southern Baja Gopher Snake

Trade Name(s): Southern Baja Gopher, Cape Gopher (snake).

Family & Scientific Name: Colubridae; *Pituophis catenifer vertebralis.*

Identifying Features: This snake is defined by tannish-orange to buff

anterolaterally, lighter yellow posteriolaterally, deep orange on the anterior dorsum fading to a lighter orange posteriorly. The head is generally a deep, unmarked orange. Dorsal blotches are darkest near the head and tail, with those of the midbody being a rich brown to maroon. The scales of species are less strongly keeled than other gopher snakes. Capable of hissing loudly when aroused.

Similar Species: See accounts for bullsnake, Sonoran gopher snake, Pacific gopher snake, and northern pine snake.

Range & Origin: La Paz, Baja California Sur and southward to the tip of the Baja peninsula. This species is available only as captive-bred specimens.

Adult Size: 4–5 feet.

Life Span: 15–20 years.

Terrarium Size: A 20-gallon, long aquarium or similar terrarium adequately houses a single adult.

Terrarium Type: Desert or scrub.

Social Structure: Adult pairs and trios may be housed safely together.

Diet: Eats mice and small rats.

Potential Problems: Captive breeding produces hardy animals that are relatively free of problems. Hatchlings may be nervous, but tame rapidly with gentle handling.

References:

Bartlett, R. D., and Patricia Bartlett. *Snakes.* Hauppauge, NY: Barron's Educational Series, Inc., 1998.

Northern Pine Snake

Trade Name(s):
Northern Pine,
Pine Snake.
Family & Scientific Name:
Colubridae;
*Pituophis
melanoleucus
melanoleucus.*
***Identifying
Features:*** This
is a large, stout-
bodied snake
with a well-
developed ros-

Adult Size:
5–7 feet.
Life Span:
15–20 years.
Terrarium Size:
Large terraria or
aquariums of 75
gallons or more
are necessary for
this impressive
species.
Terrarium Type:
Sandy woodland
or pine forest.
Social Struc-

tral scale and keeled dorsal scales.
Background varies from chalk-white to buff
or reddish-buff. Dorsal markings are black
to dark reddish brown. Animals with a reddish overcast are often marketed as "red
phase" northern pines.
Similar Species: See accounts for bullsnake and Florida pine snake.
Range & Origin: Distribution is spotty, but
includes portions of New Jersey to central
Kentucky southward to South Carolina and
Alabama. While the majority of specimens
are captive-bred, some states allow the
commercial collection and sale of wild
northern pines.

ture: Adult pairs or trios may be housed
safely together if adequate space is
provided.
Diet: Eats mice and rats.
Potential Problems: Wild-caught pine
snakes are generally irascible and can
deliver a painful bite. Most tame readily with
frequent, gentle handling. Wild-caught
snakes should be evaluated for internal and
external parasites. The large babies feed
readily on fuzzy or hopper mice.
References:
Bartlett, R. D., and Patricia Bartlett. *Snakes.*
   Hauppauge, NY: Barron's Educational
   Series, Inc., 1998.

Black Pine Snake

Trade Name(s):
Black Pine,
Loding's Pine
Snake, Lodingi.
Family & Scientific Name:
Colubridae;
Pituophis
melanoleucus
lodingi.
Identifying
Features: This
is a large, thick-
bodied snake
with an enlarged

rostral scale and keeled dorsal scales. The
background is dark brown to black, obscur-
ing the black dorsal blotches almost completely in the darkest (and most desired)
specimens. Hatchlings are more boldly patterned than adults. May hiss loudly when
disturbed.
Similar Species: See accounts for
Mexican black kingsnake and black
rat snake.
Range & Origin: Natural range is restricted
to a small area along the Florida-Alabama
state border. Protected in the wild, all speci-

mens offered for
sale should be of
captive origin.
Adult Size:
5–6 feet.
Life Span:
15–20 years.
Terrarium Size:
Large terraria
and 60-gallon
or larger
aquariums are
well-suited to
this large
species.

Terrarium Type: Sandy pineland.
Social Structure: Adult pairs or trios may
be housed safely together.
Diet: Eats mice and rats.
Potential Problems: Because of their cap-
tive origin, black pine snakes pose few
problems when maintained properly. Even
the most nervous of hatchlings tame readily
with handling.
References:
Bartlett, R. D., and Patricia Bartlett. *Snakes.*
 Hauppauge, NY: Barron's Educational
 Series, Inc., 1998.

Florida Pine Snake

Trade Name(s): Florida Pine, Southern Pine (snake).

Family & Scientific Name: Colubridae; *Pituophis melanoleucus mugitus.*

Identifying Features: A large snake with a well-developed rostral scale and keeled dorsal scales. Chalky-white, grayish, or buff background marked with brown, reddish-brown, or charcoal dorsal blotches. Blotches on the tail may approach brick red in some specimens. A patternless beige or tan phase exists as well. Hisses loudly when aroused.

Similar Species: See account for northern pine snake.

Range & Origin: Southeastern South Carolina, Georgia, and most of Florida. Protected throughout its range from commercial collection; captive-bred specimens are the rule.

Adult Size: 5–6 feet. With a record length of 90 inches, the Florida pine is the largest pine snake.

Life Span: 15–20 years.

Terrarium Size: 60-gallon or larger aquarium, or a similarly sized terrarium.

Terrarium Type: Sandy pineland or scrub.

Social Structure: Adult pairs or trios may be housed safely together if provided with adequate space.

Diet: Eats mice and rats.

Potential Problems: May be nervous and nippy at first, but tames readily with handling. Problems are rare if captive-bred hatchlings are maintained properly.

References:

Bartlett, R. D., and Patricia Bartlett. *Snakes.* Hauppauge, NY: Barron's Educational Series, Inc., 1998.

Red Coachwhip

Trade Name(s): Red Racer, Western Coachwhip.

Family & Scientific Name: Colubridae; *Masticophis flagellum testaceus.*

Identifying Features: This is a long, thin, smooth-scaled snake with prominent eyes. Reddish or pinkish above, often fading to a shade of tan toward the tail. Wide black, dark brown, or pink crossbands mark the neck and may be united or absent in some specimens. A dark phase is black above, pale below, and the dorsal coloration fades to salmon or red toward the tail.

Similar Species: Dark phase specimens may be confused with the black racer.

Range & Origin: Arizona, southern California, and southwestern Nevada. While most specimens are wild-caught, limited captive breeding does occur.

Adult Size: 6–9 feet.

Life Span: 8–12 years.

Terrarium Size: Truly huge enclosures are necessary for the well-being of this large, active species. Caging should be at least as long as the snake being kept inside. The width of the cage should allow the snake to turn around with ease.

Terrarium Type: Desert, grassland, or prairie.

Social Structure: Solitary, coachwhips are confirmed snake eaters.

Diet: Eats lizards, snakes, chicks, mice, and small rats.

Potential Problems: While among the calmest of the whipsnakes, recent captives are nervous and nippy. Some tame with frequent, gentle handling (gloves are recommended). Rostral abrasions are common as this active serpent searches its housing for an escape route. Parasites are almost inevitable, given this species' broad prey base. Ultraviolet light may be beneficial to this diurnal species.

References:

Mattison, Chris. *Keeping and Breeding Snakes.* London: Blandford Press, 1988.

Stebbins, Robert C. *Western Reptiles and Amphibians,* 2d ed. NY: Houghton Mifflin, 1985.

Natal Green Snake

Trade Name(s): African Green Snake.

Family & Scientific Name: Colubridae; *Philothamnus natalensis.*

Identifying Features: This is a slender snake with prominent eyes and keeled ventral and subcaudal scales. Uniformly bright green above and pale green below. Young specimens may have black crossbars on the neck.

Similar Species: See account for rough green snake.

Range & Origin: Found in portions of eastern South Africa, Zimbabwe, and Mozambique. Specimens in the pet trade are almost always wild-caught.

Adult Size: 2–3 feet.

Life Span: Unknown.

Terrarium Size: A vertically oriented terrarium, similar in dimensions to a 20-gallon, long aquarium, is recommended.

Terrarium Type: Woodland, forest, or shoreline.

Social Structure: This species is not known to eat snakes; may be housed in pairs or trios.

Diet: Eats frogs, lizards, occasionally fish.

Potential Problems: Generally heavily parasitized. Imports are often dehydrated and severely stressed from capture and transport. Successful acclimation to captivity requires a thorough veterinary examination.

References:

Branch, Bill. *Field Guide to Snakes and Other Reptiles of Southern Africa,* 2d ed. Cape Town, South Africa: Struik, 1994.

Short-nosed Parrot Snake

Trade Name(s): Parrot Snake.
Family & Scientific Name: Colubridae; Leptophis depressirostris.
Identifying Features: This snake has a tendency to indulge in widely opened mouth threat display. Mouth

interior is dark; enlarged rear teeth in the upper jaw. Snake is primarily leaf-green above with decidedly blue lips. Rather narrow, deep head; no elongated nose. Keels on paravertebral (and occasionally next lower) rows of body scales; no keels on tail scales.
Similar Species: Many green snakes in the pet trade look similar; the short-nosed parrot snake resembles the African green bush snake.
Range & Origin: Central America.
Adult Size: 4 feet.

Life Span: Unknown, but captive congenerics have lived for more than 7 years.
Terrarium Size: 40-gallon or larger.
Terrarium Type: Dry woodland or savanna.
Social Structure: Little is known about this snake, but it seems to do well in groups.
Diet: Lizards, frogs; a pink mouse may be accepted if scented with lizard. Use long forceps for feeding.
Potential Problems: This is a mildly venomous rear-fanged species. The efficacy of the venom on humans is unknown, but the venom overcomes lizards quickly. Avoid getting bitten.
References:
Savage, Jay M., and Jaime R. Villa. *Herpetofauna of Costa Rica.* Athens, Ohio: SSAR, 1986.

Rough Green Snake

Trade Name(s): Keeled Green Snake.

Family & Scientific Name: Colubridae; *Opheodrys aestivus.*

Identifying Features: A slender snake with keeled scales and prominent eyes. Olive to lime green above and cream to yellow below.

Similar Species: See account for Natal green snake.

Range & Origin: Found from New Jersey to Kansas and southward to the Gulf coast. Small populations also occur in northeastern Mexico. Most specimens in captivity are wild-caught or captive-hatched from eggs laid by wild females. Captive breeding has been accomplished, but is uncommon.

Adult Size: 2–3 feet.

Life Span: 3–5 years.

Terrarium Size: A 20-gallon, long aquarium tipped on end provides enough vertical space for a few adults.

Terrarium Type: Woodland or shoreline. Plenty of thin branches should be provided for climbing. Leafy plants will increase cage humidity and provide safe hiding spots.

Social Structure: A single male may live comfortably with 1–3 females if adequate cover and basking areas are provided.

Diet: Feed frequently, 3–4 times a week. Include gut-loaded or calcium-dusted crickets, moths, waxworms, and wild insects collected from pesticide-free areas.

Potential Problems: Attempting to keep this snake like a typical colubrid rapidly results in failure. Green snakes fare best with frequent feedings, and in naturalistic vivaria under conditions that one would associate with gecko or chameleon care. This species prefers to drink water droplets from leaves; therefore, the enclosure must be misted lightly with water on a daily basis. Inappropriate cage humidity or ventilation can lead to shedding difficulty and skin infections. Ultraviolet light is most likely important to the health of this diurnal snake.

References:

Bartlett, R. D., and Patricia Bartlett. *Snakes.* Hauppauge, NY: Barron's Educational Series, Inc., 1998.

Conant, Roger, and Joseph T. Collins. *Reptiles and Amphibians of Eastern/Central North America,* 3d ed. NY: Houghton Mifflin, 1991.

African Egg-eating Snake

Trade Name(s): Egg Eater, Rhombic Egg Eater, Common Egg Eater.

Family & Scientific Name: Colubridae; *Dasypeltis* spp.; *D. medici* is shown.

Identifying Features: This is a slender species with

heavily keeled scales and a small, rounded head. Dorsal coloration is gray to brown with a row of dark squarish blotches bordered on the sides by a series of dark, narrow bars.

Similar Species: Not easily confused with other species seen in the pet trade.

Range & Origin: Occurs naturally through much of the South African subcontinent. Most animals offered for sale are wild-caught imports.

Adult Size: Approximately 2 feet.

Life Span: Unknown.

Terrarium Size: A 10-gallon or larger aquarium or terrarium. Areas for climbing are appreciated but do not appear to be necessary.

Terrarium Type: Woodland or grassland. In the wild this species occupies a wide variety of habitats.

Social Structure: May be kept in pairs or trios.

Diet: Feeds exclusively on the eggs of birds, which are consumed whole. Once swallowed, the eggshell is broken by extensions of the neck vertebrae, and the egg crushed by the neck muscles. The empty shell is regurgitated. Wild snakes feed heavily during the nesting season in preparation for a long winter fast.

Potential Problems: Full-grown adults are capable of eating quail eggs, but may not recognize the scent of, or be able to engulf, poultry eggs found at most supermarkets. A supply of very small fresh hen or quail eggs is often necessary to meet the nutritional needs of this species. Feeding the young requires proportionately smaller eggs. A trio of zebra finches provides a steady supply of small eggs.

References:

Branch, Bill. *Field Guide to Snakes and Other Reptiles of Southern Africa,* 2d ed. Cape Town, South Africa: Struik, 1994.

Mattison, Chris. *Keeping and Breeding Snakes.* London: Blandford Press, 1988.

African House Snake

Trade Name(s): Brown House Snake, House Snake.

Family & Scientific Name: Colubridae; *Lamprophis fuliginosus.*

Identifying Features: This small colubrid has elliptical pupils and a light stripe running through the eye from the snout to the neck. A second stripe runs from the rear of the eye to the angle of the jaw. House snakes are variable, but uniform in color, ranging from black to brown, olive, terracotta, chocolate, or golden brown. The belly is opalescent white to pale yellow.

Similar Species: Few small colubrids found in captivity have elliptical pupils.

Range & Origin: Found throughout most of the South African subcontinent. The vast majority of the specimens offered for sale is captive-bred in origin.

Adult Size: 2–3½ feet. Males are considerably smaller and lighter than females.

Life Span: 12–15 years.

Terrarium Size: A 20-gallon, long aquarium,

or similar terrarium, comfortably houses a pair of adults.

Terrarium Type: Woodland or savannah. These snakes are found in varied habitats in the wild and apparently tolerate urban conditions well.

Social Structure: Adult pairs and trios may be housed safely together.

Diet: Eats mice.

Potential Problems: Few problems are associated with this species, considered to be among the best snakes for beginners. House snakes breed throughout the year, and breeding females should be watched closely to ensure that they maintain good body condition. Recent imports may be nervous and nippy.

References:

Bartlett, R. D., and Patricia Bartlett. *Snakes.* Hauppauge, NY: Barron's Educational Series, Inc., 1998.

Branch, Bill. *Field Guide to Snakes and Other Reptiles of Southern Africa,* 2d ed. Cape Town, South Africa: Struik, 1994.

Western Hognosed Snake

Trade Name(s): Western Hognose, Plains Hognose (snake), Mexican Hognose (snake), Hognose, Plains Hog, Western Hog, Mexican Hog.

Family & Scientific Name: Colubridae; *Heterodon nasicus* ssp.

Life Span: 15–20 years.

Terrarium Size: A 20-gallon, long aquarium, or similar terrarium, comfortably houses a single adult female. Males may be kept in smaller quarters.

Terrarium Type: Desert or grassland. This species likes to burrow and should be provided with a suitable substrate to allow this natural behavior.

Identifying Features: A stout-bodied snake with heavily keeled scales and an upturned rostral. Ground color may be yellow, brown, or reddish brown with a series of small, dark, rectangular dorsal blotches and round lateral blotches. A dark mask runs through each eye and across the snout. The belly is darkly pigmented. The three subspecies are all similar in color and pattern.

Similar Species: The upturned snout differentiates the plains hognose from all other commonly offered species.

Range & Origin: Collectively, the subspecies range in a wide north-south band through the Great Plains states from southern Saskatchewan and Alberta, Canada into Mexico. While wild-caught specimens are still offered, captive-bred specimens are extremely common.

Adult Size: 2–4 feet. Females are considerably larger than males, which usually do not exceed 18–22 inches.

Social Structure: Adult pairs or trios may be housed together all year.

Diet: Eats mice. Some hatchlings prefer nestling mice scented with lizards or toads.

Potential Problems: Hognose snakes have been included in the subfamily Xenodontinae—the odd-toothed snakes. They have enlarged rear teeth and a primitive venom apparatus. There is currently much debate as to whether these "harmless" snakes are truly harmless. While hognose snakes are, as a rule, very docile, some specimens display aggressive feeding behaviors and should be watched carefully to prevent an accidental bite.

References:
Bartlett, R. D., and Patricia Bartlett. *Snakes.* Hauppauge, NY: Barron's Educational Series, Inc., 1998.

Eastern Garter Snake

Trade Name(s): Eastern Garter, Common Garter.

Family & Scientific Name: Colubridae; *Thamnophis sirtalis sirtalis.*

Identifying Features: This small colubrid has strongly keeled scales. Typically, it is a dark, blackish snake patterned with three yellow, longitudinal stripes. Background color may range from olive to tan, and the stripes may vary from tan to bluish, depending upon origin and habitat. In some populations, stripes are poorly defined and replaced by a checkerboard pattern. In the red-sided garter snake (*T. sirtalis parietalis,* inset), the dark background color between the dorsal and lateral stripes is broken by vertical bars of orange or red.

Similar Species: See accounts for checkered garter snake, black-necked garter snake, and ribbon snakes.

Range & Origin: Collectively, the two subspecies are found throughout most of the eastern and central United States.

Adult Size: 2–4 feet.

Life Span: 12–15 years.

Terrarium Size: A 20-gallon, long aquarium, or similar terrarium, is recommended.

Terrarium Type: Woodland, shoreline, or prairie. A large water bowl is essential for soaking.

Social Structure: Adult pairs and trios may be housed safely together.

Diet: Frogs, toads, fish, earthworms, and nestling and fuzzy mice are all accepted. Fish fillets, cut into strips and supplemented with calcium and a multivitamin containing thiamin may also be fed. Feed frequently, 2–3 times a week.

Potential Problems: Mice usually must be scented with ectothermic prey to induce feeding in this species. Garter snakes are active, have high metabolic rates, and feed (and therefore void feces) frequently. A large water bowl should be provided, as this species likes to soak. The cage, however, must dry rapidly. Elevated humidity or poor ventilation will lead to pustular dermatitis (blister disease). Intestinal parasites are common in wild-caught snakes that feed on ectothermic prey. Wild garter snakes frequently bite, defecate, and expel foul-smelling musk when restrained or frightened. Most become tame with gentle handling.

References:

Bartlett, R. D., and Patricia Bartlett. *Snakes.* Hauppauge, NY: Barron's Educational Series, Inc., 1998.

Mattison, Chris. *Keeping and Breeding Snakes.* London: Blandford Press, 1988.

Checkered Garter Snake

Trade Name(s): Checkered Garter, Marcy's Garter (snake), Marcianus.

Family & Scientific Name: Colubridae; *Thamnophis marcianus marcianus.*

Identifying Features: This snake has small colubrid with strongly keeled scales. The green to brown background color is marked with a checkerboard of dark squares, which often invades the mid-dorsal and lateral stripes. A light crescent or triangle marks each side of the head behind the jaw. Amelanistic albinos (inset) are bred in fair numbers. Lacking black pigment, they are pink, white, and yellow.

Similar Species: See accounts for eastern garter snake, black-necked garter snake, and ribbon snakes.

Range & Origin: Most of central and western Texas, portions of New Mexico, Arizona, and extreme southeastern California. Both wild-caught and captive-bred specimens are available; this is the most commonly bred garter snake in American collections.

Adult Size: 2–4 feet.

Life Span: 12–15 years.

Terrarium Size: A 20-gallon, long aquarium or similar terrarium is ideal.

Terrarium Type: Woodland, grassland, or shoreline.

Social Structure: Adult pairs or trios may be housed safely together.

Diet: This species more readily accepts mice than other garter snakes. Frogs, toads, fish, and earthworms are also accepted.

Potential Problems: Garter snakes are active, have high metabolic rates, and feed (and therefore void feces) frequently. A large water bowl should be provided, as garter snakes like to soak. The cage must not remain wet, or pustular dermatitis (blister disease) may occur. Wild-caught specimens should have a fecal analysis performed to look for intestinal parasites. Wild garter snakes frequently bite, defecate, and expel malodorous musk when restrained or frightened. Patience and gentle handling usually are all that are necessary to tame most specimens.

References:

Bartlett, R. D., and Patricia Bartlett. *Snakes.* Hauppauge, NY: Barron's Educational Series, Inc., 1998.

Conant, Roger, and Joseph T. Collins. *Reptiles and Amphibians of Eastern/Central North America,* 3d ed. NY: Houghton Mifflin, 1991.

Black-necked Garter Snake

Trade Name(s): Black-necked Garter, Black-neck Garter (snake).

Family & Scientific Name: Colubridae; *Thamnophis cyrtopsis* ssp.

Identifying Features: A small colubrid with strongly keeled scales.

Mid-dorsal stripe is yellow to orange; lateral stripes are yellowish, cream, or tan. A pair of large black blotches, separated by the dorsal stripe, adorn the neck. The darker ground color is marked dorsolaterally with a checkerboard pattern of small dark squares.

Similar Species: See accounts for eastern garter snake, checkered garter snake, and ribbon snakes.

Range & Origin: Found throughout much of western Texas, portions of New Mexico and Arizona, and northern Mexico. Most specimens are wild-caught, but some captive breeding does occur.

Adult Size: 2–3 feet.

Life Span: 12–15 years.

Terrarium Size: A 20-gallon, long aquarium, or similar terrarium, comfortably houses an adult or two.

Terrarium Type: Grassland, prairie, or shoreline.

Social Structure: Adult pairs and trios may be housed safely together all year.

Diet: Eats frogs, toads, fish, and earthworms 2–3 times a week. Fish fillets, cut into strips and supplemented with calcium and a multivitamin containing thiamin, may also be fed. Scented nestling and fuzzy mice also may be taken by some specimens.

Potential Problems: Garter snakes are active snakes with high metabolic rates; they feed (and therefore void feces) frequently. A large water bowl should be provided, as this species likes to soak. The cage, however, must not remain wet. Elevated humidity or poor ventilation will lead to pustular dermatitis (blister disease). Wild-caught specimens should be evaluated for the presence of intestinal parasites. Wild garter snakes may bite, defecate, or expel the contents of their musk glands when frightened or restrained. Most specimens tame with gentle handling.

References:

Bartlett, R. D., and Patricia Bartlett. *Snakes.* Hauppauge, NY: Barron's Educational Series, Inc., 1998.

Mattison, Chris. *Keeping and Breeding Snakes.* London: Blandford Press, 1988.

Ribbon Snakes

Trade Name(s): Eastern Ribbon (snake), Western Ribbon (snake); each species contains four subspecies.

Family & Scientific Name: Colubridae; *Thamnophis sauritis* ssp. and *T. proximus* ssp.

Identifying Features: All

ribbon snakes are slender and have strongly keeled scales and prominent eyes. With one possible exception, all have three precisely delineated light stripes on a dark background; the dorsal stripe of the peninsula ribbon snake (*T. sauritis sackenii*) is sometimes reduced or absent. Both species have a light rectangular spot in front of each eye.

Similar Species: See account for eastern garter snake.

Range & Origin: The two species collectively range from west Texas and Nebraska, east to the coast. Ribbon snakes are absent from the northern parts of the Great Lakes states and much of Appalachia. Rarely bred in captivity; most specimens in the pet trade are wild-caught.

Adult Size: 2–3 feet.

Life Span: 8–12 years.

Terrarium Size: A 20-gallon, long aquarium, or similar terrarium, comfortably houses one to three adults.

Terrarium Type: Woodland, prairie, or

shoreline. Ribbon snakes climb if given the opportunity.

Social Structure: Adult pairs or trios may be housed safely together.

Diet: Frogs, toads, fish, and earthworms; scented nestling mice may be consumed by some specimens. Fish fillets, cut into strips and supplemented with calcium and a multivitamin containing thiamin, may also be fed. Feed 2–3 times a week.

Potential Problems: Like garter snakes, ribbon snakes are active and have high metabolic rates. Frequent feeding and frequent defecation lead to increased maintenance time when compared to other colubrids. While they show strong aquatic proclivities, ribbon snakes do not tolerate cages that are chronically wet. Blister disease is common when cage humidity is excessive. Wild-caught snakes that feed on ectothermic prey commonly harbor intestinal parasites.

References:

Bartlett, R. D., and Patricia Bartlett. *Snakes.* Hauppauge, NY: Barron's Educational Series, Inc., 1998.

Conant, Roger, and Joseph T. Collins. *Reptiles and Amphibians of Eastern/Central North America,* 3d ed. NY: Houghton Mifflin, 1991.

Water Snakes

Trade Name(s): Florida Water Snake (pictured), Mangrove Water Snake (inset); nine species and numerous subspecies of water snakes occur in North America.

Family & Scientific Name: Colubridae; *Nerodia* spp.

Identifying Features: As a general rule, water snakes are relatively large, stout-bodied snakes with strongly keeled scales. Generally clad in dull browns, grays, and greens, water snakes may be patternless, banded, blotched, saddled, or striped, depending upon the species.

Similar Species: Water snakes belong to the same subfamily (Natricinae) as garter snakes, which they only superficially resemble.

Range & Origin: The various species of water snakes occur naturally over most of the central and eastern United States and into parts of adjacent Canada and Mexico. Most specimens offered for sale are collected from the wild.

Adult Size: 2–5 feet depending upon species.

Life Span: 10–15 years.

Terrarium Size: A 20-gallon, long aquarium, or similar size terrarium, may be used to house most specimens.

Terrarium Type: Woodland or shoreline. A large water bowl should be provided for soaking.

Social Structure: Adult pairs and trios may be housed safely together.

Diet: Eats frogs and fish predominantly. Fish fillets cut into strips and supplemented with calcium and a multivitamin containing thiamin may also be fed.

Potential Problems: Like garter snakes, water snakes are active, have high metabolic rates, and feed (and therefore void feces) frequently. A large water bowl should be provided, as water snakes like to soak. The cage, however, must dry rapidly. Elevated humidity or poor ventilation will lead to pustular dermatitis (blister disease). Wild-caught snakes that feed on ectothermic prey often harbor intestinal parasites. Most species of water snake are nervous and irritable; some bite ferociously.

References:

Conant, Roger, and Joseph T. Collins. *Reptiles and Amphibians of Eastern/Central North America,* 3d ed. NY: Houghton Mifflin, 1991.

Mattison, Chris. *Keeping and Breeding Snakes.* London: Blandford Press, 1988.

Lizards

Lizards are second only to snakes in hobbyist popularity. Therefore, more than a dozen lizard families appear in this section. Among these are the Old World agamids, true chameleons, plated lizards and girdle-tails, monitors, and lacertids; the primarily New World iguanians; and the skinks, eyelidded geckos, true geckos, and anguids that occur widely in both Old and New Worlds.

Some agamids and iguanids are specialist feeders on ants and are difficult to keep. Green iguanas are herbivores, but most lizards are either omnivorous (spiny-tailed lizards, spiny-tailed iguanas) or insectivorous, and when provided with a healthy diet, vitamin-mineral (D_3 and calcium are especially important) supplements, and full spectrum lighting (the latter is not necessary for nocturnal species), are easily kept and very interesting. Depending on the species, lizards may be arboreal (chameleons, anoles, tree dragons), rock dwellers (spiny lizards, many geckos, girdle-tailed lizards), rainforest dwellers (green iguanas), desert inhabitants (spiny-tailed lizards, some skinks), water edge species (basilisks, water dragons), or burrowers (sandfish).

Some adult iguanas and monitors may become huge (6-feet plus) and difficult to house. Conversely, some geckos may top out at less than two inches. Most pet trade species are between these extremes. Be sure that your cages are the right size.

Many lizards change color. Most have well developed functional legs but some are legless.

The males of most lizards are very territorial, and once acclimated it is not usually possible to keep more than a single male per enclosure. Females are usually far less antagonistic, but the females of some skinks may become very aggressive prior to parturition. It is usually possible to keep one male and up to several females of most species communally.

For lizards to thrive as captives, they must be provided with rather naturalistic conditions (lighting, cage humidity, perches, or a medium for burrowing, and temperature gradients).

Some species are extensively farmed in the countries to which they are indigenous for the pet trade. Others are captive bred by hobbyists in immense numbers. However, most lizards of most species are collected from the wild.

Fresh drinking water is needed by most lizards. Many species will lap their water from a drinking bowl, but some are adapted to lapping pendulous water droplets from leaves. Be certain that the needs of your captives are met.

Mali Spiny-tailed Agama

Trade Name(s): Mali Uromastyx, (Mali) Uro, Mali Dabb Lizard, Mali Spiny-tailed Lizard, Maliensis.

Family & Scientific Name: Agamidae; *Uromastyx maliensis.*

Identifying Features: This is a robust lizard with a thick, short tail covered with whorls of enlarged, spiny scales. The blunt snout is rounded. This species is sexually dimorphic. Males have charcoal to black heads, limbs, and tails; the back is brilliantly marked with numerous irregular yellow dots and ocelli. Females are more subdued, being drab gray to brown with small, light ocelli arranged in parallel transverse rows on the neck and body.

Similar Species: See account for Moroccan spiny-tailed agama.

Range & Origin: Occurs naturally in northern Mali and extreme southwestern Algeria. Wild-caught specimens are readily available; captive breeding of this species is in its infancy at this time.

Adult Size: 10–14 inches.

Life Span: Unknown, probably longer than 12 years.

Terrarium Size: Single animals may be kept in 60-gallon or larger aquariums and similar terraria. A 4 × 2 × 2-foot area is recommended for small breeding groups.

Terrarium Type: Desert. Place rocks on tank

bottom so this burrower is not crushed as it tunnels through its substrate.

Social Structure: One male may be housed comfortably with 1 to 3 females all year.

Diet: This herbivore eats grasses, greens, and seeds in the wild. Dried lentils and fresh and dried peas are relished. Alfalfa and birdseed are also good.

Potential Problems: Recent imports are under enormous stress and are often dehydrated and infested with intestinal parasites. New acquisitions should be evaluated by a qualified veterinarian, and strict quarantine procedures should be followed during acclimation. Ultraviolet light is necessary for formation of vitamin D_3 and normal calcium metabolism. Under- or over-supplementation of calcium and/or vitamin D_3 can lead to metabolic bone disease and calcification of soft tissues. Feeding insects, and other high proteins of animal origin, may predispose spiny-tailed lizards to gout.

References:

Bartlett, R. D., and Patricia Bartlett. *Lizard Care from A to Z.* Hauppauge, NY: Barron's Educational Series, Inc., 1997.

Gray, Randall L., and Mark Walsh. "Unearthing Uromastyx: the Newly-Described Mali Spiny-tailed Lizard." *Reptiles* 6(2) (Feb. 1998): 40–43.

Moroccan Spiny-tailed Agama

Trade Name(s): Moroccan Uromastyx, Moroccan Uro, Moroccan Dabb Lizard, Acanthinurus.

Family & Scientific Name: Agamidae; *Uromastyx acanthinurus.*

Identifying Features: A

robust, stout-bodied lizard with a blunt nose and a thick tail adorned with whorls of spiny scales. The colors of males and females are similar and intensify with age. Red, orange, yellow, lime green, or a combination of these colors dapple the head, limbs, body, and tail. A busy reticular pattern of the darker background color interrupts the brilliant dorsal coloration.

Similar Species: See account for Mali spiny-tailed agama.

Range & Origin: Found throughout much of northern Africa; the colorful specimens seen in herpetoculture originate from Morocco, Algeria, Tunisia, and Mauritania. Wild-caught examples are more common than captive-bred offspring.

Adult Size: 15–17 inches.

Life Span: To approximately 20 years.

Terrarium Size: A 60-gallon or larger aquarium, or similar terrarium, is recommended for single animals. Pairs and small breeding groups require a cage that measures at least $4 \times 2 \times 2$ feet.

Terrarium Type: Desert. Place rocks on tank bottom so this burrower is not crushed as it tunnels through its substrate.

Social Structure: A male may be kept with one to three females all year.

Diet: Eats greens, grasses, hays, alfalfa, dried lentils, dried and fresh peas, birdseed.

Potential Problems: Recent imports are frequently stressed, dehydrated and infested with intestinal parasites. New acquisitions should be evaluated by a qualified herp veterinarian, and strict quarantine procedures should be followed during acclimation. Ultraviolet light is necessary for formation of vitamin D_3 and normal calcium metabolism. Under- or over-supplementation of calcium and/or vitamin D_3 can lead to problems such as metabolic bone disease and calcification of soft tissues. Feeding insects, and other foods high in proteins of animal origin, may predispose spiny-tailed lizards to gout.

References:

Bartlett, R. D., and Patricia Bartlett. *Lizard Care from A to Z.* Hauppauge, NY: Barron's Educational Series, Inc., 1997.

Gray, Randall L. "The Natural History, Husbandry, and Captive Propagation of the Moroccan Spiny-tailed Lizard, *Uromastyx acanthinurus.*" *The Vivarium* 10(1) (1998): 35–43.

Bearded Dragon

Trade Name(s):
Inland Bearded Dragon, Central Bearded Dragon, Beardie.

Family & Scientific Name: Agamidae; *Pogona vitticeps*.

Identifying Features: This is a heavy bodied lizard with a broad triangular head. Small spinose scales form a crown across the back of the head and a lateral fringe along each side of the body. A pair of dark shoulder pads is visible behind the head at the base of each forelimb. The gular beard, for which the species is named, is composed of large, conical chin scales. Dorsal coloration is tan to yellow or terra-cotta red. The dorsal pattern consists of irregular blotches arranged in two roughly parallel rows; these blotches may fuse, forming two wide stripes. The amount of pattern and overall color depends upon the individual's temperature and state of arousal. Numerous color variations are now bred in fair numbers.

Similar Species: See accounts for frilled dragon, brown water dragon, and horned lizards.

Range & Origin: The central deserts of Australia. All specimens must be of captive-bred origin.

Adult Size: 16–22 inches.

Life Span: 8–10 years.

Terrarium Size: A single adult or adult pair can be housed in a 75-gallon or larger aquarium or terrarium. Larger cages are recommended to facilitate the formation of a temperature gradient and to promote natural behaviors.

Terrarium Type: Desert or savannah.

Social Structure: Bearded dragons do well in small groups of one male and a few females. Dominance hierarchies form rapidly in captive situations.

Diet: Eats greens, vegetables, and insects. Commercial foods should be used sparingly as a part of the complete diet.

Potential Problems: These lizards are susceptible to metabolic bone disease, especially when dietary calcium and vitamin D_3, or ultraviolet light levels, are inadequate. Veterinary advice should be sought if signs of weakness, lethargy, tremors, swollen limbs, or soft jaws are observed. Juveniles feed aggressively and may bite each other if food supply is limited or if crowded conditions exist. Adults, especially males, may fight to establish their place in the dominance hierarchy.

References:

Bartlett, R. D., and Patricia Bartlett. *Lizard Care from A to Z.* Hauppauge, NY: Barron's Educational Series, Inc., 1997.

Frilled Lizard

Trade Name(s): Frilled Dragon, Frilly, Chlamydosaurus.

Family & Scientific Name: Agamidae; *Chlamydosaurus kingii.*

Identifying Features: This is a large, slender bodied lizard that is nearly two-thirds tail. The dark frill lies folded against the neck at most times, only to be extended in periods of alarm. Dorsal coloration is gray to brown with a network of darker markings that give the overall appearance of tree bark.

Similar Species: See accounts for bearded dragon, brown water dragon, and green water dragon.

Range & Origin: Northern Australia and Papua New Guinea. Wild-caught specimens originate from New Guinea. Captive-bred hatchlings may be of Australian or New Guinean descent.

Adult Size: 24–32 inches.

Life Span: 8–12 years.

Terrarium Size: A large terrarium with moderate vertical dimensions is preferred by this climbing species. Turn a 60-gallon or larger aquarium on its short end to provide the height necessary for a single adult. Pairs require 100-gallon and larger aquariums or terraria.

Terrarium Type: Woodland.

Social Structure: An adult male may be housed comfortably with a female or two.

Diet: Insects and occasional nestling mice.

Potential Problems: Dehydration may occur if this species is not misted with drinking water daily. Metabolic bone disease can be a problem if dietary and ultraviolet light requirements are not met. This active species will rapidly develop rostral abrasions if confined in too small an enclosure. Wild-caught specimens frequently harbor intestinal parasites and should be evaluated by a veterinarian as a part of the acclimation process.

References:

Bartlett, R. D., and Patricia Bartlett. *Lizard Care from A to Z.* Hauppauge, NY: Barron's Educational Series, Inc., 1997.

Green Water Dragon

Trade Name(s): Water Dragon, Chinese Water Dragon, Asian (green) Water Dragon.

Family & Scientific Name: Agamidae; *Physignathus cocincinus.*

Identifying Features: This is a robust lizard that is some

shade of green above. A well-defined vertebral crest extends from the nape to the tail. Light body bands may be present; dark tail bands are prominent in most specimens.

Similar Species: See accounts for frilled lizard, brown water dragon, and green iguana.

Range & Origin: Found throughout much of southeast Asia. Both wild-caught and captive-born examples may be found.

Adult Size: 24–30 inches.

Life Span: 12–15 years.

Terrarium Size: Large enclosures are recommended for this active species. Provide the largest cage that space and finances will permit. Terraria with a capacity of less than 75 gallons for a single adult are discouraged.

Terrarium Type: Tropical forest or river's edge.

Social Structure: Best kept singly or in a pair or trio.

Diet: Eats insects, fish, and earthworms. Some specimens eat chopped fruits, greens, and mixed vegetables. Feed mice sparingly to avoid fat deposits in the eye.

Potential Problems: The vast majority of all captive water dragons show lasting signs of rostral abrasions caused by incessant rubbing of their nose in an effort to escape their cage. Providing adequate space, climbing, and hiding areas can minimize the risk of cage trauma. Metabolic bone disease is fairly common, especially in the rapidly growing juveniles. Calcium, vitamin D_3, and ultraviolet light are essential parts of this species' care. Wild-caught adults may have difficulty adjusting to captivity and be difficult to tame; it is best to begin with a captive-bred hatchling or imported juvenile.

References:

Bartlett, R. D., and Patricia Bartlett. *Lizard Care from A to Z.* Hauppauge, NY: Barron's Educational Series, Inc., 1997.

Bartlett, R. D., and Patricia Bartlett. *Anoles, Basilisks, and Water Dragons.* Hauppauge, NY: Barron's Educational Series, Inc., 1997.

Brown Water Dragon

Trade Name(s):
Australian Water Dragon, Lesueur's Water Dragon.

Family & Scientific Name:
Agamidae; *Physignathus lesueurii.*

Identifying Features: This is a large, robust lizard with a well-

adult. Vertical, as well as horizontal, space is needed.

Terrarium Type: Temperate forest.

Social Structure: A female or two may be housed safely with a single male.

Diet: Insects, mice, and fish

developed dorsal crest extending from the neck to the tail. Overall dorsal coloration is gray to brown with light bands on the body and tail. Mature adults may have a suffusion of dark red ventrally. A dark stripe extends from behind the eye, onto the neck, behind the angle of the jaw.

Similar Species: See accounts for bearded dragon, frilled lizard, and green water dragon

Range & Origin: Temperate eastern Australia. All specimens should be of captive origin.

Adult Size: 30–36 inches.

Life Span: 12–15 years.

Terrarium Size: Large terraria are the rule for this active species. No less than 100 gallons of volume (48 inches × 24 inches × 18 inches) should be provided for a single

may all be accepted; some specimens may also eat fruits and vegetables. Feed mice sparingly to avoid fat build-up in the eyes.

Potential Problems: Provide appropriate calcium, vitamin D_3, and ultraviolet light to help reduce the risk of metabolic bone disease. Cage-related trauma does not appear to be as common in this species of water dragon. However, this fact may be a function of its relative abundance in captivity when compared to its green relatives.

References:

Bartlett, R. D., and Patricia Bartlett. *Anoles, Basilisks, and Water Dragons.* Hauppauge, NY: Barron's Educational Series, Inc., 1997.

Bartlett, R. D., and Patricia Bartlett. *Lizard Care from A to Z.* Hauppauge, NY: Barron's Educational Series, Inc., 1997.

Red-headed Agama

Trade Name(s): Red-headed Agama, Agama (agama).

Family & Scientific Name: Agamidae; *Agama agama.*

Identifying Features: This is a strongly built lizard with a vertebral crest and round tail. This species is dimorphic in coloration. Mature males in breeding coloration are loudly colored with orange heads, bluish-gray to charcoal backs, and an orange vertebral stripe. Variable amounts of green, yellow, and blue highlights are also present. Females, juveniles, and subordinate or immature males are more subdued and clad in earthen tones.

Similar Species: A male in breeding coloration is unmistakable.

Range & Origin: Naturally occurs in east Africa. Most specimens offered for sale are collected from the wild.

Adult Size: 12–14 inches.

Life Span: 6–10 years.

Terrarium Size: A 75- to 100-gallon aquarium, or similar terrarium, can easily house a small breeding group.

Terrarium Type: Desert, ruin, or rocky ledge. Numerous outcroppings and crags should be formed to provide basking and hiding areas.

Social Structure: Wild populations are typically composed of smaller groups consisting of a dominant male and a few to several females. This may be duplicated in captivity.

Diet: Eats various insects.

Potential Problems: Wild-caught animals frequently have internal and/or external parasites. Recent imports may be dehydrated or suffering from the stress of capture and transport. This species prefers to drink water that accumulates on rocks after misting. Providing an ultraviolet light source and properly preparing insect prey by gut-loading, or dusting with a calcium supplement, can help prevent metabolic bone disease.

References:

Rogner, Manfred. *Lizards: Husbandry and Reproduction in the Vivarium.* Malabar, FL: Kreiger, 1997.

Himalayan Tree Dragons

Trade Name(s): Splendid Tree Dragon, Splendid Japalure, Striped Japalure.

Family & Scientific Name: Agamidae: *Japalura* sp.; *J. swinhonis* (shown) and *J. flaviceps* may also be available.

Identifying Features: Rough scalation; those in the pet trade have brown coloration; low nuchal and vertebral crest. These lizards have a variable light dorsolateral to lateral stripe and a variably defined light mustache marking. Overlapping identification characteristics make species identification very difficult once the exact origin of the lizards has been lost. *J. swinhonis* tends to have a broad and well-defined, albeit jagged-edged, lateral stripe. The stripe of *J. flaviceps* tends to be more dorsolateral and less well-defined.

Similar Species: All other brown members of this genus.

Range & Origin: Southwestern China.

Adult Size: Total length is about 10 inches. Snout-vent length is 3½ inches.

Life Span: Unknown; some species with similar habits and habitats from closely allied genera have documented captive life spans of nearly 3 years.

Terrarium Size: One or a pair of these

lizards may be maintained in a 20-gallon or larger terrarium with diagonally oriented upright perches.

Terrarium Type: These montane lizards need a cool, humid tank (68–74°F) with an illuminated hotspot of about 85°F. They are arboreal.

Social Structure: Acclimated males are territorial. One male may be kept with one or more females in a tank with sufficient space. Numerous visual barriers help prevent overt aggression.

Diet: These lizards eat many kinds of gut-loaded insects. Crickets and silkworms are among their favorites.

Potential Problems: It is not always easy to acclimate high altitude lizards to low altitude caging conditions. Many lizards become stressed when temperature and humidity are incorrect and by being crowded at wholesalers. Purchase only alert, bright-eyed lizards that you see feed.

References:

Smith, Malcolm A. *The Fauna of British India, Reptilia and Amphibia, Vol. II—Sauria.* Hollywood, FL: Ralph Curtis Books, 1973.

Zhao, Er-Mi, and Kraig Adler. *Herpetology of China.* Oxford, Ohio: SSAR, 1993.

Green Iguana

Trade Name(s): Iguana, Common Iguana, Blue Iguana, Giant Green Iguana.

Family & Scientific Name: Iguanidae; *Iguana iguana.*

Identifying Features: This is a solidly built bright green lizard with a laterally compressed tail and a prominent dorsal crest. Hatchlings and young adults have a series of dark vertical bars on the trunk near the legs. Adult males in breeding coloration may be suffused with orange over all or part of the body. The tails of all ages are banded with black. Adults bear a dewlap, or flap of skin, beneath the lower jaw. Small, horn-like protuberances may adorn the nose.

Similar Species: See accounts for green water dragon, rhinoceros iguana, brown basilisk, and green basilisk.

Range & Origin: Naturally occurs throughout much of Latin America. The majority of iguanas seen in the pet trade are bred on farms in El Salvador and Costa Rica, wild-caught imports and domestically captive-bred specimens are also available.

Adult Size: 6 feet or more.

Life Span: 15–20 years.

Terrarium Size: The cute baby iguanas sold in pet stores rapidly outgrow most aquariums. Adult iguanas require very large enclosures. Minimum suggested size for adult iguanas is 6 feet long × 30 inches wide × 6 feet high. Custom construction is often required for cages of these dimensions.

Terrarium Type: Tropical forest.

Social Structure: Iguanas are solitary and territorial lizards. Males housed together may fight savagely.

Diet: This lizard is strictly herbivorous. Greens of several varieties (collard, kale, mustard, turnip, beets) should form the bulk of the diet. Additional foods that are high in fiber and have adequate calcium: phosphorus ratio include grape, hibiscus and mulberry leaves; hibiscus flowers; cilantro leaves and stems, bok choy, cabbage, romaine, and leaf lettuce; endive, and escarole. A small portion of the diet (20 percent or less) may be composed of fruits and hard vegetables. Variety is the key to good nutrition. Unlike the nutrient requirements of domestic pets, those of iguanas are not fully known. It is best, therefore, to use "complete" commercial diets only sparingly in combination with a varied diet of produce. Food should be dusted with a calcium supplement, or a crushed calcium carbonate antacid, one to two times weekly.

Potential Problems: Calcium deficiency is very common in green iguanas of all ages. Typical signs of metabolic bone disease—including weakness, swollen limbs, and soft jaw and skull bones—are typical in young

specimens. Calcium deficiency in adults is characterized by neuromuscular signs such as weakness, tremors, trembling of toes or limbs, and seizures. These conditions can be fatal and should be addressed by a qualified reptile veterinarian. Excessive animal protein in the diet may result in kidney and reproductive diseases. Cuts and abrasions frequently occur in improperly housed iguanas. Those given free range in the home may spread salmonella or cause fires due to fallen lamps. Broken bones are common in specimens permitted free range in the home. Large iguanas, especially males in breeding season, can deliver a painful bite and are potentially dangerous animals. Iguanas are avid baskers and must be provided with an ultraviolet light source; exposure to natural sunlight is ideal for this purpose. Zoos and herpetological societies are overwhelmed with offers of iguanas that have grown too large or too aggressive to house or handle. Carefully consider the nutritional and housing requirements of an iguana throughout its life before bringing that cute baby home from the pet store.

References:

Bartlett, R. D., and Patricia Bartlett. *Iguanas.* Hauppauge, NY: Barron's Educational Series, Inc., 1995.

Bartlett, R. D., and Patricia Bartlett. *Lizard Care from A to Z.* Hauppauge, NY: Barron's Educational Series, Inc., 1997.

Rhinoceros Iguana

Trade Name(s): Hispaniolan Rhinoceros Iguana, Rhino Iguana, Rhino.

Family & Scientific Name: Iguanidae; *Cyclura cornuta cornuta.*

Identifying Features: This is a large and impressive iguana with a prominent dorsal crest and large dewlap. Dorsal coloration ranges from gray to bluish gray. Prominent nasal horns are most noticeable in older males. Dark lateral bands are most evident in young specimens.

Similar Species: See accounts for green iguana and Mexican spiny-tailed iguana.

Range & Origin: The Caribbean island of Hispaniola. This species is actively bred in many zoos and private collections.

Adult Size: These heavy bodied iguanas often look larger than their 4-foot length.

Life Span: 15–20 years.

Terrarium Size: Large terraria measuring at least 6 feet × 6 feet × 30 inches wide are necessary for adult specimens. Hatchlings and juveniles may be housed in smaller terraria and aquariums.

Terrarium Type: Rocky scrub.

Social Structure: Solitary and territorial. Extremely large enclosures are required to house multiple animals comfortably.

Diet: Leafy greens, similar to those for green iguanas, are recommended. An occasional invertebrate meal is accepted.

Potential Problems: Rhino iguanas are no less susceptible to the effects of calcium deficiency than their green cousins. Provide adequate dietary calcium, vitamin D_3, and ultraviolet light. Traumatic injuries including rostral abrasions are seen frequently. Their powerful jaws can give a severe bite.

References:

Bartlett, R. D., and Patricia Bartlett. *Iguanas.* Hauppauge, NY: Barron's Educational Series, Inc., 1995.

Bartlett, R. D., and Patricia Bartlett. *Lizard Care from A to Z.* Hauppauge, NY: Barron's Educational Series, Inc., 1997.

Mexican Spiny-tailed Iguana

Trade Name(s): Spiny-tail Iguana, Ctenosaur.

Family & Scientific Name: Iguanidae; *Ctenosaura pectinata.*

Identifying Features: This is a streamlined iguana with a somewhat flattened, elongated head, and prominent dorsal crest.

The tail is armored with whorls of low spines. Adults are bluish-gray to black; hatchlings and juveniles are gray to buff with dark lateral banding. The dark tail bands of the young are sometimes visible on adults as well.

Similar Species: See accounts for rhinoceros iguana and Honduran club-tailed iguana.

Range & Origin: Sinaloa to Oaxaca on Mexico's Pacific coast. Feral populations exist in parts of Florida and Texas. The vast majority of specimens in the pet trade are collected from the wild.

Adult Size: 3–4 feet.

Life Span: 12–15 years.

Terrarium Size: A large terrarium measuring 2 × 4 × 4 feet houses a single adult. This species is less arboreal than the green iguana.

Terrarium Type: Forest or scrub.

Social Structure: Solitary and territorial.

Males housed together typically fight for dominance.

Diet: This species seems to be more omnivorous than the green iguana. Greens, vegetables, fruits, insects, and young mice may all be accepted.

Potential Problems: Calcium deficiency is less common in species that include whole vertebrate prey in their diet. Gut-loading insects, or dusting insects or vegetables, can help increase dietary calcium intake. An ultraviolet light source should be provided. This species may be aggressive, and frequent gentle handling is recommended until they become accustomed to human contact. Active and strong, spiny-tailed iguanas frequently abrade their noses in captivity. Both internal and external parasites are common.

References:

Bartlett, R. D., and Patricia Bartlett. *Iguanas.* Hauppauge, NY: Barron's Educational Series, Inc., 1995.

Bartlett, R. D., and Patricia Bartlett. *Lizard Care from A to Z.* Hauppauge, NY: Barron's Educational Series, Inc., 1997.

Rogner, Manfred. *Lizards: Husbandry and Reproduction in the Vivarium.* Malabar, FL: Kreiger, 1997.

Honduran Club-tailed Iguana

Trade Name(s): Dwarf Spiny-tailed Iguana.

Family & Scientific Name: Iguanidae; *Ctenosaura (Enyliosaurus) quinquecarinata.*

Identifying Features: This lizard has a tan ground color and blue flecks posterodorsally 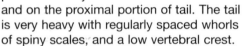 and on the proximal portion of tail. The tail is very heavy with regularly spaced whorls of spiny scales, and a low vertebral crest.

Similar Species: This is the only species of dwarfed, club-tailed iguana commonly available in the pet trade.

Range & Origin: Southern Mexico to Nicaragua.

Adult Size: Commonly to 14 inches; occasionally to 17 inches.

Life Span: Unknown; captive congenerics have lived more than 20 years.

Terrarium Size: One or two adults may be kept in a 40-gallon tank or cage; larger quarters are better.

Terrarium Type: Dry savanna with absorbent substrate and a dish of clean water.

Social Structure: Males are not communal with other males, but can be kept with one or more females.

Diet: It is omnivorous. Gut-loaded insects, fruits, and dark green leafy vegetables are eaten.

Potential Problems: This is normally a hardy lizard, but some specimens are stressed by hunger, dehydration, and overcrowding at the wholesalers. Purchase only heavy, alert, lizards with bright eyes. Try to see the lizard feed before you buy.

References:

Bartlett, R. D., and Patricia Bartlett. *Iguanas.* Hauppauge, NY: Barron's Educational Series, Inc., 1995.

Desert Iguana

Trade Name(s): Dipsosaurus, Dipso.

Family & Scientific Name: Iguanidae; *Dipsosaurus dorsalis.*

Identifying Features: This is a slender, streamlined iguana with a rounded snout and round tail.

The vertebral crest is low, being most prominent on the tail. The tail is protected by scales arranged in whorls. Ground color is sandy tan to gray, often with a wash of brown or brownish red on the sides. Light ocelli on the anterior trunk give way to wavy lines posteriorly. The tail is encircled with numerous rings composed of small dark spots.

Similar Species: See accounts for chuckwalla, collared lizards, leopard lizard, and northern curly-tailed lizard.

Range & Origin: Southwestern United States and adjacent Mexico.

Adult Size: 10–14 inches.

Life Span: 10–15 years.

Terrarium Size: Long terraria are appreciated by this active species. Seventy-five-gallon and larger aquariums provide adequate floor space.

Terrarium Type: Desert. Provide plenty of sand for burrowing, but put the rocks in before the sand so the lizard cannot burrow under them.

Social Structure: A small group consisting of a single male and two or three females may be housed safely together.

Diet: This herbivore should be provided a diet of mixed greens and shredded vegetables.

Potential Problems: This sun-loving lizard is active only during the hottest parts of the year. Inadequate temperatures lead to poor appetite and failure to thrive. The preferred active temperature of wild specimens is nearly 100°F; temperature gradients should allow this temperature to be achieved in captivity. Calcium deficiency and metabolic bone disease are best prevented through dietary management and the provision of ultraviolet lighting.

References:

Bartlett, R. D., and Patricia Bartlett. *Iguanas.* Hauppauge, NY: Barron's Educational Series, Inc., 1995.

Bartlett, R. D., and Patricia Bartlett. *Lizard Care from A to Z.* Hauppauge, NY: Barron's Educational Series, Inc., 1997.

Rogner, Manfred. *Lizards: Husbandry and Reproduction in the Vivarium.* Malabar, FL: Kreiger, 1997.

Chuckwalla

Trade Name(s): Chuck, Chuckie.
Family & Scientific Name: Iguanidae; *Sauromalus obesus*.
Identifying Features: This pot-bellied iguanid varies in coloration depending upon age, sex, and geographic origin.

Young and female chuckwallas are generally drab gray, buff, or brown with distinct to barely visible dorsal crossbands. The tail is banded with alternating dark and light rings. Males of most populations are more colorful, often having a dark head, a paler trunk that may be tan, yellow, orange, or red, and a cream, yellow, orange, or red tail. A beautiful red-tailed black variant occurs near Phoenix, Arizona.

Similar Species: See accounts for desert iguana, collared lizards, and leopard lizard.

Range & Origin: Southwestern United States and northern Mexico, including Baja California and several coastal islands. Most of the chuckwallas offered for sale are captured from the wild. The red-tailed black phase mentioned above is found only within the confines of a natural preserve, and is strictly protected from commercialization.

Adult Size: 14–18 inches.
Life Span: 12–15 years.

Terrarium Size: A 60-gallon aquarium or terrarium comfortably houses a single adult or a pair of adults.

Terrarium Type: Rock-strewn desert. Basking rocks with crevices for hiding should be provided.

Social Structure: A single wild male oversees a territory that overlaps with those of a few females. Similar groups may be kept in captivity.

Diet: This is a greens-based diet of vegetables similar to that recommended for the green iguana.

Potential Problems: High temperatures and ultraviolet light are essential for captive specimens. Active temperature in the wild approaches 100°F; provide a thermal gradient to allow the chuckwalla to achieve its optimal temperature. Calcium deficiency can be seen in specimens provided with too little dietary calcium and inadequate exposure to ultraviolet light.

References:

Bartlett, R. D., and Patricia Bartlett. *Iguanas.* Hauppauge, NY: Barron's Educational Series, Inc., 1995.

Bartlett, R. D., and Patricia Bartlett. *Lizard Care from A to Z.* Hauppauge, NY: Barron's Educational Series, Inc., 1997.

Collared Lizards

Trade Name(s): Collared, Crotaphytus; specific and subspecific common names include common, eastern, Sonoran, western, Chihuahuan, yellow-headed, Baja, and Great Basin collared lizards.

Family & Scientific Name: Iguanidae; *Crotaphytus collaris*, *Crotaphytus insularis*.

Identifying Features: This small, squatty lizard is almost toadlike in appearance. It is named for the paired, prominent dark collars that incompletely encircle the neck. The two species (and their numerous subspecies) vary somewhat in coloration. The ground color may be greenish, bluish, olive, brown, or yellowish. The young are prominently crossbanded; these markings fade with age. The colors of breeding males and gravid females are the most vibrant.

Similar Species: See account for leopard lizard.

Range & Origin: Much of the Great Plains and desert southwest, from Arkansas and Missouri west to Utah and Arizona, and south into Mexico. Most pet trade specimens are wild in origin; captive breeding is becoming more common.

Adult Size: 8–12 inches.

Life Span: 5–10 years.

Terrarium Size: A single adult specimen may be housed in a 20-gallon, long aquarium.

Terrarium Type: Desert, grassland, or prairie.

Social Structure: Males will fight when housed together, but will usually share their quarters with a female or two. Specimens of this lizard-eating species should be matched for size if they are to be housed together.

Diet: Eats gut-loaded or dusted insects and small lizards.

Potential Problems: Some recently captured collared lizards show a strong preference for lizard prey. Fearless, the collared lizard encounters aggressors mouth first; their bite, however, amounts to little more than a firm pinch. Intestinal parasites and Trombiculid (chigger) mites are common.

References:
Bartlett, R. D., and Patricia Bartlett. *Lizard Care from A to Z*. Hauppauge, NY: Barron's Educational Series, Inc., 1997.

Leopard Lizard

Trade Name(s): Long-nosed Leopard Lizard.

Family & Scientific Name: Iguanidae; *Gambelia wislizenii*.

Identifying Features: Shaped something like a stretched collared lizard, the leopard lizard is clad in shades of brown marked with darker bars and spots. The tail is ringed with light and dark bands. Coloration is brightest in breeding females.

Similar Species: See account for collared lizards.

Range & Origin: Western and southwestern states from Oregon and Idaho to eastern California and western Texas.

Adult Size: 10–14 inches.

Life Span: 6–10 years.

Terrarium Size: An aquarium or terrarium with running room is recommended. 55-gallon and larger aquariums are ideal.

Terrarium Type: Desert or arid grassland.

Social Structure: Small groups consisting of a single male, and two or three similarly sized females may be housed together. This lizard eater will occasionally consume smaller specimens placed in its cage.

Diet: Eats gut-loaded or dusted insects and lizards.

Potential Problems: Intestinal parasites are frequently found in this lizard-eating species. Ultraviolet light and adequate dietary calcium must be provided.

References:

Bartlett, R. D., and Patricia Bartlett. *Lizard Care from A to Z.* Hauppauge, NY: Barron's Educational Series, Inc., 1997.

Horned Lizards

Trade Name(s):
Horned Toad,
Horny Toad,
Round-tailed
Horned Lizard,
Desert Horned
Lizard.

Family & Scientific Name:
Iguanidae;
Phrynosoma modestum,
Phrynosoma platyrhinos.

Adult Size: 3–6 inches.

Life Span: 3–5 years. Captive longevity is often much less.

Terrarium Size: A 20-gallon, long aquarium or larger terrarium is recommended.

Terrarium Type: Desert or grassland.

Identifying Features: Small, flat, and toadlike the various species of horned lizards are characterized by a crown of spines and the large, spiny tubercles scattered among the smaller scales of their bodies. They are clad in grays, browns, and reds that aid them in blending into their surroundings.

Similar Species: Horned lizards are not easily confused with other species.

Range & Origin: The numerous species of horned lizards occur through most of the western United States. Their collective range extends from southern Alberta, Canada to the tip of Baja California and deep into mainland Mexico. The two species listed above are frequently available as wild-caught specimens.

Social Structure: Solitary.

Diet: Wild specimens feed chiefly on ants. Captives sometimes accept other insect prey.

Potential Problems: Due to their special dietary needs, horned lizards make a poor choice as a pet. None of the species is easily kept. These lizards are best enjoyed in their natural habitat.

References:

Bartlett, R. D., and Patricia Bartlett. *Lizard Care from A to Z.* Hauppauge, NY: Barron's Educational Series, Inc., 1997.

Rogner, Manfred. *Lizards: Husbandry and Reproduction in the Vivarium.* Malabar, FL: Kreiger, 1997.

Green Anole

Trade Name(s):
Carolina Anole, American Chameleon, Chameleon, Anole.

Family & Scientific Name: Iguanidae; *Anolis carolinensis.*

Identifying Features:
A small, slim lizard with an elongated, wedge-shaped head. Specialized lamellae on the toes allow anoles to climb sheer surfaces, including glass. Capable of limited color changes, green anoles are more closely related to the green iguana than they are to true chameleons. They are uniformly green, brown, or some shade in between depending upon temperature and stress level. Males have a pink or red (rarely white or greenish white) dewlap that is extended during territorial and breeding displays.

Similar Species: See accounts for brown anole and knight anole.

Range & Origin: Southeastern states from North Carolina to Texas. Most of the wild-caught anoles in the pet trade originate from Louisiana and Florida.

Adult Size: 4–6 inches.

Life Span: 2–5 years.

Terrarium Size: A 10-gallon aquarium turned on end provides adequate vertical space for a single adult.

Terrarium Type: Woodland.

Social Structure: Males are very territorial, but may be housed safely with one to three females, provided there is adequate space for basking.

Diet: Eats gut-loaded or calcium dusted insects.

Potential Problems: Dehydration and stress from handling, overcrowding, and poor care are all very common in pet store anoles. Bite wounds and abscesses are frequently seen in animals housed in high densities in the pet trade. These basking lizards require proper thermal gradients and ultraviolet light. Water should be provided by daily misting, but do not allow the cage to remain wet. Improper cage humidity can predispose anoles to skin infections.

References:
Bartlett, R. D., and Patricia Bartlett. *Lizard Care from A to Z.* Hauppauge, NY: Barron's Educational Series, Inc., 1997.

Brown Anole

Trade Name(s):
Bahaman Anole, Anole.
Family & Scientific Name: Iguanidae; *Anolis sagrei*.
Identifying Features:
This is a medium-sized anole. Males are some shade of brown or reddish brown. The orange-edged red dewlap is extended during territorial and courtship displays. A light vertebral strip may be present in males, but is most prominent in females and juveniles. The edges of this stripe are generally dark and scalloped.
Similar Species: See account for green anole.
Range & Origin: Native to the West Indies, the brown anole is well-established in Florida and parts of Texas. Specimens offered for sale are wild-caught with few exceptions.
Adult Size: 6–8 inches.
Life Span: 3–5 years.
Terrarium Size: A 20-gallon, high aquarium

provides adequate horizontal and vertical space for a male and one or two females.
Terrarium Type: Forest edge or woodland.
Social Structure:
Males are very territorial. A single male may reside with one or a few females if numerous basking sites are provided.
Diet: Eats gut-loaded or calcium dusted insects.
Potential Problems:
Dehydration, stress, and injuries due to overcrowding are the principal problems encountered with pet store anoles. Provide water by misting the leaves of terrarium plants to encourage drinking. Adequate thermal gradients and ultraviolet lighting are necessary for successful maintenance.
References:
Bartlett, R. D., and Patricia Bartlett. *Lizard Care from A to Z.* Hauppauge, NY: Barron's Educational Series, Inc., 1997.

Knight Anole

Trade Name(s): Cuban Anole.
Family & Scientific Name: Polychrotidae; *Anolis equestris equestris.*
Identifying Features: The large size, massive head, huge coral pink dewlap (on both males and females) and yellow shoulder stripes are diagnostic.

Similar Species: None.
Range & Origin: Cuba; firmly established in Dade County, Florida from which those seen in the pet trade are collected. Occasionally bred in captivity.
Adult Size: 14–16½ inches.
Life Span: 16+ years.
Terrarium Size: Although not overly active, these anoles should be given a large terrarium or cage. A pair of adults can be kept in a 75-gallon terrarium if it is oriented vertically. Ours thrived in large outside wood and wire cages that were 6-feet high × 4-feet long × 2.5-feet wide.
Terrarium Type: These are undemanding anoles, but do best if cage humidity is fairly high. Several horizontal perches of at least the body diameter of the anoles should be provided at varying levels in the cage. A vining foliage plant (pothos is an excellent choice) can serving as a drinking "fountain;" mist every other day. A substrate of leaf litter, or nonaromatic mulch, also helps hold a high humidity.
Social Structure: Males fight with other males. A pair, or a single male with several females, usually coexist well.
Diet: This big anole eats a wide variety of insects, some blossoms and fruits, and may occasionally eat a pinky mouse. Dust insects with vitamin D_3-calcium powder twice weekly for babies and ovulating females, once weekly otherwise.
Potential Problems: Providing this lizard is kept adequately hydrated and given D_3-calcium supplements, it is an easily maintained species.
References:

Bartlett, R. D., and Patricia Bartlett. *Anoles, Basilisks, and Water Dragons.* Hauppauge, NY: Barron's Educational Series, Inc., 1997.

Bartlett, R. D., and Patricia Bartlett. *Lizard Care from A to Z.* Hauppauge, NY: Barron's Educational Series, Inc., 1997.

Northern Brown Basilisk

Trade Name(s):
Brown Basilisk.

Family & Scientific Name:
Corytophanidae; *Basiliscus vittatus.*

Identifying Features:
These lizards have brown coloration with a brown to yellow(ish) lateral stripe on each side. Males have a high head crest and a low vertebral crest. Females are similarly colored, but lack the crests.

Similar Species: The southern brown basilisk, but this lizard is rare in the pet trade, and has more extensive cresting on the back and on the tail.

Range & Origin: Mexico to Colombia; now well-established in Miami. This species is bred by some hobbyists, but most pet trade specimens are now collected from Miami canals.

Adult Size: Males to about 24 inches; females much smaller.

Life Span: To about 10 years.

Terrarium Size: These active lizards can be difficult to cage properly. Because they often continually run into the glass of a terrarium, or rub their nose against wire if in a mesh cage, it is hard to know how much space to provide them. Adult males are the most nervous. Some keepers feel it better to tightly constrain a basilisk, to prevent it from getting enough momentum to badly injure itself when it hits the glass. We advocate larger cages (50–75 gallon capacity), but suggest they be provided with many visual barriers. Paper or opaque cloth should be taped to the glass on at least three sides of the cage/terrarium.

Terrarium Type: A humid aquarium with a large water receptacle is needed. A substrate of nonaromatic mulch is fine. Provide horizontal perches of at least the diameter of the lizard's body. Tough-leafed vining plants (for example, pothos, Monstera) create visual barriers.

Social Structure: Males fight with other males, but a single male, and from one to several females, coexist well.

Diet: Feed a variety of insects and an occasional blossom. Dust insects with vitamin D_3-calcium powder twice weekly for babies and ovulating females, once weekly otherwise.

Potential Problems: Relatively hardy, but see the cautionary note in "Terrarium Size," in this account.

References:

Bartlett, R. D., and Patricia Bartlett. *Lizard Care from A to Z.* Hauppauge, NY: Barron's Educational Series, Inc., 1997.

Bartlett, R. D., and Patricia Bartlett. *Anoles, Basilisks, and Water Dragons.* Hauppauge, NY: Barron's Educational Series, Inc., 1997.

Green (Plumed) Basilisk

Trade Name(s): Same.

Family & Scientific Name: Corytophanidae, *Basiliscus plumifrons.*

Identifying Features: Have green to blue-green coloration dark cross-bands. Males have a high head crest with a plume-like front lobe, another high vertebral crest, and an equally high caudal crest. Females are similarly colored, but lack the crests.

Similar Species: None.

Range & Origin: Central America. This species is now bred in considerable numbers, but many pet trade specimens are still collected from the wild.

Adult Size: Males to about 24 inches; females much smaller.

Life Span: To more than 13 years.

Terrarium Size: Adult, wild-caught males of this active lizard can be difficult to cage properly. They often run into the glass of a terrarium or rub their nose against wire if in a mesh cage. We advocate large cages (50–75-gallon capacity or larger), but suggest cages be provided with many visual barriers. Paper or opaque cloth should be taped to the glass on at least three sides of the cage/terrarium.

Terrarium Type: A humid aquarium with a large water receptacle should be provided. A substrate of nonaromatic mulch is fine. Horizontal perches of at least the diameter of the lizard's body should be provided. The inclusion of tough-leafed vining plants (for example, pothos, Monstera) creates visual barriers.

Social Structure: Males fight with other males, but a single male, and from one to several females, coexist well.

Diet: A variety of insects and an occasional blossom will be eaten. Dust insects with vitamin D_3-calcium powder twice weekly for babies and ovulating females, once weekly otherwise.

Potential Problems: Relatively hardy, but see the cautionary note in "Terrarium Size," in this account.

References:

Bartlett, R. D., and Patricia Bartlett. *Lizard Care from A to Z.* Hauppauge, NY: Barron's Educational Series, Inc., 1997.

Bartlett, R. D., and Patricia Bartlett. *Anoles, Basilisks, and Water Dragons.* Hauppauge, NY: Barron's Educational Series, Inc., 1997.

Desert Spiny Lizard

Trade Name(s):
Desert Swift.
Family & Scientific Name:
Phrynosomatidae; *Sceloporus magister* ssp.
Identifying Features:
Rather than a collar, this species has a black triangle on each side of the neck. The

ground color is tan, olive, olive-yellow, gray, or brown. Irregular, often obscure, darker crossbands are present on the back and tail. Adult males have a blue patch on each side of the belly. The scales are very spiny.
Similar Species: Most other large species of spiny lizard are differentiated from this species by having a black collar.
Range & Origin: Western United States and Mexico.
Adult Size: To about 10 inches.
Life Span: From 3–6+ years.
Terrarium Size: 1–3 specimens can be maintained in a 29-gallon capacity terrarium.
Terrarium Type: Aridland to semiaridland. The substrate should consist of fine, smooth (desert, not sharp silica) sand. Leaf litter (we use the fallen leaves of live oaks) should be

spread on top of the sand. Aridland plants may be incorporated. Diagonal and horizontal perches, at least twice the diameter of the lizard's body, should be incorporated into the design. One end of one perch should be illuminated and warmed from above.
Social Structure: Usually communal, some males may fight during the breeding season and require temporary isolation.
Diet: A variety of insects is eaten by this hardy species. Dust insects with vitamin D_3-calcium powder twice weekly for babies and ovulating females, once weekly otherwise.
Potential Problems: If kept dry (but provided with clean drinking water), this is a hardy and almost trouble-free lizard.
References:
Bartlett, R. D., and Patricia Bartlett. *Lizard Care from A to Z.* Hauppauge, NY: Barron's Educational Series, Inc., 1997.
Bartlett, R. D., and Patricia Bartlett. *Terrarium and Cage Construction and Care.* Hauppauge, NY: Barron's Educational Series, Inc., 1999.

Emerald Swift

Trade Name(s): Green Swift.
Family & Scientific Name: Phrynosomatidae; *Sceloporus malachiticus.*
Identifying Features: Males are emerald green with darker markings, orange and black throat, blue belly patches, and turquoise tail. Females are duller. They have spiny scalation.

Similar Species: None.
Range & Origin: Cloud forests of southern Mexico and Central America. Virtually all specimens in the pet trade are collected from the wild.
Adult Size: To about 7 inches.
Life Span: Potential unknown. This species has proven a delicate captive with an unnaturally high mortality. Most examples live for less than a year.
Terrarium Size: One or a pair can be maintained in a 20–29-gallon capacity terrarium.
Terrarium Type: Cloud forests are typified by variable periods of intense sunshine, perpetual breezes, reduced vision while clouds pass through, variable temperatures, and usually a high relative humidity. In these habitats emerald swifts climb agilely about on trees and boulders. Use a humidity holding substrate such as Perlite-free potting soil, nonaromatic mulch, or leaf litter. (We use the fallen leaves of live oaks.) The incorporation of a live pothos, or similar plant, helps elevate cage humidity and provide visual barriers. Diagonal and horizontal perches, at least twice the diameter of the lizard's body, should be provided. The terrarium should be bright but cool (70–75°F) except for one end of one perch, which should be illuminated and warmed to about 95°F from above.
Social Structure: This is a territorial species. One male or a pair may be maintained in each cage.
Diet: A variety of insects is eaten by these hardy lizards. Dust insects with vitamin D_3-calcium powder twice weekly for babies and ovulating females, once weekly otherwise.
Potential Problems: Very little is known with certainty about the keeping of emerald swifts. To date, they have proven among the most difficult of lizards to successfully maintain.

References:

Bartlett, R. D., and Patricia Bartlett. *Lizard Care from A to Z.* Hauppauge, NY: Barron's Educational Series, Inc., 1997.

Bartlett, R. D., and Patricia Bartlett. *Terrarium and Cage Construction and Care.* Hauppauge, NY: Barron's Educational Series, Inc., 1999.

Northern Curly-tailed Lizard

Trade Name(s): Bahaman Curly-tailed Lizard.

Family & Scientific Name: Tropiduridae; *Leiocephalus carinatus armouri.*

Identifying Features: In general appearance this lizard looks much like a heavy bodied

spiny lizard with a serrate row of vertebral scales. This low crest extends from nape to well on to the tail. When the lizard is startled, the tip of the tail curls upwards.

Similar Species: This is the only non-red-sided curly tailed lizard now in the pet trade.

Range & Origin: Bahamas. Now well-established in Broward and Dade counties, Florida. Specimens collected from Florida supply the pet trade.

Adult Size: 8½–10 inches. Males tend to be the larger sex.

Life Span: To more than 10 years.

Terrarium Size: 1–3 specimens can be maintained in a 29-gallon capacity terrarium.

Terrarium Type: Although preferring a semi-aridland terrarium, this lizard can withstand high cage humidity. The substrate should consist of fine, smooth (desert, not sharp silica) sand. Aridland plants may be incorporated. This lizard climbs agilely on rocks incorporated into the setup. One rock should be illuminated and warmed from above.

Social Structure: A single male and one or more females usually coexist well.

Diet: A variety of insects, as well as some blossoms and fruits, is eaten by this hardy species. Dust insects with vitamin D_3-calcium powder twice weekly for babies and ovulating females, once weekly otherwise.

Potential Problems: If kept dry (but provide with clean drinking water), this is a hardy and almost trouble-free lizard.

References:

Bartlett, R. D., and Patricia Bartlett. *Lizard Care from A to Z.* Hauppauge, NY: Barron's Educational Series, Inc., 1997.

Bartlett, R. D., and Patricia Bartlett. *Terrarium and Cage Construction and Care.* Hauppauge, NY: Barron's Educational Series, Inc., 1999.

Monkey-tailed Skink

Trade Name(s): Solomon Island Giant Skink, Prehensile-tailed Skink.

Family & Scientific Name: Scincidae; *Corucia zebrata.*

Identifying Features: This is a large, heavy bodied skink with olive green scales, light crossbands, a long, strongly prehensile tail, a large triangular head, and usually, a willingness to bite.

Similar Species: None.

Range & Origin: Solomon Islands. Very few are domestically bred, but most are collected from the wild for the pet trade.

Adult Size: 18–24 inches.

Life Span: To about 25 years.

Terrarium Size: These are very arboreal, nocturnal, lizards. A single baby can be kept in a 10-gallon terrarium, or a cage with about the same dimensions. An adult should have a vertically oriented terrarium with a minimum capacity of 40 gallons (or a cage of equal size).

Terrarium Type: A high humidity is important. The substrate may be Perlite-free potting soil, mulch, or leaf litter. A bowl of drinking water and tubes of corkbark (or a similar hide-box) must be continually available. These large lizards are quiescent by day, but become active at dusk.

Social Structure: They are communal providing there are sufficient hides and other visual barriers, and sufficient space. Females become quarrelsome when gravid and may be actively aggressive immediately following parturition. At this time it is keeper beware!

Diet: This big skink eats a wide variety of fruits, blossoms, greens. Dust the food with vitamin D_3-calcium powder twice weekly for babies and ovulating females, once weekly otherwise. Vitamins and minerals are very important to these lizards.

Potential Problems: If not provided with sufficient vitamin D_3 and calcium, fast growing babies are very prone to metabolic bone disease. This rapidly manifests itself by causing weakened limbs and kinked backs.

References:

Bartlett, R. D., and Patricia Bartlett. *Lizard Care from A to Z.* Hauppauge, NY: Barron's Educational Series, Inc., 1997.

Bartlett, R. D., and Patricia Bartlett. *Terrarium and Cage Construction and Care.* Hauppauge, NY: Barron's Educational Series, Inc., 1999.

Northern Blue-tongued Skink

Trade Name(s): Blue-tongue.

Family & Scientific Name: Scincidae; *Tiliqua intermedia*.

Identifying Features: This is a large, heavy bodied skink with keeled scales, dark crossbands, often pink to orange coloring on its sides, and no ocular stripe.

Similar Species: Eastern blue-tongue skink has a dark eyestripe.

Range & Origin: Australia. Some are domestically bred, but many are imported for the pet trade from New Guinea breeding farms.

Adult Size: 12–15 inches.

Life Span: To more than 20 years.

Terrarium Size: A single baby can be kept in a 10-gallon terrarium, or a sweater box with about the same floor space. An adult should have a terrarium with a minimum capacity of 40 gallons (or a cage of equal size).

Terrarium Type: Variable, as long as the substrate is not wet and a bowl of drinking water is continually available. A substrate of paper towels, reptile bedding, or mulch will do fine.

Social Structure: Solitary. Even babies fight savagely. Females, normally less quarrelsome than the males, become especially so when gravid or immediately following parturition.

Diet: This big skink eats a wide variety of fruits, blossoms, and other vegetation, as well as insects, and an occasional pinky mouse. Dust insects with vitamin D_3-calcium powder twice weekly for babies and ovulating females, once weekly otherwise. Vitamins and minerals are very important to these lizards.

Potential Problems: If not provided with sufficient vitamin D_3 and calcium, fast growing babies are very prone to metabolic bone disease. This rapidly manifests itself by causing weakened limbs and kinked backs. If kept communally, this lizard may fight savagely, tearing off the limbs and tailtip of any cagemates.

References:

Bartlett, R. D., and Patricia Bartlett. *Lizard Care from A to Z.* Hauppauge, NY: Barron's Educational Series, Inc., 1997.

Bartlett, R. D., and Patricia Bartlett. *Terrarium and Cage Construction and Care.* Hauppauge, NY: Barron's Educational Series, Inc., 1999.

Broad-headed Skink

Trade Name(s):
Greater Five-lined Skink.
Family & Scientific Name:
Scincidae;
Eumeces laticeps.
Identifying Features: This skink is distinguished by large adult size and shiny grayish-brown to brown

body. During the breeding season adult males have an enlarged temporal area and a fire-orange head. Females often retain vestiges of the striped juvenile pattern. Juveniles have a black body with either 5 or 7 narrow, yellow stripes. Nonbreeding adults are much less colorful. A row of wide scales is along the underside of the tail.
Similar Species: Common five-lined skink is smaller and usually has wider lines. Southeastern five-lined skink is smaller and lacks the widened scales beneath the tail.
Range & Origin: Southeastern United States. All specimens available in the pet trade are collected from the wild.
Adult Size: To 12 inches.
Life Span: To more than 10 years.
Terrarium Size: 1–3 adults can be maintained in a 29-gallon capacity terrarium.
Terrarium Type: Dry woodland. The substrate should consist of Perlite-free potting soil, or merely soil scraped from the yard.

Leaf litter (we use the fallen leaves of live oaks) should be spread on top of the soil. Suitable plants may be incorporated. This skink uses diagonal and horizontal perches if they are at least twice the diameter of the lizard's body.
One end of the terrarium should be illuminated and warmed from above.
Social Structure: Males fight savagely with other males, but a single male coexists well with 1–3 females.
Diet: A variety of insects is eaten by this hardy species. They also eat some blossoms and fruit. Captives occasionally eat a little low-fat canned catfood. Dust insects with vitamin D_3-calcium powder twice weekly for babies and ovulating females, once weekly otherwise.
Potential Problems: If properly cared for, this is a hardy lizard that should give its owner no problems.
References:
Bartlett, R. D., and Patricia Bartlett. *Lizard Care from A to Z.* Hauppauge, NY: Barron's Educational Series, Inc., 1997.
Bartlett, R. D., and Patricia Bartlett. *Terrarium and Cage Construction and Care.* Hauppauge, NY: Barron's Educational Series, Inc., 1999.

Fire Skink

Trade Name(s): Same.

Family & Scientific Name: Scincidae; *Lygosoma (=Riopa) fernandi.*

Identifying Features: The warm brown dorsum, bright red sides with black and white vertical bars,

and black and white striped chin, are distinctive.

Similar Species: The red-sided skink is far less colorful and cleanly marked.

Range & Origin: Tropical West Africa. All specimens in the pet trade are collected from the wild.

Adult Size: 9–12 inches.

Life Span: 10+ years.

Terrarium Size: From one specimen to a trio can be kept in a 20-gallon, long terrarium. A greater number of specimens requires a larger tank.

Terrarium Type: This is a forest-edge and damp-savanna species. The terrarium substrate should consist of several inches of barely dampened soil, over which a layer of leaf litter is strewn. Flat basking rocks, illuminated and warmed from above, will be used by these lizards.

Social Structure: Usually communal, some large males may fight during the breeding season and require isolation.

Diet: Earthworms are a favored food. In addition to a variety of insects, some finely chopped fruit, and the fruit-honey day gecko mixture will all be consumed. Dust insects with vitamin D_3-calcium powder twice weekly for baby skinks and ovulating females, once weekly otherwise.

Potential Problems: If kept dry (but provided with clean drinking water), this is a hardy and trouble-free lizard.

References:

Bartlett, R. D., and Patricia Bartlett. *Lizard Care from A to Z.* Hauppauge, NY: Barron's Educational Series, Inc., 1997.

Bartlett, R. D., and Patricia Bartlett. *Terrarium and Cage Construction and Care.* Hauppauge, NY: Barron's Educational Series, Inc., 1999.

Red-sided Skink

Trade Name(s): Mistakenly called Fire Skink.

Family & Scientific Name: Scincidae; *Mabuya perotetti.*

Identifying Features: Warm brown back, red sides spangled with white.

Similar Species: Fire skink has red sides bearing well-separated black and white bars.

Range & Origin: Tropical West Africa. All red-sided skinks available in the pet trade are collected from the wild.

Adult Size: 8–10½ inches.

Life Span: 5+ years; 10+ years should be an attainable longevity.

Terrarium Size: From one specimen to a trio can be kept in a 20-gallon, long terrarium. A greater number of specimens requires a larger tank.

Terrarium Type: This is a savanna species that apparently enters somewhat drier areas than the fire skink. The terrarium substrate should consist of several inches of almost dry, sandy soil over which a layer of leaf litter is strewn. Flat basking rocks, illuminated and warmed from above, will be used by these lizards. A water dish is important.

Social Structure: Usually communal, some large males may fight during the breeding season and require isolation.

Diet: In addition to a variety of insects, some finely chopped fruit, and the fruit-honey day gecko mixture (equal parts baby food fruit, honey, and water) will all be consumed. Dust insects with vitamin D_3-calcium powder twice weekly for baby skinks and ovulating females, once weekly otherwise.

Potential Problems: Many imported red-sided skinks are dehydrated, have not eaten in some time, and are severely stressed.

References:

Bartlett, R. D., and Patricia Bartlett. *Lizard Care from A to Z.* Hauppauge, NY: Barron's Educational Series, Inc., 1997.

Bartlett, R. D., and Patricia Bartlett. *Terrarium and Cage Construction and Care.* Hauppauge, NY: Barron's Educational Series, Inc., 1999.

Red-eyed Crocodile Skink

Trade Name(s): Same.

Family & Scientific Name: Scincidae; *Tribolonotus gracilis*.

Identifying Features: This skink has a bony casque on the back of the head, very rough dorsal scales, and orange orbits.

Similar Species: *T. novaeguinae* is very similar, but lacks orange around the eyes. Philippine water skinks, *Tropidophorus* sp., are more elongated and lack the casqued head.

Range & Origin: New Guinea. This is not yet a commonly seen skink in the pet trade. Of those available, many are wild collected, but a few are now captive-bred.

Adult Size: To 6½ inches.

Life Span: Not yet determined. It is likely that with proper care, a minimum lifespan of 10 years is achievable.

Terrarium Size: This is a quiet, nocturnal, skink. From one specimen to a trio can be kept in a 20-gallon, long terrarium. A greater number of specimens requires a larger tank.

Terrarium Type: This is a cool forest and stream-edge species. The terrarium substrate should consist of several inches of slightly moistened soil, over which a layer of leaf litter is strewn. Hiding areas, and a receptacle of water in which this lizard may occasionally submerge, should be provided.

Social Structure: Usually communal, some large males may fight during the breeding season and require isolation.

Diet: Earthworms are a favored food. In addition, a variety of insects, some finely chopped fruit, and the fruit-honey day gecko mixture will all be sampled. Dust insects with vitamin D_3-calcium powder twice weekly for baby skinks and ovulating females, once weekly otherwise.

Potential Problems: Daytime terrarium temperatures should not rise above the low 70s. Nighttime temperatures can be a few degrees cooler. Providing these lizards are kept cool and allowed access to water, few problems will be encountered.

References:

Bartlett, R. D., and Patricia Bartlett. *Lizard Care from A to Z.* Hauppauge, NY: Barron's Educational Series, Inc., 1997.

Bartlett, R. D., and Patricia Bartlett. *Terrarium and Cage Construction and Care.* Hauppauge, NY: Barron's Educational Series, Inc., 1999.

Common Sandfish & Red Sandfish

Trade Name(s): Egyptian Sandfish and Arabian Sandfish.

Family & Scientific Name: Scincidae; *Scincus scincus* (common sandfish); *S. mitranus* (red sandfish).

Identifying Features: Flattened snout, small eyes, fringed toes.
S. scincus is clad in scales of cream and has well-defined and well separated gray dorsal crossbands. *S. mitranus* has a definite reddish suffusion to all scales.

Similar Species: None currently in the pet trade.

Range & Origin: Egypt and Arabia. All pet trade specimens of both species are wild collected.

Adult Size: To about 6 inches.

Life Span: 6 to 10 years, perhaps longer.

Terrarium Size: 1–3 specimens can be maintained in a 15–20-gallon capacity terrarium. If a larger group is kept, the terrarium size should be increased.

Terrarium Type: This is an aridland species. The substrate should consist of several inches of fine, smooth (desert, not sharp silica) sand. The lowest levels of the sand should be kept barely dampened by trickling water into a small diameter (½-inch) PVC pipe pushed to the tank bottom. Desert plants may be incorporated. This is a burrowing skink that will seldom be seen on the surface. The sand should be illuminated and warmed (to about 120°F on one end of the terrarium) from above.

Social Structure: Usually communal, some large males may fight during the breeding season and require isolation.

Diet: A variety of insects, especially burrowing forms such as king mealworms, is eagerly accepted. Some finely chopped fruit and the fruit-honey day gecko mixture will be consumed. Dust insects with vitamin D_3-calcium powder twice weekly for babies and ovulating females, once weekly otherwise.

Potential Problems: If kept warm enough, this is a hardy and trouble-free lizard. Although they seldom drink, a shallow dish of fresh water should be available.

References:
Bartlett, R. D., and Patricia Bartlett. *Lizard Care from A to Z.* Hauppauge, NY: Barron's Educational Series, Inc., 1997.
Bartlett, R. D., and Patricia Bartlett. *Terrarium and Cage Construction and Care.* Hauppauge, NY: Barron's Educational Series, Inc., 1999.

Slender Glass Lizard

Trade Name(s):
Glass Snakes.
Family & Scientific Name:
Anguidae;
*Ophisaurus
attenuatus* ssp.
**Identifying
Features:**
These lizards
are very attenuate, have no
legs, and have
functional eyelids. There are
stripes both above and below the lateral
fold.

Similar Species: Other species of glass
lizards lack stripes below the lateral fold.
Range & Origin: Eastern United States. All
specimens in the pet trade are collected
from the wild.
Adult Size: 30–36 inches.
Life Span: 5+ years; 10+ years should be
an attainable longevity.
Terrarium Size: A single specimen can be
kept in a 20-gallon long terrarium. Two or
more specimens should have a 40–75-
gallon terrarium.
Terrarium Type: This is a dry woodland and
savanna species. The terrarium substrate
should consist of several inches of almost
dry, sandy soil
over which a
layer of leaf litter
is strewn. Hides
should be provided. One end
of the terrarium
should be illuminated and
warmed from
above.
Social Structure: Usually
communal.
Diet: A variety of
insects, crickets, mealworms, waxworms,
grasshoppers, and roaches are readily
accepted. Dust insects with vitamin D_3-
calcium powder twice weekly for baby glass
lizards and ovulating females, once weekly
otherwise.
Potential Problems: When properly fed,
hydrated, and warmed these are hardy, relatively trouble-free lizards.
References:
Bartlett, R. D., and Patricia Bartlett. *Lizard
Care from A to Z.* Hauppauge, NY:
Barron's Educational Series, Inc., 1997.
Bartlett, R. D., and Patricia Bartlett. *Terrarium and Cage Construction and Care.*
Hauppauge, NY: Barron's Educational
Series, Inc., 1999.

Southern Alligator Lizard

Trade Name(s): Same.

Family & Scientific Name: Anguidae; *Elgaria multicarinata* ssp.

Identifying Features: They have short but functional legs, attenuate form, and a lengthwise skin fold on each lower side. Dark stripes along centers of belly scales are visible.

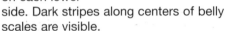

Similar Species: Northern alligator lizards are less elongated and have the dark belly stripes between the scale rows. Texas alligator lizards have a white mottled gray belly and may have dark lines along the centers of the belly scales.

Range & Origin: Pacific coast of the United States and Baja California. All specimens in the pet trade are collected from the wild.

Adult Size: 12–14 inches.

Life Span: To 10+ years.

Terrarium Size: One or two specimens can be kept in a 20-gallon, long terrarium. Three or more specimens should have a 40–75-gallon terrarium.

Terrarium Type: This is a dry woodland and semiaridland species. The terrarium substrate should consist of several inches of almost dry, sandy soil, over which a layer of leaf litter is strewn. Hides should be provided. One end of the terrarium should be illuminated and warmed from above.

Social Structure: Usually communal.

Diet: A variety of insects, crickets, mealworms, waxworms, grasshoppers, and roaches are readily accepted. Dust insects with vitamin D_3-calcium powder twice weekly for baby glass lizards and ovulating females, once weekly otherwise.

Potential Problems: When properly fed, hydrated, and warmed these are hardy, relatively trouble-free lizards.

References:

Bartlett, R. D., and Patricia Bartlett. *Lizard Care from A to Z.* Hauppauge, NY: Barron's Educational Series, Inc., 1997.

Bartlett, R. D., and Patricia Bartlett. *Terrarium and Cage Construction and Care.* Hauppauge, NY: Barron's Educational Series, Inc., 1999.

Four-lined Plated Lizard

Trade Name(s): Same.

Family & Scientific Name: *Zonosaurus quadrilineatus.*

Identifying Features: These lizards have a moderate size, shiny scales, and four cream to yellow lines on a dark body.

Similar Species: Other Malagasy species may have three or five light lines.

Range & Origin: Madagascar. The pet trade is dependent upon wild collected specimens.

Adult Size: 15 inches.

Life Span: To 24+ years.

Terrarium Size: One or two specimens can dwell in a 40–75-gallon terrarium. Three or more specimens need a 75–100-gallon terrarium.

Terrarium Type: Dry savanna or aridland setup is fine. Preferentially, this species of plated lizard dwells in dry scrublands. Captives seem to do well when provided with slabs of corkbark on which they may bask and between which they may hide. A leaf-litter or dry mulch substrate, deep enough for burrowing is useful.

Social Structure: These lizards are communal.

Diet: In addition to a variety of insects, some finely chopped fruit and the fruit-honey day gecko mixture will be consumed. Dust insects with vitamin D_3-calcium powder twice weekly for baby skinks and ovulating females, once weekly otherwise.

Potential Problems: This is a hardy, easily kept, and trouble-free lizard.

References:

Bartlett, R. D., and Patricia Bartlett. *Lizard Care from A to Z.* Hauppauge, NY: Barron's Educational Series, Inc., 1997.

Bartlett, R. D., and Patricia Bartlett. *Terrarium and Cage Construction and Care.* Hauppauge, NY: Barron's Educational Series, Inc., 1999.

Rough-scaled Plated Lizard

Trade Name(s):
Same.
Family & Scientific Name:
Gerrhosauridae;
Gerrhosaurus major.
Identifying Features: This olive-tan to olive-brown lizard is heavy-bodied and has a tail of moderate length. The

scales are heavily keeled (especially so on the tail), but not truly spinose.

Similar Species: The giant plated lizard is larger, more flattened in appearance, and has a well-defined light stripe along each side.

Range & Origin: Africa. The pet trade is dependent upon wild collected specimens.

Adult Size: 15 inches.

Life Span: To 24+ years.

Terrarium Size: One or two specimens can dwell in a 50–75-gallon capacity terrarium. Three or more specimens need a 75–150-gallon terrarium.

Terrarium Type: Dry savanna or aridland setup is fine. Preferentially, this species of plated lizard dwells on escarpments and amid boulders, seeking safety in rock crevices. This is a difficult habitat to simulate. Captives seem to do well when provided with slabs of corkbark on which they may bask and between which they may hide.

Social Structure: These lizards are communal.

Diet: In addition to a variety of insects, some finely chopped fruit and the fruit-honey day gecko mixture will all be consumed. Dust insects with vitamin D_3-calcium powder twice weekly for babies and ovulating females, once weekly otherwise.

Potential Problems: This is a hardy, easily kept, and almost trouble-free lizard.

References:

Bartlett, R. D., and Patricia Bartlett. *Lizard Care from A to Z.* Hauppauge, NY: Barron's Educational Series, Inc., 1997.

Bartlett, R. D., and Patricia Bartlett. *Terrarium and Cage Construction and Care.* Hauppauge, NY: Barron's Educational Series, Inc., 1999.

Girdle-tailed (Armadillo) Lizards

Trade Name(s): Same.

Family & Scientific Name: Cordylidae; *Cordylus warreni* ssp. (Warren's girdle-tailed lizard) and *C. tropidosternum* ssp. (tropical girdle-tailed lizard).

Identifying Features: The subspecies of *C.*

warreni are flattened lizards that are adapted to life on and between rocks. They vary in dorsal color from black (most races) to brown (Berberton and orange-bellied races) with small light patches. All have enlarged spines around the back of the head and on the neck, sides, and tail. *C. tropidosternum* is less flattened, and less spinose on the head, neck, and sides, but does have enlarged, spiny tail scales. They are clad in scales that vary from rich brown to olive-brown.

Similar Species: Several other species of girdle-tailed lizards are occasionally available. Rely on your dealer for identification.

Range & Origin: Southern Africa. The pet trade is dependent upon wild collected specimens.

Adult Size: Warren's girdle-tail varies from 8½–12 inches in length. The tropical girdle-tail tops out at about 6½ inches.

Life Span: 7–12+ years.

Terrarium Size: Up to a trio of *C. warreni* may be kept in a 40-gallon or larger terrarium. A 20-gallon, long terrarium will suffice for up to a trio of the smaller *T. tropidosternum*.

Terrarium Type: Dry savanna terraria are suitable. The several subspecies of Warren's girdle-tailed lizard prefer simulated rock outcrops with crevices into which they can move when startled. The races of the tropical girdle-tailed lizard utilize corkbark tubes and stacked plaques.

Social Structure: With sufficient visual barriers, these species usually do well communally in a large cage.

Diet: In addition to a variety of insects, some finely chopped fruit and the fruit-honey day gecko mixture will all be consumed. Dust insects with vitamin D_3-calcium powder twice weekly for baby skinks and ovulating females, once weekly otherwise.

Potential Problems: None, providing basic needs for housing and food are met.

References:

Bartlett, R. D., and Patricia Bartlett. *Lizard Care from A to Z.* Hauppauge, NY: Barron's Educational Series, Inc., 1997.

Bartlett, R. D., and Patricia Bartlett. *Terrarium and Cage Construction and Care.* Hauppauge, NY: Barron's Educational Series, Inc., 1999.

Leopard Gecko

Trade Name(s): Same. Hobbyists have coined several catchy names, such as "blizzard lizard," for certain color morphs.

Family & Scientific Name: Eublepharidae; *Eublepharis macularius.*

Identifying Features: The wild color and pattern is yellow with a variable pattern (banded in babies, reticulated in adults) of dark pigment. There are now many additional morphs, including but not limited to, albinos, leucistic, striped, very yellow, and very dark.

Similar Species: The African fat-tailed gecko is brown and gray and usually retains very precise bands throughout its life.

Range & Origin: India, Pakistan. Although a few specimens are still wild collected for the pet industry, most of the tens of thousands of babies sold annually are captive-bred and hatched.

Adult Size: Commonly 6½–8 inches. Occasionally to about 10 inches.

Life Span: 25–30 years.

Terrarium Size: A single male or a pair may be maintained in a 10- or 15-gallon capacity terrarium. If additional specimens are to be kept as a group, the size of the terrarium should be increased.

Terrarium Type: These are arid-land geckos that thrive in a desert or dry-savanna terrarium. A substrate of a few inches of sand or sandy soil will suffice. Ample hiding areas should be provided.

Social Structure: Males fight with other males, but coexist well with one or more females.

Diet: A variety of gut-loaded insects should be offered, but an occasional pinky mouse will be eaten. Fruit-honey gecko food mixture will be lapped. Dust insects with vitamin D_3-calcium powder twice weekly for baby geckos and ovulating females, once weekly otherwise.

Potential Problems: This is one of the hardiest of lizards. No problems are commonly seen.

References:

Bartlett, R. D., and Patricia Bartlett. *Geckos.* Hauppauge, NY: Barron's Educational Series, Inc., 1995.

Bartlett, R. D., and Patricia Bartlett. *Leopard and Fat-tailed Geckos.* Hauppauge, NY: Barron's Educational Series, Inc., 1999.

Fat-tailed Gecko

Trade Name(s): Same.

Family & Scientific Name: Eublepharidae; *Hemitheconyx caudicinctus*

Identifying Features: Precise brown and grayish tan bands are retained throughout the life of this lizard.

Designer colors—albinos, leucistics, and those with reddish ground color—are now available. A naturally occurring phase with a white vertebral stripe (as well as the bands), is commonly encountered.

Similar Species: The pattern of the brown and yellow leopard gecko becomes reticulated with age.

Range & Origin: Tropical western Africa. Wild collected specimens continue to be imported, but this species is now captive-bred in the thousands annually.

Adult Size: 6–9 inches.

Life Span: 14–20 years.

Terrarium Size: A single male or a pair may be maintained in a 10- or 15-gallon capacity terrarium. If additional specimens are to be kept as a group, the size of the terrarium should be increased.

Terrarium Type: These geckos require the slightest bit of moisture in the substrate. A substrate of a few inches of cypress mulch (or other nonaromatic mulch) seems ideal. Ample hiding areas should be provided.

Social Structure: Males fight with other males, but coexist well with one or more females.

Diet: Primarily, a variety of gut-loaded insects, but an occasional pinky mouse will be eaten, and fruit-honey gecko food mixture will be lapped. Dust insects with vitamin D_3-calcium powder twice weekly for baby geckos and ovulating females, once weekly otherwise.

Potential Problems: Imported specimens are often dehydrated, starved, and harbor an untenable load of endoparasites. Even with veterinarian intervention, many die. On the other hand, captive produced fat-tailed geckos are very hardy and require little in the way of specialized care. Buy captive-bred!

References:

Bartlett, R. D., and Patricia Bartlett. *Geckos.* Hauppauge, NY: Barron's Educational Series, Inc., 1995.

Bartlett, R. D., and Patricia Bartlett. *Leopard and Fat-tailed Geckos.* Hauppauge, NY: Barron's Educational Series, Inc., 1999.

Dwarf Fat-tailed Gecko

Trade Name(s): Same.

Family & Scientific Name: Eublepharidae; *Holodactylus africanus.*

Identifying Features: This is a strange little burrowing gecko that appears occasionally in

the pet trade. It is big-headed, thin-bodied, and stumpy-tailed. Like many other of the eublepharines, it is clad in bands of tan and brown. Persistently nocturnal, the heavily lidded eyes of this gecko are often squinted almost shut during the hours of daylight.

Similar Species: None.

Range & Origin: Eastern Africa. All pet trade specimens are collected from the wild.

Adult Size: 3½–4 inches.

Life Span: Unknown. These little burrowing lizards have proven delicate until acclimated. To date the mortality has been unnaturally high. There has now been some captive breeding, and captive lifespans are up to 4+ years. It is expected that a longevity of 5–10 years eventually will be realized.

Terrarium Size: 10–15-gallon capacity.

Terrarium Type: Rocky desert or dry savanna. Be certain that rocks or other cage furniture cannot shift and injure the lizards. The substrate should be several inches deep to allow the lizards to burrow. The bottom layers of sand should be barely dampened. This can be accomplished by pushing a small diameter PVC pipe through the layers of sand to the terrarium's bottom glass. Then dribble small amounts of water into the pipe. The water will percolate out along the bottom of the tank, moistening the bottom layers, and leaving the top layers dry.

Social Structure: Males may be antagonistic. A single male coexists well with any number of females. The terrarium must be large enough to accommodate all comfortably.

Diet: Feed daily. Small crickets, termites, baby mealworms, and all similar insects are accepted. Insects should be gut-loaded. Dust insects with vitamin D_3-calcium powder twice weekly for baby geckos and ovulating females, once weekly otherwise. Also offer fruit-honey gecko mixture.

Potential Problems: Fresh imports are delicate and many have died. Once acclimated, they are hardy. The few captive-bred and hatched young that are available seem even hardier.

References:

Bartlett, R. D., and Patricia Bartlett. *Geckos.* Hauppauge, NY: Barron's Educational Series, Inc., 1995.

Bartlett, R. D., and Patricia Bartlett. *Leopard and Fat-tailed Geckos.* Hauppauge, NY: Barron's Educational Series, Inc., 1999.

Madagascar Green Day Geckos (small)

Trade Name(s): There are perhaps, two dozen species of small Green Day Geckos now being sold in the pet trade. Each has its own common and scientific name. Among these are such species as the Golddust, the Seipp's, and the Neon Day Geckos. Rely on your dealer for accurate identification.

Family & Scientific Name: Gekkonidae; *Phelsuma* species.

Identifying Features: Most species have a Kelly green back and sides with a varying number of orange dorsal dots or spots. The neon day gecko differs by having a turquoise tail and a chartreuse head. A wide dark stripe runs along each side.

Similar Species: The various day geckos of the genus *Phelsuma* are the only bright green day geckos regularly seen in the pet trade.

Range & Origin: Madagascar and Indian Ocean Islands. A fair proportion of many species are now captive-bred.

Adult Size: From 3 inches (neon day gecko)–5 inches (golddust day gecko).

Life Span: 6–15+ years.

Terrarium Size: One or two of the smallest species can be housed in a 5–10-gallon tank. Double the tank size for the larger forms, or if you intend to keep 3 or 4 specimens.

Terrarium Type: Variable, but relatively simple is often the best. A substrate of leaf litter, diagonal and horizontal perches (at least of the diameter of the lizard's body), hiding areas (corkbark tubes or plaques are fine), an egg deposition site (if necessary), and a live vining plant (pothos is one of the most easily kept) can be incorporated into a very suitable terrarium.

Social Structure: Males fight each other. A single male and from one to several females usually are perfectly compatible.

Diet: A variety of insects and continual access to a fruit-honey mixture are the suggested diet. Viatmin D_3-calcium additives should either be dusted on the insects or mixed into the fruit-honey formula. Feed vitamin additives for baby geckos and ovulating females twice weekly; for other geckos once weekly will suffice.

Potential Problems: These lizards drink pendant droplets of water misted on to the terrarium sides and foliage. They readily autotomize their tail. Do not grasp any day gecko by the tail. The very delicate skin is easily torn during normal handling. Move lizards of this genus by shepherding them into a jar or other receptacle.

References:

Bartlett, R. D., and Patricia Bartlett. *Day Geckos.* Hauppauge, NY: Barron's Educational Series, Inc., (forthcoming).

Bartlett, R. D., and Patricia Bartlett. *Geckos.* Hauppauge, NY: Barron's Educational Series, Inc., 1995.

Madagascar Green Day & Standing's Day Geckos (large)

Trade Name(s):
In addition to Standing's Day Gecko, there are four subspecies of the giant day gecko that appear in the pet trade. Each of these has its own common and scientific name.

Family & Scientific Name:
Gekkonidae; Giant day gecko, *Phelsuma madagascariensis* ssp. (pictured); Standing's day gecko, *P. standingi.*

Identifying Features: The various subspecies of the giant day gecko have a Kelly green back and sides with a varying number of orange dots or spots dorsally. The Standing's day gecko has a pale green back with dark reticulations.

Similar Species: The various day geckos of the genus *Phelsuma* are the only bright green day geckos regularly seen in the pet trade.

Range & Origin: Madagascar. Although many of the specimens available are collected from the wild, both of these species are now being bred extensively in captivity.

Adult Size: 9–11½ inches.

Life Span: 6–15+ years.

Terrarium Size:
One or two specimens can be housed in a 20-gallon tank. Double the tank size if you intend to keep three or four specimens.

Terrarium Type:
Variable, but relatively simple is often the best. A substrate of leaf litter, diagonal and horizontal perches (at least of the diameter of the lizard's body), hiding areas (cork-bark tubes or plaques are fine), an egg deposition site (if necessary), and a live vining plant (pothos is one of the most easily kept) can be incorporated into a very suitable terrarium.

Social Structure: Males fight savagely with other males. A single male, and from one to several females, usually are perfectly compatible.

Diet: A variety of insects and continual access to the fruit-honey mixture (see page 100) are the suggested diet for this gecko. Vitamin D_3-calcium additives should either be dusted on the insects or mixed into the fruit-honey formula. Twice weekly vitamin additives for baby geckos and ovulating females are suggested; for other geckos once weekly will suffice.

Potential Problems: These beautiful lizards drink pendant droplets of water misted on to the terrarium side and foliage. They readily autotomize their tail. Do not grasp any day gecko by the tail. Day geckos have very delicate skin that is easily torn during normal handling. If it is necessary to move lizards of this genus around, do so by shepherding them into a jar or other receptacle. Do not grasp them by hand.

References:

Bartlett, R. D., and Patricia Bartlett. *Day Geckos.* Hauppauge, NY: Barron's Educational Series, Inc., (forthcoming).

Bartlett, R. D., and Patricia Bartlett. *Geckos.* Hauppauge, NY: Barron's Educational Series, Inc., 1995.

Green-eyed Gecko

Trade Name(s):
Jade-eyed
Gecko.
Family & Scientific Name:
Gekkonidae;
Gekko smithii.
***Identifying
Features:*** Gray
color, jade green
eyes, large size
but moderately
slender, large
toepads, somewhat tuberculate skin.

Similar Species: No other large pet trade
gecko with toepads has jade green eyes.
Range & Origin: Southeast Asia and
Malaysia. Except in very rare instances, pet
trade specimens are wild collected imports.
Adult Size: 10–12 inches.
Life Span: 7+ years; 10–20 years should be
an attainable age.
Terrarium Size: For one or for a pair of
adults, a vertically oriented 20-gallon long
tank will suffice.
Terrarium Type: A leafy or soil substrate
and tubes of corkbark for hiding will suffice.

Misting every
other day provides drinking
water and cage
moisture.
Social Structure: Males fight
persistently with
other males.
A pair, trio, or
single male
with a group of
females, coexist
well.
Diet: Primarily, a
variety of gut-loaded insects, but an occasional pinky mouse will be eaten, and the
fruit-honey gecko food mixture will be
lapped. Dust insects with vitamin D_3-
calcium powder twice weekly for baby
geckos and ovulating females, once
weekly otherwise.
Potential Problems: Like most geckos, this
species prefers to lap pendulous water
droplets from cage furniture and plants.
References:
Bartlett, R. D., and Patricia Bartlett. *Geckos.*
  Hauppauge, NY: Barron's Educational
  Series, Inc., 1995.

Tokay Gecko

Trade Name(s): Same.

Family & Scientific Name: Gekkonidae; *Gekko gecko*.

Identifying Features: Gray color with peach, tan, or orange spots that often contain a skin tubercle. They have yellow eyes, large in size, but moderately slender (some old captives are very heavy bodied), large toepads, and somewhat tuberculate skin. Very ready to bite an intruder.

Similar Species: No other large pet trade gecko with toepads has orange(ish) spots.

Range & Origin: Southeast Asia and Malaysia. Except in very rare instances, pet trade specimens are wild collected imports.

Adult Size: 10–12 inches.

Life Span: 23+ years.

Terrarium Size: For one or for a pair of adults, a vertically oriented 30-gallon, long tank will suffice.

Terrarium Type: A leafy or soil substrate and tubes of corkbark for hiding are ideal.

Social Structure: Males are very aggressive toward each other. A pair, trio, or single male with a group of females coexist well.

Diet: Primarily, a variety of gut-loaded insects, but an occasional pinky mouse will be eaten, and the fruit-honey gecko food mixture will be lapped. Dust insects with vitamin D_3-calcium powder twice weekly for baby geckos and ovulating females, once weekly otherwise.

Potential Problems: Like most geckos, this species prefers to lap pendulous water droplets from cage furniture and plants. Do not allow it to become dehydrated. It will drink from a dish if the water is moving and if the dish is elevated somewhat.

References:

Bartlett, R. D., and Patricia Bartlett. *Geckos.* Hauppauge, NY: Barron's Educational Series, Inc., 1995.

Vietnam Golden (Lemon) Gecko

Trade Name(s): Lemon Gecko, Yellow Gecko.

Family & Scientific Name: Gekkonidae; *Gekko ulikovskii.*

Identifying Features: A large, smooth-skinned gecko with huge toepads and a yellow to olive-gold blush over much of its body.

Similar Species: Green-eyed gecko has jade green eyes. Tokay gecko has much wartier skin.

Range & Origin: Vietnam. All pet trade specimens are wild collected.

Adult Size: 8–10 inches.

Life Span: Unknown, but 10+ years (perhaps to 20 years) should be possible.

Terrarium Size: For one or for a pair of adults, a vertically oriented 20-gallon, long tank will suffice.

Terrarium Type: A leafy or soil substrate, and tubes of corkbark for hiding, will suffice. Ambient moisture and drinking water can be provided by misting every other day or by a dish of moving water (use an air stone or a drip feeder for the water.)

Social Structure: Males fight persistently with other males. A pair, trio, or single male with a group of females coexist well.

Diet: Primarily, a variety of gut-loaded insects, but an occasional pinky mouse will be eaten, and the fruit-honey gecko food mixture (see page 100) will be lapped. Dust insects with vitamin D_3-calcium powder twice weekly for baby geckos and ovulating females, once weekly otherwise.

Potential Problems: Like most geckos, this species prefers to lap pendulous water droplets from cage furniture and plants. Do not allow it to dehydrate.

References:

Bartlett, R. D., and Patricia Bartlett. *Geckos.* Hauppauge, NY: Barron's Educational Series, Inc., 1995.

Skunk Gecko

Trade Name(s): Lined Gecko.

Family & Scientific Name: Gekkonidae; *Gekko vittatus.*

Identifying Features: Brown color, gold eyes, large size, and large toepads; generally there are light spots on the upper surface of the tail.

Similar Species: No other large pet trade gecko with toepads has the vertebral stripe.

Range & Origin: Southeast Asia and Malaysia. Except in very rare instances, pet trade specimens are wild collected imports.

Adult Size: 10–12 inches.

Life Span: 7+ years; 10–20 years should be an attainable age.

Terrarium Size: For one or for a pair of adults, a vertically oriented 20-gallon, long tank will suffice.

Terrarium Type: A leafy or soil substrate and tubes of corkbark for hiding will suffice.

Social Structure: Males are aggressive and fight persistently with other males. A pair, trio, or single male with a group of females coexist well.

Diet: Primarily, a variety of gut-loaded insects, but an occasional pinky mouse will be eaten, and the fruit-honey gecko food mixture will be lapped. Dust insects with vitamin D_3-calcium powder twice weekly for baby geckos and ovulating females, once weekly otherwise.

Potential Problems: Like most geckos, this species prefers to lap pendulous water droplets from cage furniture and plants. Do not allow it to become dehydrated.

References:

Bartlett, R. D., and Patricia Bartlett. *Geckos.* Hauppauge, NY: Barron's Educational Series, Inc., 1995.

New Caledonian Crested Gecko

Trade Name(s): Same. Also Eyelash Gecko.

Family & Scientific Name: *Rhacodactylus ciliatus.*

Identifying Features: This distinctive gecko is of moderate size, has a fringe of pointed scales over each eye,

and a serrate crest extending rearward from each eye to the base of the tail.

Similar Species: None.

Range & Origin: New Caledonia. Most examples now in the pet trade are captive-bred and hatched.

Adult Size: 6–7 inches long.

Life Span: 5+ years; more than 15 is probably an attainable goal.

Terrarium Size: A single example of this arboreal gecko can be maintained in a 10-gallon terrarium. We prefer to expand to a 15-gallon for a pair and a 20-gallon, long for a trio.

Terrarium Type: A forest and scrub gecko, this species prefers a humid cage and both diagonal and horizontal limbs (at least twice the diameter of the body of the lizard)

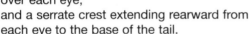

for perching. It should be discouraged from hanging on the glass in a head-down position since this seems to permanently kink the tail to one side.

Social Structure: Although a relatively easygoing gecko, males do fight. However, a single male, and from one to several females, coexist well.

Diet: A variety of insects and continual access to the fruit-honey mixture are the suggested diet for this gecko. Vitamin D_3-calcium additives should either be dusted on the insects or mixed into the fruit-honey formula. Twice weekly vitamin additives for baby geckos and ovulating females are suggested; for other geckos once weekly will suffice.

Potential Problems: This is a very hardy and largely trouble-free gecko.

References:

Bartlett, R. D., and Patricia Bartlett. *Geckos.* Hauppauge, NY: Barron's Educational Series, Inc., 1995.

New Caledonian Gargoyle Gecko

Trade Name(s): Same.

Family & Scientific Name: Gekkonidae; *Rhacodactylus auriculatus*.

Identifying Features: This moderately sized gecko has both a striped and a mottled form. Both have a brownish to grayish ground color with darker striping or poorly defined crossbands. It has large toepads, a slightly upturned nose, and a slender tail.

Similar Species: The similarly sized *R. serasinorum* (no common name) is very rarely seen, but occasionally available. It, too, has a banded form that is more precisely marked than the gargoyle gecko. The striped form of *R. serasinorum* has a posteriorly directed white bridle on the back of the head and nape.

Range & Origin: New Caledonia. Most examples now in the pet trade are captive-bred and hatched.

Adult Size: 6–7 inches long.

Life Span: 5+ years; more than 15 years is probably an attainable goal.

Terrarium Size: A single example of this arboreal gecko can be maintained in a 10-gallon terrarium. We prefer to expand to a 15-gallon for a pair and a 20-gallon, long for a trio.

Terrarium Type: A forest and scrub gecko, this species prefers a humid cage and both diagonal and horizontal limbs (at least twice the diameter of the body of the lizard) for perching. Mist every other day for water.

Social Structure: This is a relatively easy-going gecko, but males do fight. However, a single male and from one to several females coexist well.

Diet: A variety of insects and continual access to the fruit-honey mixture are the suggested diet for this gecko. Vitamin D_3-calcium additives should either be dusted on the insects or mixed into the fruit-honey formula. Twice weekly vitamin additives for baby geckos and ovulating females are suggested; for other geckos once weekly will suffice.

Potential Problems: This is a very hardy and a largely trouble-free gecko.

References:

Bartlett, R. D., and Patricia Bartlett. *Geckos.* Hauppauge, NY: Barron's Educational Series, Inc., 1995.

New Caledonian Giant Gecko

Trade Name(s): Same.

Family & Scientific Name: Gekkonidae; *Rhacodactylus leachianus*.

Identifying Features: Adults are huge, heavy bodied, and short tailed. They have a tan to brownish or brownish-gray

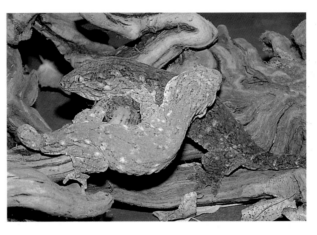

ground color with irregular crossbands of lighter spots. The eyes look proportionately small; it has large toepads and a slender tail that is round in cross section.

Similar Species: *R. trachyrhynchos* and *R. chahoua* are almost as large as the giant gecko, but remain very rarely seen in the pet trade. At the moment, neither has been given a common name.

Range & Origin: New Caledonia. There are several morphs from several islands surrounding the main island. Most examples now in the pet trade are captive-bred and hatched.

Adult Size: Up to a very heavy-bodied 14 inches long.

Life Span: 8+ years; between 15 and 20 years is probably an attainable goal.

Terrarium Size: A single example or pair of this arboreal gecko can be maintained in a 40-gallon terrarium. For three or more we suggest a minimum of a 75-gallon capacity terrarium.

Terrarium Type: A forest and scrub gecko, this species prefers a humid cage and both diagonal and horizontal limbs (at least twice the diameter of the body of the lizard) for perching.

Social Structure: Males fight. However, a single male, and from one to several females, coexist well.

Diet: A variety of insects and continual access to the fruit-honey mixture, are the suggested diet for this gecko. Vitamin D_3-calcium additives should either be dusted on the insects or mixed into the fruit-honey formula. Twice weekly vitamin additives for baby geckos and ovulating females are suggested; for other geckos once weekly will suffice.

Potential Problems: This is a very hardy and largely trouble-free gecko.

References:

Bartlett, R. D., and Patricia Bartlett. *Geckos.* Hauppauge, NY: Barron's Educational Series, Inc., 1995.

Mauretanian Gecko

Trade Name(s):
Same. Also,
Moorish Gecko,
Crocodile
Gecko.
Family & Scientific Name:
Gekkonidae;
Tarentola mauretanica.
Identifying Features: This
is a very rough-
scaled arboreal
gecko with

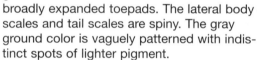

broadly expanded toepads. The lateral body scales and tail scales are spiny. The gray ground color is vaguely patterned with indistinct spots of lighter pigment.

Similar Species: None.

Range & Origin: Common from the vicinity of the Mediterranean Sea to North Africa. It is now also established in south Florida. Most of the examples now in the pet trade have been collected from the wild in North Africa.

Adult Size: To about 6 inches.

Life Span: 14+ years.

Terrarium Size: A 15–20-gallon capacity terrarium houses one, or a pair, of these lizards. If a larger group is to be kept, the size of the terrarium should be increased.

Terrarium Type: In the wild, this gecko dwells on walls, cliff faces, and rock out-croppings. A terrarium that simulates this habitat is appreciated. However, captive Mauretanian geckos also utilize vertical and diagonal corkbark plaques.

Social Structure: As with almost all geckos, males are aggressive to other males. This is especially true during the breeding season. However, one male and up to several females, can live communally.

Diet: These geckos readily eat most kinds of non-noxious insects. Crickets, meal-worms, waxworms, silkworms, and other such insects are accepted. Dust insects with vitamin D_3-calcium powder twice weekly for baby geckos and ovulating females, once weekly otherwise. Also offer the fruit-honey gecko mixture.

Potential Problems: This is a very hardy and comparatively problem-free species.

References:

Bartlett, R. D., and Patricia Bartlett. *Geckos.* Hauppauge, NY: Barron's Educational Series, Inc., 1995.

White-spotted Gecko

Trade Name(s): Same.

Family & Scientific Name: Gekkonidae; *Tarentola annularis.*

Identifying Features: There are four white spots on the shoulders.

Similar Species: None with these markings.

Range & Origin: North Africa. Tenuously established in south Florida. All specimens in the pet trade are collected from the wild.

Adult Size: To about 6 inches.

Life Span: 10+ years.

Terrarium Size: Although alert, these lizards are not overly active. A 15–20-gallon capacity terrarium houses one, or a pair, of these lizards. If a larger group is to be kept, the size of the terrarium should be increased.

Terrarium Type: In the wild, this gecko dwells on walls, cliff faces, and rock outcroppings. A terrarium that simulates this habitat is appreciated. However, captive white-spotted geckos also utilize vertical and diagonal corkbark plaques.

Social Structure: As with almost all geckos, males are aggressive to other males. This is especially true during the breeding season. However, one male and up to several females, can live communally.

Diet: These geckos readily eat most kinds of non-noxious insects. Crickets, mealworms, waxworms, silkworms, and other such insects are accepted. Dust insects with vitamin D_3-calcium powder twice weekly for baby geckos and ovulating females, once weekly otherwise. Also offer the fruit-honey gecko mixture.

Potential Problems: This is a very hardy and comparatively problem-free species.

References:

Bartlett, R. D., and Patricia Bartlett. *Geckos.* Hauppauge, NY: Barron's Educational Series, Inc., 1995.

Common Flying Gecko

Trade Name(s): Same.

Family & Scientific Name: Gekkonidae; *Ptychozoon* sp., usually *P. lionatum.*

Identifying Features: The grayish color, small size, fringed chin, body and limbs, and strongly

scalloped tail fringes, quickly identify this gecko to genus. Species identifications are considerably more difficult.

Similar Species: There are several other species of flying geckos, none of which is commonly seen in the pet trade—at least at this time. They are so similar that they are difficult to identify to species.

Range & Origin: Thailand and Burma. Most of the specimens now available in the pet trade are collected from the wild.

Terrarium Size: A 20-gallon capacity, vertically oriented, terrarium houses one, or several of these lizards. If more than four are to be kept, the size of the terrarium should be increased.

Terrarium Type: In the wild, this is an arboreal gecko, seeking seclusion behind loosened bark, in cracks in the trunk, or similar habitats. A terrarium that simulates this habitat is appreciated. Corkbark tubes or plaques can be used to make the hiding areas. Mist the enclosure to provide a water source.

Social Structure: Even the males of this gecko are comparatively benign. As long as numerous hiding places, visual barriers, and an adequately large terrarium are provided, this species may be kept communally.

Diet: These geckos readily eat most kinds of non-noxious insects. Small crickets, waxworms, mealworms, and silkworms are among the insects readily accepted. Dust insects with vitamin D_3-calcium powder twice weekly for baby geckos and ovulating females, once weekly otherwise. Also offer the fruit-honey gecko mixture.

Potential Problems: Once acclimated, as long as it is kept adequately hydrated, this is a very hardy and comparatively problem-free species.

References:

Bartlett, R. D., and Patricia Bartlett. *Geckos.* Hauppauge, NY: Barron's Educational Series, Inc., 1995.

Frog-eyed Gecko

Trade Name(s): Same; there are several species in the genus. These are also sometimes referred to as Skink Geckos and Sand Geckos.

Family & Scientific Name: Gekkonidae; *Teratoscincus* sp., usually *T. scincus.*

Identifying Features: Very large head, large lidless eyes, short tail with enlarged, raspy, scales dorsally (most species), sand to dusky colored, often with light vertebral and darker paravertebral stripes. No toepads.

Similar Species: There are several species of frog-eyed geckos currently on the market.

Range & Origin: Southern Asia to western China. Although these are now being captive-bred with some regularity, a preponderance of the available specimens are wild collected.

Adult Size: 4–6¼ inches.

Life Span: 15+ years.

Terrarium Size: For one or a pair of adults, a horizontally oriented 20-gallon, long tank will suffice.

Terrarium Type: Rocky aridland or dry savanna terrarium with a substrate of several inches of sand is best. Be sure the rocks cannot shift and harm the lizards. These lizards have a very permeable skin. Although dwellers of the aridlands, they require a little moisture in the lower levels of sand. Push a small diameter pipe through the sand to the bottom of the tank, then slowly trickle water into the pipe. The water will percolate outward along the bottom of the tank, moistening the lowest layers of sand.

Social Structure: Males are not communal. Pairs and additional females can be maintained together.

Diet: Primarily consists of insects and land snails, but an occasional large specimen will accept a pinky mouse and all lap the fruit-honey mixture. Females especially need land snails in their diet. Dust insects with vitamin D_3-calcium powder twice weekly for baby geckos and ovulating females, once weekly otherwise.

Potential Problems: Many imported specimens are dehydrated and starving when received. Avoid these. The tail can be very easily broken off. Do not grasp any gecko by the tail. Frog-eyed geckos have delicate skin that is easily torn during normal handling. Move these lizards by shepherding them into a jar or other receptacle. Do not grasp them by hand.

References:

Bartlett, R. D., and Patricia Bartlett. *Geckos.* Hauppauge, NY: Barron's Educational Series, Inc., 1995.

Henkel's Leaf-tailed Gecko

Trade Name(s): Same. Also Madagascar Leaf-tailed Gecko.

Family & Scientific Name: Gekkonidae; *Uroplatus henkeli.*

Identifying Features: Grayish color (sometimes with cross-

bands); elongated slender body; large head; flattened leaf-like tail; very large toepads. Fringes of scales along legs, lower jaw, and sides of body.

Similar Species: The fringed leaf-tailed gecko is externally similar, but genetically different, and comes from eastern Madagascar. Rely on your dealer for accurate identification.

Range & Origin: Northwestern Madagascar. Although this is the species of leaf-tailed gecko most often bred in captivity, most specimens seen in the pet trade have still been collected from the wild.

Adult Size: About 10 inches.

Life Span: 2–6 (perhaps more) years.

Terrarium Size: Quiet, usually hanging in head-down position by day, these lizards actively hunt at night. One or a pair can be kept in a 29-gallon capacity terrarium. A 50–75-gallon capacity tank houses three or more of these geckos.

Terrarium Type: These are forest geckos that spend the day hanging head-down on small diameter tree trunks. There, they are remark-

ably well camouflaged. A humid, vertically oriented, woodland terrarium or wire cage containing a few upright limbs about three inches in diameter will suffice. One or a pair of geckos can be housed in a 20-gallon, long tank; larger capacity (40–75 gallons) tanks should be used for a larger group.

Social Structure: Males may skirmish with other males, but if the cage is large, has visual barriers, and ample hiding places (like cork-bark tubes) they usually will coexist. Females and juveniles can be kept communally.

Diet: Crickets, king mealworms, grasshoppers, roaches, silkworms, and waxworms, are all eagerly accepted. Leaf-tailed geckos also lap at the fruit-honey mixture traditionally given day geckos. Dust insects with vitamin D_3-calcium powder twice weekly for baby geckos and ovulating females, once weekly otherwise. Mist the cage every other day.

Potential Problems: Once acclimated, this is a hardy gecko species.

References:

Bartlett, R. D., and Patricia Bartlett. *Day Geckos.* Hauppauge, NY: Barron's Educational Series, Inc., (forthcoming).

Bartlett, R. D., and Patricia Bartlett. *Geckos.* Hauppauge, NY: Barron's Educational Series, Inc., 1995.

Namib Web-footed Gecko

Trade Name(s): Same. Also, African Web-footed Gecko, Kalahari Web-footed Gecko.

Family & Scientific Name: Gekkonidae; *Palmatogecko rangei.*

Identifying Features: This is a small gecko of the fog-shrouded, yielding desert sands. Its webbed feet (all four) help support it when it is moving on the surface, and help it to burrow. The large eyes are lidless, the nose sharply pointed, and the body skin, translucent.

Similar Species: No other gecko has all four feet webbed.

Range & Origin: The Namib Desert of southwestern Africa. Pet trade specimens are wild collected. A very few of these geckos are now being captive-bred.

Adult Size: Total length of 4–5 inches.

Life Span: From 1 to several years.

Terrarium Size: Pairs or trios of this small gecko can be maintained in a 10- or 15-gallon terrarium.

Terrarium Type: Desert with several inches of sand for the substrate. These little geckos will construct long burrows. The bottom layers of the sand should be kept barely moistened. This can be accomplished by trickling water into a small diameter pipe that has been pushed all of the way to the very bottom of the tank.

Social Structure: Males may squabble, but otherwise this gecko can be kept communally.

Diet: Eats tiny insects. Termites are especially relished.

Potential Problems: Providing suitably sized insects are given for food, this gecko is relatively trouble free. Dust insects with vitamin D_3-calcium powder twice weekly for babies and ovulating females, once weekly otherwise.

References:

Bartlett, R. D., and Patricia Bartlett. *Day Geckos.* Hauppauge, NY: Barron's Educational Series, Inc., (forthcoming).

Bartlett, R. D., and Patricia Bartlett. *Geckos.* Hauppauge, NY: Barron's Educational Series, Inc., 1995.

Ocelot Gecko

Trade Name(s): Ocelot Gecko, Madagascar Ground Gecko.

Family & Scientific Name: Gekkonidae; *Paroedura pictus.*

Identifying Features: This species is precisely banded from hatching to young adult-

hood, but then the bands tend to break up and the pattern becomes more reticulate. It may or may not have a distinct vertebral stripe. The lamellae under the toes are in 4–6 rows. The head is broad and very distinct from the neck. This is a terrestrial gecko.

Similar Species: Several other species of *Paroedura* are very similar to the ocelot gecko in external appearance. The one that most closely resembles it is *P. bastardi*, a more arboreal species with the subdigital lamellae in only two rows.

Range & Origin: Madagascar. Some are still imported, but most pet trade ocelot geckos are now captive-bred and hatched.

Adult Size: 4½–6 inches.

Life Span: 10+ years.

Terrarium Size: 15–20-gallon, long for a pair or trio; 40-gallon for a larger group.

Terrarium Type: Dry savanna or semiaridland setup. A substrate of sand, dry mulch, or dried leaves works well.

Social Structure: It is best not to keep more than a single male in any group. He, with one, two, or more, females will do well communally.

Diet: A wide variety of insects—crickets, mealworms, and occasional waxworms, and silkworms—are readily accepted. Ocelot geckos also lap at the fruit-honey mixture provided for day geckos. Dust insects with vitamin D_3-calcium powder twice weekly for babies and ovulating females, once weekly otherwise.

Potential Problems: Providing that you start with a healthy specimen (and captive-born are the best), you should have no problems with this lizard.

References:

Bartlett, R. D., and Patricia Bartlett. *Day Geckos.* Hauppauge, NY: Barron's Educational Series, Inc., (forthcoming).

Bartlett, R. D., and Patricia Bartlett. *Geckos.* Hauppauge, NY: Barron's Educational Series, Inc., 1995.

Savanna Monitor

Trade Name(s): Same.

Family & Scientific Name: Varanidae; *Varanus exanthematicus.*

Identifying Features: This is a tan to gray monitor with a regular and busy pattern of dark-edged light ocelli on the back, sides, and anterior tail. A short, dark, postocular bar terminates just posterior to the posteriormost head scales. The nape (nuchal) scales are prominently enlarged.

Similar Species: The white-throated monitor is very similar but has a sparser pattern of ocelli on the back and the ocular stripe extends rearward to the shoulder and the nape scales are only moderately enlarged.

Range & Origin: Eastern and southern Africa. Pet trade specimens are wild collected or farmed.

Adult Size: Although some may be adult at about 2½ feet in length, others exceed 4½ feet, and a very few near 6 feet.

Life Span: 6 years reported. With proper care the lifespan should exceed 10 years.

Terrarium Size: One or two babies can be housed temporarily in a 20-gallon, long terrarium. One or two adults should be given floor space of no less than 100 square feet.

Terrarium Type: The common name of this monitor is descriptive. They are creatures of the dry African savannas where heat and UV radiation rule summer days. They bask in the morning, often attaining a body temperature of more than 100°F, then forage and seek the cooling shade later. A plain cage (or a dedicated room) is probably the best for this, and other large monitors.

Social Structure: Babies can be kept together. Keep larger specimens singly.

Diet: Although captive savanna monitors readily eat lab rodents, it is now known that this high-fat diet soon leads to obesity and lethargy. A varied diet, high in insects, crayfish, and other low fat foods, is best. Canned monitor foods, if not too high in animal protein, can help fill this monitor's large appetite. Feed vitamin D_3-calcium powder into the diet twice weekly for babies and ovulating females, once weekly otherwise.

Potential Problems: If provided with insufficient vitamin D_3 and calcium, fast growing savanna monitors can develop MBD (metabolic bone disease). Some imported specimens are starved and dehydrated when received. Avoid purchasing these, even as a kindness. Large monitors may be cannibalistic. Segregate the sizes. Male monitors may fight other males savagely. Keep these separated.

References:
Bartlett, R. D., and Patricia Bartlett. *Monitors, Tegus, and Related Lizards.* Hauppauge, NY: Barron's Educational Series, Inc., 1996.

Water Monitor

Trade Name(s): Same.

Family & Scientific Name: Varanidae; *Varanus salvator* ssp.

Identifying Features: There are several subspecies of water monitor that are imported for the pet trade. The color may vary from olive gray or olive black with an orangish blush on the chin, face, (lips dark barred) and neck, to nearly black with regular crossrows of small yellow spots. The nostrils are closer to the tip of the snout than the eye. The tail is laterally flattened for swimming.

Similar Species: Nile monitors can look very similar to the water monitor. However, the nostrils of the Nile monitor are about equidistant between the eye and the tip of the snout.

Range & Origin: Asia, Malaysia, Indonesia. All specimens available in the pet trade are wild collected imports.

Adult Size: To more than 8 feet.

Life Span: 14+ years.

Terrarium Size: One or two babies can be housed temporarily in a 20-gallon, long terrarium. One or two adults should be given a floor space of no less than 100 square feet.

Terrarium Type: This aquatic monitor, with sufficient handling and attention, becomes very tame in captivity. In the wild, they bask in the morning on river and pond banks, or partially exposed in the shallows, often attaining a body temperature of more than 100°F. To cool down they either plunge into, or seek deeper, water. They may forage either in or out of the water. A large cage (or a dedicated room) is probably the best for this and other large monitor species.

Social Structure: Babies can be kept together. Keep larger specimens singly.

Diet: Although captive water monitors often readily eat lab rodents, it is now known that this diet soon leads to obesity and lethargy. A varied diet, high in insects, small fish, crustaceans, and other low fat foods, is best. Incorporate vitamin D_3-calcium powder into the diet twice weekly for babies and ovulating females, once weekly otherwise.

Potential Problems: If deficient in vitamin D_3 and calcium, fast growing water monitors can develop MBD (metabolic bone disease). Some imports are starved and dehydrated when received. Avoid purchasing these, even as a kindness. To keep these monitors communally, it is always best to segregate them by size. Male monitors may fight other males savagely, and may kill females during breeding, especially when the females cannot escape.

References:

Bartlett, R. D., and Patricia Bartlett. *Monitors, Tegus, and Related Lizards.* Hauppauge, NY: Barron's Educational Series, Inc., 1996.

Black-throated Monitor/ White-throated Monitor

Trade Name(s): Same.

Family & Scientific Name: Varanidae; *Varanus albigularis.*

Identifying Features: This is a dark monitor with a well-spaced but regular pattern of

dark-edged light ocelli on the back and sides, and a light-barred dark tail. The post-ocular bar extends rearward to the shoulder. The nape scales are not greatly enlarged. The throat may be either black or white.

Similar Species: The savanna monitor is very similar but has light body color and a very busy pattern of light ocelli on the back, sides, and anterior tail.

Range & Origin: Eastern and southern Africa. Pet trade specimens are wild collected or, more rarely, farmed.

Adult Size: This heavy bodied monitor is adult at 4½–6 feet.

Life Span: 8+ years; more than 10 years should be attainable.

Terrarium Size: One or two babies can be housed temporarily in a 20-gallon, long terrarium. One or two adults should be given a floor space of no less than 100 square feet.

Terrarium Type: The common name of this monitor is descriptive. They are creatures of the dry African savannas. They bask in the

morning, often attaining a body temperature of more than 100°F, then forage and seek the cooling shade later in the day. A large cage (or a dedicated room) is probably the best for this species.

Social Structure: Babies can be kept together. Keep larger specimens singly.

Diet: Although white-throated monitors readily eat lab rodents, it is now known that this high-fat diet quickly leads to obesity and lethargy. A varied diet, high in insects, crayfish, and other low fat foods, is by far the best. Incorporate vitamin D_3-calcium powder into the diet twice weekly for babies and ovulating females, once weekly otherwise.

Potential Problems: If deficient in vitamin D_3 and calcium, fast growing white-throated monitors can develop MBD (metabolic bone disease). Some imports are starved and dehydrated when received. Avoid purchasing these, even as a kindness. Large monitors may be cannibalistic. Segregate the sizes. Male monitors may fight other males savagely. Keep these separated.

References:

Bartlett, R. D., and Patricia Bartlett. *Monitors, Tegus, and Related Lizards.* Hauppauge, NY: Barron's Educational Series, Inc., 1996.

Nile Monitor

Trade Name(s): Same.

Family & Scientific Name: Varanidae; *Varanus niloticus.*

Identifying Features: This monitor has a black body with yellow spotting on the legs, and yellow flecks between regularly spaced, but well separated, crossrows of large yellow ocelli. The tail is laterally flattened and strongly banded with black and yellow. Nostrils are about equidistant between tip of snout and eye.

Similar Species: The Asian water monitor can be similar in coloration and general appearance, but the nostrils are much closer to the tip of the snout than the eye.

Range & Origin: Africa, south of the Sahara.

Adult Size: 5½–6½ feet.

Life Span: 10–20 years.

Terrarium Size: One or two babies can be housed temporarily in a 20-gallon, long terrarium. One or two adults should be given a floor space of no less than 100 square feet.

Terrarium Type: This is a persistently aquatic monitor that often does not tame well. In the wild, they bask in the morning on river- and pond banks, or partially exposed in the shallows. To cool down they either plunge into the water or seek shade on the bank. They may forage either in or out of the water. A large cage (or a dedicated room) is probably the best for this, and other large, monitor species.

Social Structure: Babies can be kept together. Larger specimens are best kept singly.

Diet: Although captive Nile monitors often readily eat lab rodents, it is now known that this high fat diet soon leads to obesity and lethargy. A varied diet, high in insects, small fish, crustaceans, and other low fat content foods, is by far the best. Incorporate vitamin D_3-calcium powder into the diet twice weekly for babies and ovulating females, once weekly otherwise.

Potential Problems: If deficient in vitamin D_3 and calcium, fast growing Nile monitors can develop MBD (metabolic bone disease). Some imported specimens are starved and dehydrated when received. Avoid purchasing these, even as a humanitarian gesture. If trying to keep these monitors communally, it is always best to segregate them by size. Male monitors may fight other males savagely. Keep these separated.

References:
Bartlett, R. D., and Patricia Bartlett. *Monitors, Tegus, and Related Lizards.* Hauppauge, NY: Barron's Educational Series, Inc., 1996.

Storr's Monitor

Trade Name(s): Same.

Family & Scientific Name: Varanidae; *Varanus storri.*

Identifying Features: A small reddish monitor (often lighter middorsally) that has sparse dark dorsal reticulations, and a short, spiny tail.

Similar Species: None in the pet trade.

Range & Origin: Australia. All specimens available in the pet trade are captive-bred and hatched by European or American hobbyists.

Adult Size: 12–14 inches; occasionally to 16 inches.

Life Span: 6–10 years; perhaps longer.

Terrarium Size: The small adult size of this monitor allows a relatively small cage to be used. For a pair, a 75-gallon capacity terrarium (or a cage of equal size) will suffice. If a larger number of lizards are kept, a 100–150-gallon terrarium should be provided.

Terrarium Type: This is a semiaridland and dry savanna monitor. They are often found in the grasses in or near boulder fields. Nevertheless, Storr's monitors are somewhat tolerant of high humidity and frequent rains. We bred them outside in southwest Florida. Yet, we recommend a low humidity dry savanna setup with a several inch deep sandy soil substrate, diagonal basking logs, and many visual barriers.

Social Structure: Males fight with other males. Unless the cage is very large and amply supplied with visual barriers, only one male should be kept per cage. However, a single male and from one to several females usually are compatible.

Diet: A wide variety of insects are readily accepted. Among others, roaches, cicadas, grasshoppers, locusts, crickets, and king mealworms are eaten. Small lizards are also run down and eaten.

Potential Problems: This is a very hardy lizard that should not present any problems.

References:
Bartlett, R. D., and Patricia Bartlett. *Monitors, Tegus, and Related Lizards.* Hauppauge, NY: Barron's Educational Series, Inc., 1996.

Ridge-tailed Monitor

Trade Name(s):
Same.
Family & Scientific Name:
Varanidae;
Varanus acanthurus.
Identifying Features:
These monitors have myriad light spots against tan, brown, or reddish dorsal ground color, and a light belly and facial stripes. The spines on tail are arranged in lengthwise ridges.

Similar Species: Storr's monitors lack light spots.

Range & Origin: Australia; specimens available in the pet trade are captive-bred and hatched.

Adult Size: To about 20 inches; usually a few inches shorter.

Life Span: 10–15 years.

Terrarium Size: Although babies can be kept in smaller tanks, a pair or trio of adults require a 50–75-gallon capacity terrarium.

Terrarium Type:
This semiarid-land to aridland lizard dwells in rocky outcroppings where it seeks seclusion in crevices. This habitat is easily duplicated in the terrarium, but be certain that the rocks can't shift and crush the monitors.

Social Structure: Males can be aggressive with other males, but pairs and trios are communal.

Diet: Insects and other lizards, and sometimes low fat canned cat food. Dust insects with vitamin D_3-calcium powder twice weekly for babies and ovulating females, once weekly otherwise.

Potential Problems: This is usually a healthy, hardy, and problem-free lizard.

References:
Bartlett, R. D., and Patricia Bartlett. *Monitors, Tegus, and Related Lizards.* Hauppauge, NY: Barron's Educational Series, Inc., 1996.

Dumeril's Monitor

Trade Name(s): Same.

Family & Scientific Name: Varanidae; *Varanus dumerilii.*

Identifying Features: With their brilliant orange head and black and yellow banded body and tail, hatchlings are spectacular and unmistakable. However, the brilliance soon dulls, and juvenile and larger Dumeril's monitors are a deep brown, broadly banded with a lighter brown on the body. The tail often loses even vestiges of bands. There is a broad dark eyestripe that extends back onto the anterior neck. The lips are vertically banded.

Similar Species: The rough-necked monitor has a very elongated, bird-like snout and narrow body and tail bands.

Range & Origin: Malaysia (Sarawak).

Adult Size: 32–38 inches.

Life Span: To 10+ years.

Terrarium Size: One or two hatchlings can be kept in a 20- or 29-gallon terrarium, but as their size increases, so too, must the terrarium size. One or two adults should be kept in nothing smaller than a 150-gallon terrarium, a 220-gallon terrarium is even better or cage of equal size (30 × 36 × 72 inches).

Terrarium Type: This monitor is an arboreal forest species and should have large, humid, vertically oriented terraria or cages with horizontal and diagonal limbs.

Social Structure: Although these monitors are not overly aggressive, they are easily startled, and often fare better when kept singly. Once acclimated, providing the cage is large enough and visual barriers are ample, a pair or a trio may be kept together.

Diet: Insects, snails, and small rodents—with the emphasis on insects and snails—are accepted by these monitors. Once acclimated, some accept commercial monitor diets and canned cat food. Dust insects with vitamin D_3-calcium powder twice weekly for babies and ovulating females, once weekly otherwise.

Potential Problems: Many imports are dehydrated, starving, and heavily laden with endoparasites. Because some of these monitors are slow to begin eating after capture and unable to overcome their accentuated load of gut parasites on their own, it is sometimes necessary to entubate soft foods and seek veterinary help to overcome the problems. Most drink readily.

References:
Bartlett, R. D., and Patricia Bartlett. *Monitors, Tegus, and Related Lizards.* Hauppauge, NY: Barron's Educational Series, Inc., 1996.

Green Tree Monitor

Trade Name(s): Emerald Monitor.

Family & Scientific Name: Varanidae; *Varanus prasinus.*

Identifying Features: Very slender head and body and a very attenuate, prehensile tail. This is the only truly green monitor currently in the pet trade.

Similar Species: None.

Range & Origin: New Guinea.

Adult Size: 28–36 inches.

Life Span: To 15+ years.

Terrarium Size: Vertically oriented 75-gallon terrarium for one green tree monitor, a 150- or 220-gallon size (or equal-sized cage) for two or more.

Terrarium Type: This is an arboreal monitor of highly humid rain forests. High cage humidity and limbs, both horizontal and diagonal, for climbing are essential.

Social Structure: Males may fight occasionally, but a single male, and one or more females, usually are compatible.

Diet: Mainly insects and other lizards, and sometimes low fat canned cat food. Dust insects with vitamin D_3-calcium powder twice weekly for babies and ovulating females, once weekly otherwise.

Potential Problems: Most emerald monitors are collected from the wild. Many bear heavy loads of endoparasites, are severely dehydrated and are starving. With a severely weakened specimen, it may be necessary to entubate soft foods while seeking the advice of a veterinarian.

References:

Bartlett, R. D., and Patricia Bartlett. *Monitors, Tegus, and Related Lizards.* Hauppauge, NY: Barron's Educational Series, Inc., 1996.

Veiled Chameleon

Trade Name(s): Yemen Chameleon.

Family & Scientific Name: Chameleonidae; *Chamaeleo calyptratus calyptratus.*

Identifying Features: They are large in size. They have a very high bluish-green head casque, no middorsal sail, horns, or other adornments. Males have distinct calcars (heel spurs) that are apparent at birth.

Similar Species: Many chameleons are similar in appearance, but few have the extravagant casque of the veiled chameleon.

Range & Origin: Yemen. Some adults are still collected from the wild and imported for the pet trade, but this species is now captive-bred by the thousands annually.

Adult Size: Females to 14 inches; males 18–24 inches.

Life Span: 3–5 years.

Terrarium Size: From one to several babies can be housed temporarily in a 15-gallon terrarium with leafy branches and/or potted vining plants. The minimum cage size for an adult pair should be 2 × 2 × 3 feet. Larger is better. Ours have thrived and bred in upright cages 6 × 4 × 2½ feet.

Terrarium Type: A semiarid setup is ideal. Potted plants, such as *Ficus benjamina,* provide visual barriers, add some humidity, and provide aerial pathways. The veiled chameleon prefers the air exchange in a wire cage over the comparative stillness of an aquarium with a screen top. Mist the leaves and branches once or twice daily to allow the lizards to drink.

Social Structure: Males must be kept out of the sight of other males. However, a pair or one male and two females usually coexist well in a large cage with visual barriers present.

Diet: Crickets, king mealworms, grasshoppers, roaches, silkworms, and waxworms are all eagerly accepted. Blossoms and leaves, including dandelions, hibiscus, ficus, romaine, and escarole are also relished. Dust insects with vitamin D_3-calcium powder twice weekly for baby chameleons and ovulating females, once weekly otherwise.

Potential Problems: Males often stress-out if another male is visible. Females may become fatally eggbound. Since veiled chameleons usually only drink pendant water droplets from leaves and limbs, dehydration is possible if the cage is not misted sufficiently.

References:

Bartlett, R. D., and Patricia Bartlett. *Chameleons.* Hauppauge, NY: Barron's Educational Series, Inc., 1995.

Le Berre, Francois. *The New Chameleon Handbook.* Hauppauge, NY: Barron's Educational Series, Inc., 1995.

Flap-necked Chameleon/
Graceful Chameleon

Trade Name(s):
Same.
Family & Scientific Name:
Chameleonidae;
Chamaeleo
dilepis (*C. gracilis*, inset).
Identifying
Features:
These are two
commonly
seen African
chameleons.
The flap-necked
chameleon *(C.*
dilepis), shown

above, has well-developed occipital lobes
(the flaps on the side of the head). Males
have tarsal spurs and orange skin between
the throat scales. The graceful chameleon
(C. gracilis), shown on page 138, lacks neck
flaps and has only a low vertebral and throat
crest.

Similar Species: Senegal chameleons look
so much like the graceful chameleon that in
this case you should rely on your dealer for
identification.

Range & Origin: Both are African species.
Those available in the pet trade are wild collected specimens. These species are seldom bred in captivity.

Adult Size: To 12 or 14 inches.

Life Span: 1–3½ years. These are both delicate species that have a high and unnatural
mortality when taken captive.

Terrarium Size:
From one to sev-
eral babies can
be housed tem-
porarily in a 15-
gallon terrarium
with leafy
branches and/or
potted vining
plants. The *mini-*
mum cage size
for an adult pair
should be 2 × 2
× 3 feet. Larger
is better. We
suggest a verti-
cal orientation.

Terrarium Type: Either a humid or a dry
savanna setup will suffice. Potted plants
such as *Ficus benjamina* provide visual barriers, add some humidity, and provide aerial
pathways for these arboreal lizards. Like all
chameleons, these two species seem to do
better when in a wire cage than when in a
glass terrarium with a screen top. Mist the
leaves and branches once or twice daily to
allow the lizards to drink the pendant
droplets.

Social Structure: Only a single male per
cage, but a male and one or two females
often coexist peacefully, especially in a large
cage with many visual barriers.

Diet: A variety of insects including crickets,
king mealworms, grasshoppers, roaches,
silkworms, and waxworms are all eagerly
accepted. Dust insects with vitamin

D$_3$-calcium powder twice weekly for baby chameleons and ovulating females, once weekly otherwise.

Potential Problems: Males are very territorial and should be kept out of each other's sight. Stressed imports may

have an untenable number of endoparasites and subcutaneous nematodes. Veterinary intervention may be necessary. Since these creatures usually only drink pendant water droplets from leaves and limbs, dehydration is possible if the cage is not misted sufficiently.

References:

Bartlett, R. D., and Patricia Bartlett. *Chameleons.* Hauppauge, NY: Barron's Educational Series, Inc., 1995.

Le Berre, Francois. *The New Chameleon Handbook.* Hauppauge, NY: Barron's Educational Series, Inc., 1995.

Four-horned Chameleon

Trade Name(s):
Same.
Family & Scientific Name:
Chameleonidae;
*Chamaeleo
quadricornis.*
*Identifying
Features:*
These have a
sail on the tail
and four noticeable and two
very small horns on the snout.

small chameleon seems to do better in a wire cage than in a glass terrarium with a screen top (although the latter holds high humidity better). Mist the leaves and branches frequently both to provide humidity and to allow the lizards to drink.

Similar Species: The sail-finned chameleon has only two large nose horns.

Range & Origin: Cameroon, West Africa. The vast majority of the four-horned chameleons that appear in the pet trade are collected from the wild. An increasing number are now being captive-bred.

Adult Size: This is a fairly small chameleon species. Adult males are 9–12 inches in length. Females are somewhat smaller and have smaller horns and fin.

Life Span: 2–5 years.

Terrarium Size: From one to several babies can be housed temporarily in a 15-gallon terrarium with leafy branches and/or potted vining plants. The minimum cage size for an adult pair or trio should be 2 × 2 × 3 feet. Larger is better. Vertical orientation is suggested.

Terrarium Type: Cool (60–74°F) and humid describes the terrarium type best suited for this pretty chameleon. Potted plants such as *Ficus benjamina* provide visual barriers, add some humidity, and provide aerial pathways. This

Social Structure: Only a single male per cage, but a male and one or two females often coexist peacefully, especially in a large cage with many visual barriers.

Diet: Crickets, king mealworms, grasshoppers, roaches, silkworms, and waxworms are all eagerly accepted. Dust insects with vitamin D_3-calcium powder twice weekly for baby chameleons and ovulating females, once weekly otherwise.

Potential Problems: Providing you give this chameleon the cool temperature and high humidity it needs, this is an easily kept species. Since these creatures usually only drink pendant water droplets from leaves and limbs, dehydration is possible if the cage is not misted sufficiently.

References:
Bartlett, R. D., and Patricia Bartlett.
  Chameleons. Hauppauge, NY: Barron's
  Educational Series, Inc., 1995.
Le Berre, Francois. *The New Chameleon
  Handbook.* Hauppauge, NY: Barron's
  Educational Series, Inc., 1995.

Cameroon Sail-finned Chameleon

Trade Name(s): Mountain Chameleon.

Family & Scientific Name: Chameleonidae; *Chamaeleo montium.*

Identifying Features: Males have a sailfin on their tail and two large horns on the snout. Females lack the horns and the fin is smaller.

Similar Species: The four-horned chameleon is similar in overall appearance, but has six small, rather than two large horns.

Range & Origin: Cameroon, West Africa. The vast majority of the sail-finned chameleons that appear in the pet trade are collected from the wild. An increasing number are now being captive-bred.

Adult Size: This is a fairly small chameleon species. Adult males are 9–12 inches in length. Females are somewhat smaller.

Life Span: 2–5 years.

Terrarium Size: From one to several babies can be housed temporarily in a 15-gallon terrarium with leafy branches and/or potted vining plants. The minimum cage size for an adult pair or trio should be 2 × 2 × 3 feet. Larger is better. A vertical orientation is suggested.

Terrarium Type: Cool (60–74°F) and humid describes the terrarium type best suited for this pretty chameleon. Potted plants such as *Ficus benjamina* provide visual barriers, add some humidity, and provide aerial pathways.

This small chameleon seems to do better in a wire cage than in a glass terrarium with a screen top (although the latter holds high humidity better). Mist the leaves and branches frequently both to provide humidity and to allow the lizards to drink.

Social Structure: Only a single male per cage, but a male and one or two females often coexist peacefully, especially in a large cage with many visual barriers.

Diet: Crickets, king mealworms, grasshoppers, roaches, silkworms, and waxworms are all eagerly accepted. Dust insects with vitamin D_3-calcium powder twice weekly for baby chameleons and ovulating females, once weekly otherwise.

Potential Problems: Providing you give this chameleon the cool temperature and high humidity it needs, this is an easily kept species. Since these creatures usually only drink pendant water droplets from leaves and limbs, dehydration is possible if the cage is not misted sufficiently.

References:

Bartlett, R. D., and Patricia Bartlett. *Chameleons.* Hauppauge, NY: Barron's Educational Series, Inc., 1995.

Le Berre, Francois. *The New Chameleon Handbook.* Hauppauge, NY: Barron's Educational Series, Inc., 1995.

Panther Chameleon

Trade Name(s): Same.

Family & Scientific Name: Chameleonidae; *Furcifer pardalis.*

Identifying Features: This is a beautiful and variably colored species. Green, brown, red, orange, or turquoise may be the base color. A distinct parietal crest terminates at the elevated rear edge of the casque. There are also pronounced lateral (supraorbital) crests that continue on to the snout.

Similar Species: Although all chameleons with minimal adornment could be called similar, the facial and crown cresting pattern of the panther chameleon should render it easily identifiable.

Range & Origin: Madagascar. Most pet trade specimens are collected from the wild, but an ever increasing number are being captive-bred.

Adult Size: Females to 14 inches; males to 20 inches.

Life Span: 2–5 years.

Terrarium Size: From one to several babies can be housed temporarily in a 15-gallon terrarium with leafy branches and/or potted vining plants. The minimum cage size for an adult pair should be 2 × 2 × 3 feet. Larger is better. Vertical orientation is suggested. In their large (6 × 4 × 2½ feet), vertical, outside cages, our panther chameleons lived well and bred repeatedly.

Terrarium Type: A warm and humid setup seems best for this species. Potted plants such as *Ficus benjamina* provide visual barriers, add some humidity, and provide aerial pathways for these arboreal lizards. Like most chameleons, the panther chameleon seems to do better when in a wire cage with ready air exchange than when in a glass terrarium with a screen top. Mist the leaves and branches once or twice daily to allow the lizards to drink the pendant droplets.

Social Structure: Only a single male per cage, but a male and one or two females often coexist peacefully, especially in a large cage with many visual barriers.

Diet: A variety of insects including crickets, king mealworms, grasshoppers, roaches, silkworms, and waxworms are all eagerly accepted. Dust insects with vitamin D_3-calcium powder twice weekly for baby chameleons and ovulating females, once weekly otherwise.

Potential Problems: Males are moderately territorial. Stressed imports may have an untenable number of endoparasites. Veterinary intervention may be necessary to purge these. Since chameleons usually only drink pendant water droplets from leaves and limbs, dehydration is possible if their cage plantings are not misted sufficiently.

References:

Bartlett, R. D., and Patricia Bartlett. *Chameleons.* Hauppauge, NY: Barron's Educational Series, Inc., 1995.

Le Berre, Francois. *The New Chameleon Handbook.* Hauppauge, NY: Barron's Educational Series, Inc., 1995.

Jackson's Chameleon

Trade Name(s):
Three-horned
Chameleon.
Family & Scientific Name:
Chameleonidae;
Chamaeleo jacksoni xantholophus.
Identifying Features: There are
many three-

between 66°F
(nights) and 80°F
(days) seems best
for this species.
Potted *Ficus
benjamina* and
hibiscus provide
visual barriers,
add some humidity, and provide
aerial pathways.
Like most

horned chameleons, but the slightly upturned
horns and parietal crest, and the lack of
occipital lobes, of the Jackson's chameleon
are distinctive.
Similar Species: The two upper horns of
Johnston's chameleon are slightly down-
turned and it lacks a parietal crest. The
Poroto Mountain chameleon has three short
horns and occipital lobes.
Range & Origin: Kenya; other races from
elsewhere in eastern Africa. Some adults
come from the African wilds; many are collected from the Hawaiian Islands where they
are established; a few are captive-bred and
born.
Adult Size: 12–15 inches.
Life Span: 3–8+ years.
Terrarium Size: From one to several babies
can be housed temporarily in a vertical 15-
gallon terrarium with leafy branches and vining plants. The minimum cage size for an
adult pair should be 2 × 2 × 3 feet. Larger is
better. Ours have done very well, living for
years and breeding repeatedly, in their large
(6 × 4 × 2½ feet), vertical, outside cages.
Terrarium Type: A humid setup maintained

chameleons, Jackson's chameleon seems to
do better in a wire cage with ready air
exchange than in a glass terrarium with a
screen top. Mist the leaves and branches
once or twice daily to allow the lizards to drink.
Social Structure: Only a single male per
cage, but a male and one or two females
often coexist peacefully, especially in a large
cage with many visual barriers.
Diet: Crickets, king mealworms, grasshoppers, roaches, silkworms, and waxworms, are
all eagerly accepted. Dust insects with vitamin D_3-calcium powder twice weekly for
baby chameleons and ovulating females,
once weekly otherwise.
Potential Problems: Provided they are kept
amply hydrated and not subjected to excessive heat, Jackson's chameleon is a hardy
and relatively trouble-free species.
References:
Bartlett, R. D., and Patricia Bartlett.
 Chameleons. Hauppauge, NY: Barron's
 Educational Series, Inc., 1995.
Le Berre, Francois. *The New Chameleon
 Handbook.* Hauppauge, NY: Barron's
 Educational Series, Inc., 1995.

Leaf Chameleons

Trade Name(s):
Same.
Family & Scientific Name:
Chameleonidae;
Brookesia
superciliaris and
B. perarmata
(shown).
Identifying
Features:
These are small
chameleons with
barely prehensile

Terrarium Type:
B. superciliaris is
associated with
damp forest
habitats. A
woodland terrarium seems suitable for these. *B.
perarmata* seem
more tied to
drier, rocky areas
where they clamber about in low,
thorny, vegeta-

tails. Except for its rows of paravertebral spines, the horned leaf chameleon*, B. superciliaris,* is smooth-skinned and has large, flattened, supraorbital projections and a laterally compressed, deep body. The armored leaf chameleon bears scaly spines and spiny rosettes on its sides and back, as well as spinous lateral crests and fringed occipital lobes.

Similar Species: Other leaf chameleons do not have as deep a body, have an even shorter tail, or are less spinose.

Range & Origin: Madagascar; all available in the pet trade are wild collected.

Adult Size: 3½–4¼ inches.

Life Span: Unknown. Most specimens live for from several months to somewhat less than two years. As we fine-tune husbandry techniques, from two to four (or more) years may be possible.

Terrarium Size: 10–20-gallon capacity terraria are ample for one or several specimens. A 30–40-gallon terrarium would harbor up to a half dozen leaf chameleons.

tion. A dry savanna or semiarid terrarium would seem more in line for this species.

Social Structure: Leaf chameleons do not seem overly aggressive. If visual barriers are present, they seem to do reasonably well communally in spacious terraria.

Diet: A variety of tiny insects including pinhead to one-eighth inch grown crickets, tiny mealworms, nymphal grasshoppers, newly hatched silkworms, and ants are accepted. Dust insects with vitamin D_3-calcium powder twice weekly for baby chameleons and ovulating females, once weekly otherwise.

Potential Problems: Very little is yet known about the chameleons in this genus. Providing food and water requirements are met, they seem hardy.

References:

Bartlett, R. D., and Patricia Bartlett.
Chameleons. Hauppauge, NY: Barron's
Educational Series, Inc., 1995.
Le Berre, Francois. *The New Chameleon
Handbook.* Hauppauge, NY: Barron's
Educational Series, Inc., 1995.

Black and Gold Tegu

Trade Name(s): Common Tegu, Black and Yellow Tegu, Colombian Tegu.

Family & Scientific Name: Teiidae; *Tupinambis teguixin.*

Identifying Features: Large-headed, shiny-scaled, and huge, this, the most commonly seen of the tegus, is clad in black scales and patterned with a series of gold crossbands.

Similar Species: The red tegu is black and red(dish); the Argentine tegu is black and white.

Range & Origin: Northern South America. Virtually all available in the pet trade are collected from the wild.

Adult Size: 30–36 inches, of which more than half is tail length.

Life Span: 10–20 years.

Terrarium Size: 1–3 babies can be housed in 20–40-gallon terraria. One or two adults require caging with a minimum floor space of 4 × 8 feet.

Terrarium Type: These rain forest lizards thermoregulate at the edges of clearings and trails. They enjoy high humidity, but do not enjoy being wet. A woodland terrarium would suffice for smaller specimens, but because they are large, heavy, and active diggers, all but the sturdiest plantings are quickly trampled. Large, suitably appointed cages are better.

Social Structure: As long as they are not crowded, juveniles can be kept communally. Adults can be aggressive toward one another, but pairs or trios can often be kept in cages that are large enough and contain a series of visual barriers.

Diet: Insects, some mice, some baby chicks, canned dog food, and a variety of fruit should be offered these lizards. A steady diet of mice and chicks can quickly lead to obesity, and hence is contraindicated. The diet should contain a large proportion of insects. Babies and ovulating females should have their feed insects dusted with vitamin D_3-calcium powder twice weekly. Otherwise, dust the insects once every week or two.

Potential Problems: Occasional specimens bear heavy loads of endoparasites and require veterinary intervention to be restored to health. However, most black and gold tegus are in reasonable health, and make hardy, long-lived, if occasionally surly, pets.

References:

Bartlett, R. D., and Patricia Bartlett. *Monitors, Tegus, and Related Lizards.* Hauppauge, NY: Barron's Educational Series, Inc., 1996.

Black and White Tegu

Trade Name(s): Argentine Tegu.
Family & Scientific Name: Teiidae; *Tupinambis merianae*.
Identifying Features: Large-headed, very heavy bodied, and shiny scaled, the pattern of white crossbands that typifies this tegu is usually extensive. Juveniles have green anteriorly on the back.
Similar Species: The names of black and gold and black and red accurately indicate the difference in the other pet trade tegus.
Range & Origin: Southern South America; occasional imports are available in the pet trade, but most that are offered are captive-bred and hatched babies.
Adult Size: A heavy bodied 2½ to about 4 feet in total length. The tail makes up more than one half of the total length.
Life Span: 10–20 years.
Terrarium Size: 1–3 babies can be housed in 20–40-gallon terraria. One or two adults will require caging with a minimum floor space of 4 × 8 feet.
Terrarium Type: This is a savanna, chaco, thornscrub forest lizard that thermoregulates at the edges of clearings and trails. Dry savanna and semiaridland terraria can be used to house juveniles. Because they are large, heavy, and active diggers, all but the sturdiest plantings are quickly trampled. Large, suitably appointed cages are best for adults.
Social Structure: As long as they are not crowded, juveniles can be kept communally. Adults can be aggressive to one another, but pairs or trios can often be kept in cages that are large enough and contain a series of visual barriers.
Diet: Insects, some mice, some baby chicks, canned dog food, and a variety of fruit should be offered these lizards. A steady diet of mice and chicks can quickly lead to obesity, and hence is contraindicated. The diet should contain a large proportion of insects. Babies and ovulating females should have their feed insects dusted with vitamin D_3-calcium powder twice weekly. Otherwise, dust the insects once every week or two.
Potential Problems: Occasional specimens bear heavy loads of endoparasites and require veterinary intervention to be restored to health. However, most black and gold tegus are in reasonable health, and make hardy, long-lived, if occasionally surly, pets.
References:

Bartlett, R. D., and Patricia Bartlett. *Monitors, Tegus, and Related Lizards.* Hauppauge, NY: Barron's Educational Series, Inc., 1996.

Red Tegu

Trade Name(s): Same.

Family & Scientific Name: Teiidae; *Tupinambis rufescens.*

Identifying Features: Large-headed, very heavy bodied, and shiny scaled, the amount of pale pink to bright red is usually greater than the black ground color.

Similar Species: See accounts for the black and gold and black and white tegu.

Range & Origin: Argentina, Paraguay; occasional imports are available, but captive-bred and hatched babies make up most of the number available in the pet trade.

Adult Size: 2½ to nearly 4 feet in total length. These are very heavy bodied, impressively pretty lizards.

Life Span: 10–20, or more, years.

Terrarium Size: One to three babies can be housed in 20–40-gallon terraria. One or two adults will require caging with a minimum floor space of 4 × 8 feet.

Terrarium Type: These scrubforest, savanna, chaco lizards thermoregulate at the edges of clearings and trails. A woodland terrarium would suffice for smaller specimens, but because they are large, heavy, and active diggers, all but the sturdiest plantings are quickly trampled. Large, suitably appointed cages are better.

Social Structure: As long as they are not crowded, juveniles can be kept communally. Adults can be aggressive to one another, but pairs or trios often can be kept in cages that are large enough and contain a series of visual barriers.

Diet: Insects, some mice, some baby chicks, canned dog food, and a variety of fruit should be offered these lizards. A steady diet of mice and chicks can quickly lead to obesity, and hence is contraindicated. The diet should contain a large proportion of insects. Babies and ovulating females should have their feed insects dusted with vitamin D_3-calcium powder twice weekly. Otherwise, dust the insects once every week or two.

Potential Problems: Occasional specimens bear heavy loads of endoparasites and require veterinary intervention to be restored to health. However, most red and black tegus are in reasonable health, and make hardy, long-lived, if occasionally surly, pets.

References:
Bartlett, R. D., and Patricia Bartlett. *Monitors, Tegus, and Related Lizards.* Hauppauge, NY: Barron's Educational Series, Inc., 1996.

Chilean Dwarf Tegu

Trade Name(s): Dwarf Tegu.

Family & Scientific Name: Teiidae; *Callopistes maculatus.*

Identifying Features: This beautiful lizard has a warm brown back patterned with well separated lines of light-edged dark ocelli,

grayish sides, limbs, and tail, all bearing dark spots or reticulations, and a whitish (juveniles, females, nonbreeding males) to salmon throat (breeding males).

Similar Species: None with this pattern and color.

Range & Origin: Northern Argentina and Chile; all available in the pet trade are collected from the wild.

Adult Size: 14–16 inches, occasionally slightly larger.

Life Span: To date the husbandry for these lizards is not well known. There is an unnaturally high mortality. Many succumb within the first 6 months of captivity. We hypothesize that a lifespan of 2–10 years eventually should be possible.

Terrarium Size: One, or a pair, can be housed in a 40-gallon terrarium.

Terrarium Type: This is an Andean lizard that thermoregulates at clearing edge, at rockedge, or along the edges of trails. They are adapted to cool temperatures. A dry savanna terrarium should suffice.

Social Structure: Males or females kept singly seem to fare the best as captives. If two males or two females are housed together, one usually does poorly. A male and female have survived captivity for more than a year while housed together. We have not noticed physical skirmishes, but body language seems to quickly establish a pattern of dominance.

Diet: Insects, a very occasional pinky mouse, and an occasional blossom have been eaten by these lizards. Some captives have accepted canned cat food. Babies and ovulating females should have their feed insects dusted with vitamin D_3-calcium powder twice weekly. Otherwise, dust the insects once every week or two.

Potential Problems: Although some specimens bear heavy loads of endoparasites, others, apparently healthy when imported, die for no apparent reason. Much research is still needed for these interesting and pretty lizards.

References:

Bartlett, R. D., and Patricia Bartlett. *Monitors, Tegus, and Related Lizards.* Hauppauge, NY: Barron's Educational Series, Inc., 1996.

Giant Ameiva

Trade Name(s): Giant Whiptail, Green Whiptail, Jungle Runner.

Family & Scientific Name: Teiidae; *Ameiva ameiva.*

Identifying Features: Two distinctly different color morphs. One is dusky colored—almost charcoal—with blue spots on the sides. The other has a tan face and chin and tail and green back and sides. Never striped or with longitudinal lines of spots.

Similar Species: Most small teiids are somewhat similar. Compare the ameiva with the photo in this account.

Range & Origin: Tropical Latin America, Dade County, Florida. Specimens available in the pet trade are collected from the wild. Very few are captive-bred.

Adult Size: 14–18 inches, of which nearly two-thirds is tail length.

Life Span: 2–6 years.

Terrarium Size: Several babies can be housed in a 20-gallon terrarium. One or two adults require a 50–75-gallon terrarium.

Terrarium Type: This is a lizard both of forestedge and of semiarid to arid areas. It can withstand periodic drought but can also tolerate considerable humidity and ground moisture. It thermoregulates in clearings or along the edges of trails. It seems to do best in a dry savanna terrarium and enjoys digging in a sandy soil substrate.

Social Structure: Juveniles and females coexist well in groups; adult males may be antagonistic.

Diet: Insects are readily accepted. A very occasional pinky mouse, and an occasional blossom and canned cat food have also been eaten by these lizards.

Potential Problems: If provided with sufficient heat (a hot spot of 100–115°F), adequate food and fresh water, this is a hardy, and largely trouble-free lizard. Babies and ovulating females should have their feed insects dusted with vitamin D_3-calcium powder twice weekly. Otherwise, dust the insects once every week or two.

References:

Bartlett, R. D., and Patricia Bartlett. *Monitors, Tegus, and Related Lizards.* Hauppauge, NY: Barron's Educational Series, Inc., 1996.

Rainbow Lizard (and other whiptails)

Trade Name(s): Variable by species.

Family & Scientific Name: Teiidae; *Cnemidophorus lemniscatus* (rainbow lizard); *Cnemidophorus* species (other racerunners and whiptails).

Identifying Features: Most

species—even those with dorsal crossbars—have some degree of lineate pattern. There usually are six or seven stripes dorsally. The male rainbow lizard is the most brightly colored, but others like the Texas whiptail have blue sides and salmon throat. Females (of bisexual species) are less colorful than the males. Some species are unisexual and reproduce by parthenogenesis. Colors of all are most vivid during the breeding season. There are eight rows of large belly scales.

Similar Species: Ameivas have 10–12 rows of belly scales and often lack a well defined lineate pattern dorsally.

Range & Origin: South America (rainbow lizard). North, Central, and South America (other species). All available in the pet trade are captured from the wild.

Adult Size: Variable by species, from 6–14

inches of which two-thirds is tail length.

Life Span: 1–4 years.

Terrarium Size: These are active, fast-moving lizards. One to several of all species could be kept in a 40-gallon tank.

Terrarium Type: Dry savanna, semiaridland terrarium setups are best. These lizards enjoy digging through sandy substrates. Provide a hot spot of 105–120°F for thermoregulation.

Social Structure: Breeding males may fight with other males. Juveniles and females usually are compatible.

Diet: A variety of insects, some blossoms, and the fruit-honey mixture are accepted by these lizards.

Potential Problems: Insufficient heat and light can cause lethargy and an unwillingness to eat. When properly set up, these usually are hardy and problem-free lizards.

References:

Bartlett, R. D., and Patricia Bartlett. *Lizard Care from A to Z.* Hauppauge, NY: Barron's Educational Series, Inc., 1997.

Jeweled Lizard

Trade Name(s): Eyed Lizard, Eyed Lacerta.

Family & Scientific Name: Lacertidae; *Lacerta lepida*.

Identifying Features: Males are greenish to bright green and have blue spots along the sides. Females and juveniles are tan to gray and have dark-edged light ocelli on the sides and back.

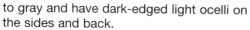

Similar Species: None in the American pet trade.

Range & Origin: Southern Europe. Most specimens in the pet trade are bred in Europe or America .

Adult Size: 16–28 inches of which about two-thirds is tail length. Males are noticeably larger than females.

Life Span: 6–15 years.

Terrarium Size: From one to several babies can be kept in a 20-gallon, long terrarium.

A pair or trio of large adults should have a 75–100-gallon terrarium.

Terrarium Type: Dry savanna or semiaridland terrarium. These lizards enjoy digging through a sandy soil substrate.

Social Structure: Large males fight with each other. Pairs, trios, or groups of juveniles can be housed safely communally.

Diet: Offer a wide variety of insects, an occasional pink mouse, blossoms, and the fruit-honey mixture.

Potential Problems: If kept warm enough (hot spot of 100–115°F) these are generally hardy, trouble-free lizards.

References:

Bartlett, R. D., and Patricia Bartlett. *Lizard Care from A to Z.* Hauppauge, NY: Barron's Educational Series, Inc., 1997.

European Green Lizard

Trade Name(s):
Green Lizard,
Emerald Lizard.
Family & Scientific Name:
Lacertidae; *Lacerta viridis.*
Identifying Features: Males
are bright green,
sometimes with
some evidence
of dark reticulations. Females
and juveniles
are tan to gray.

Similar Species: Emerald swift has spiny scales.

Range & Origin: Widely distributed in Europe. Most specimens in the pet trade are bred in Europe or America by hobbyists.

Adult Size: 10–12 inches of which about two-thirds is tail length. Males are somewhat larger than females.

Life Span: 3–8 years.

Terrarium Size: From one to several babies can be kept in a 20-gallon, long terrarium. A pair or trio of large adults should have a 40-gallon or larger terrarium.

Terrarium Type:
Dry savanna or
semiaridland terrarium. These
lizards enjoy digging through a
sandy soil substrate.
Social Structure: Large
males fight with
each other.
Pairs, trios, or
groups of juveniles can be
housed safely communally.

Diet: A wide variety of insects, an occasional blossom, and the fruit-honey mixture are all accepted.

Potential Problems: If kept warm and dry enough (hot spot of 100–115°F) these are generally hardy, trouble-free lizards. Dampness can cause potentially fatal skin disorders.

References:
Bartlett, R. D., and Patricia Bartlett. *Lizard Care from A to Z.* Hauppauge, NY: Barron's Educational Series, Inc., 1997.

European Wall Lizard

Trade Name(s): Same.

Family & Scientific Name: Lacertidae; *Podarcis muralis.*

Identifying Features: These lizards have a flattened head and body that allow fast access to narrow rock crevices. They have brownish backs, with blue spotted gray sides, and are small in size.

Similar Species: Many members of this genus are confusingly similar, but this is the only one to appear with any regularity in the American pet trade.

Range & Origin: Much of Europe; introduced to Cincinnati, Ohio and adjacent Kentucky. Most specimens seen in the American pet trade are collected from the wild.

Adult Size: 6–7½ inches. Tail slightly less than two-thirds of the total length.

Life Span: 2–5 years.

Terrarium Size: From one to several adults can be kept in a 20-gallon, long to 40-gallon terrarium.

Terrarium Type: Dry savanna or semiaridland with secure, but creviced, rock ledges between which the lizards can slip when frightened or resting.

Social Structure: They can live communally.

Diet: Small insects and the fruit-honey mixture are accepted.

Potential Problems: If fed properly and kept warm (hot spot of 100–115°F) these are hardy and trouble-free lizards.

References:
Bartlett, R. D., and Patricia Bartlett. *Lizard Care from A to Z.* Hauppauge, NY: Barron's Educational Series, Inc., 1997.

Long-tailed Grass Lizard

Trade Name(s): Striped Grass Lizard, Asian Grass Lizard.

Family & Scientific Name: Lacertidae; *Takydromus sexlineatus.*

Identifying Features: These lizards are extremely slender, have a long prehensile tail, six thin dark stripes on back, and climb well.

Similar Species: See account for alligator lizards.

Range & Origin: Asia. Collected from the wild for the pet trade.

Adult Size: 9–12 inches, most of which is tail length.

Life Span: Unknown, but probably several years.

Terrarium Size: 15 gallon or greater capacity terrarium for 2–4 lizards.

Terrarium Type: Dry savanna terrarium well planted with erect grasses or low plants.

Social Structure: Males can be aggressive to other males. One male and from one to several females usually coexist well.

Diet: A variety of insects, including crickets, mealworms, giant mealworms, grasshoppers, sowbugs, and spiders is accepted. These lizards also lap the fruit-honey mixture typically used for day geckos.

Potential Problems: If properly hydrated and provided with small insects for food, this is a hardy lizard.

References:

Bartlett, R. D., and Patricia Bartlett. *Terrarium and Cage Construction and Care.* Hauppauge, NY: Barron's Educational Series, Inc., 1999.

Blue-tailed Tree Lizard

Trade Name(s):
Same.
Family & Scientific Name:
Lacertidae;
Holaspis
guentheri.
**Identifying
Features:** This
lizard has four
yellow stripes
on a greatly flat-
tened body and
head, a broad
interorbital line,

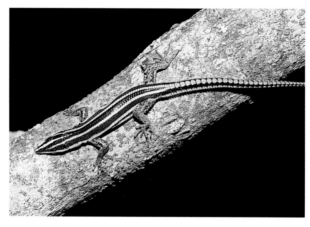

Terrarium Type:
Dry savanna;
semiaridland.
**Social Struc-
ture:** Communal,
but males may
be antagonistic.
A single male
coexists well
with one or
more females.
Diet: Spiders
and ants are
eaten in the
wild; captives

and a sky blue tail with a fringe of yellow
scales along each side.
Similar Species: None.
Range & Origin: South Africa. Pet trade
specimens are collected from the wild.
Adult Size: Total length of about 4 inches.
Life Span: Unknown.
Terrarium Size: One to four specimens live
well in a vertically oriented 15-gallon or
larger terrarium. Provide several diagonal or
vertical tree limbs of considerable (3–6 inch)
diameter, if possible with loose bark under
which the lizards can hide.

also eat pinhead crickets and baby mealworms. They may lap at the fruit-honey mixture traditionally used for day geckos.
Potential Problems: Providing small
enough insects are offered as food, this is
a hardy lizard. It drinks water droplets
misted onto the limbs and branches of its
terrarium.
References:
Bartlett, R. D., and Patricia Bartlett. *Terrarium and Cage Construction and Care.*
Hauppauge, NY: Barron's Educational
Series, Inc., 1999.

Tortoises and Turtles

Just as all chickens are birds but not all birds are chickens, all tortoises are turtles, but not all turtles are tortoises.

With few exceptions, tortoises are dry land turtles with a highly domed upper shell and with elephantine feet. The forelimbs are often clad in very large, overlapping, scales. Most of these wonderfully responsive, popular creatures are adapted to life in sunlit glades or arid environments. Most have strongly herbivorous dietary tendencies. They range in size from the few inches in length and few grams in weight of the Egyptian tortoise to the several hundred pounds and yard-long shell of the Galapagos and Aldabra tortoises.

Most other turtles are basking, semi-aquatic to mostly aquatic, species. Among the popular pet types, the box turtles are terrestrial exceptions. Most of these—the emydines (basking turtles), kinosternids (mud and musk turtles), pleurodines (side-necked turtles) and the various soft-shelled turtles—enter the pet trade as silver-dollar-sized hatchlings, this despite federal law that requires a minimum shell size of four inches. Many attain an adult length of eight to 20 inches. As hatchlings and juveniles, turtles are easily housed. As adults they are far more difficult to accommodate.

The soft-shelled turtles have a leather-covering rather than rigid plates on their shell. These persistently aquatic, long-necked, often short-tempered, turtles like to burrow into river or pond edge sand or muck where they wait in ambush for passing fish, tadpoles, or insects. Large softshells can bite painfully hard. Handle them carefully!

The most bizarre appearing turtle is the curiously fringed, aquatic, matamata. It catches its fish repast by suddenly darting its head forward and expanding its throat. The resulting vacuum draws the fish into the turtle's capacious maw. Although fully aquatic, the matamata is not a powerful swimmer and should be maintained in only a few inches of water or, if deeper, with tangles of driftwood that reach the surface.

The water in which any turtle swims must be kept clean and largely bacteria free. A healthy, varied diet must be provided. In most cases this will include healthy greens (mustard, collard, turnip, dandelion greens, some romaine lettuce [and be advised—iceberg lettuce is not a healthy green!]) as well as some animal protein (prepared turtle chows, catfish or trout chow, lowfat cat food, live bait minnows). Feeding a diet heavy in frozen fish can create a thiamine deficiency. Vitamins A and D_3, and calcium are necessary dietary components, and are especially important to fast growing babies and ovulating females.

Turtles can transmit Salmonella. Wash your hands carefully before and after handling one.

Leopard Tortoise

Trade Name(s): Same.

Family & Scientific Name: Testudinidae; *Geochelone pardalis* ssp.

Identifying Features: Very highly domed straw yellow carapace with variable dark, usually radiating, markings.

Hatchlings have a dark center in each carapacial scute and a black spot on each side of each marginal scute.

Similar Species: None.

Range & Origin: Sub-Saharan Africa. Many are now captive-bred and hatched, but large numbers of imports are still offered in the pet trade.

Adult Size: 12–20 (or more) inches. Adults may attain a weight of 30–45 pounds; record is 96 pounds.

Life Span: A minimum of 20 years, and probably more than 50.

Terrarium Size: Although small specimens can be maintained in suitably sized terraria, adults are so large that other caging arrangements must be made. Take this into consideration when purchasing or selling these pretty tortoises.

Terrarium Type: Whether terrarium or cage, this must be a dry savanna, semi-arid, or aridland setup.

Social Structure: Sexually mature males may be aggressive to each other and may even butt the legs of their keepers. However, one male and from one to several females, or a group of juveniles may be housed safely together.

Diet: Primarily vegetarian. Healthy greens, some fruit, and very little animal protein (low fat dog food) are eaten eagerly. Prepared tortoise diet can be offered, but we suggest it not be the only food offered.

Potential Problems: Captive-born babies are very hardy and if kept at reasonably low humidity, properly hydrated, and fed a healthy, varied, diet, they usually present no problems. Imported specimens may be dehydrated and harbor endoparasites. Veterinary assessment and treatment may be necessary.

References:

Bartlett, R. D., and Patricia Bartlett. *Turtles and Tortoises.* Hauppauge, NY: Barron's Educational Series, Inc., 1996.

African Spurred Tortoise

Trade Name(s): Same; African Spur-thighed Tortoise.

Family & Scientific Name: Testudinidae; *Geochelone sulcata.*

Identifying Features: This is a species with few truly noticeable identifying features. Adults and babies are tan to pale brown. Adults have each carapacial scute sculptured with growth rings, the outermost of which is of a darker color. Carapace is high-domed, but flattened centrally. The marginals are very deep and posteriorly flared. The forelimbs bear enlarged scales on the anterior surfaces. The head of the adult is proportionately narrow.

Similar Species: Few tortoises are this bland when adult.

Range & Origin: Africa, along the southern edge of the Sahara Desert. This has proven a prolific, easily bred tortoise. Virtually all hatchlings offered in the pet trade are captive-bred and hatched. A few specimens continue to be collected from the wild and imported.

Adult Size: Males may attain a shell length of 2½ feet and a weight of more than 100 pounds. Females are smaller.

Life Span: More than a half century.

Terrarium Size: Although babies can be housed in a terrarium, adults need a room-sized cage at the very least.

Terrarium Type: This is a semi-arid and aridland species.

Social Structure: Adult males can be aggressive toward each other, and in their persistent efforts to breed, may bully females. However, in most cases, one male and several females may be housed communally. Juveniles are fully compatible.

Diet: Primarily vegetarian. Healthy greens, some fruit, and very little animal protein (low fat dog food) are eaten eagerly. Prepared tortoise diet can be offered, but we suggest it not be the only food offered.

Potential Problems: Captive-born babies are very hardy if kept at reasonably low humidity, properly hydrated, and fed a healthy, varied, diet. This fast-growing tortoise can get *very* large at maturity. Imported specimens may be dehydrated and harbor endoparasites. Veterinary assessment and treatment for imports may be necessary.

References:

Bartlett, R. D., and Patricia Bartlett. *Turtles and Tortoises.* Hauppauge, NY: Barron's Educational Series, Inc., 1996.

Hermann's Tortoise

Trade Name(s): European Tortoise.

Family & Scientific Name: Testudinidae; *Testudo hermanni* ssp.

Identifying Features: These tortoises have a very high domed carapace and a straw yellow carapace with some amount of dark pigment on the anterior of each scute. The plastron is weakly hinged posteriorly (between the abdominal and the femoral scutes). The tail is tipped with large, horny scales and there are no enlarged spurs on the thighs.

Similar Species: The Greek tortoise has enlarged spurs on the thigh and lacks horny scales on the tailtip. The Central Asian tortoise has only four claws on the forefeet.

Range & Origin: Southern Europe. Most specimens now available in the pet trade are the results of American and European captive breeding projects.

Adult Size: 5½–7 inches. Rarely to 8 inches.

Life Span: 25–35 (or more) years.

Terrarium Size: From one to several hatchlings can be maintained in a 15–20-gallon capacity terrarium. A pair of adults should have at least the floor space provided by a 75-gallon capacity (2 × 4 feet) terrarium.

Terrarium Type: Dry savanna or semiaridland terrarium or cage.

Social Structure: Communal, but breeding males need to be watched for aggressive tendencies.

Diet: Primarily vegetarian, with healthy greens being the preferred food. Some fruit, and *very little* animal protein (prepared tortoise food or low fat dog food) is also eaten. Food should be dusted biweekly (most adults), or once or twice weekly (hatchlings and ovulating females) with a good quality vitamin-mineral powder.

Potential Problems: Captive-bred specimens usually are trouble-free.

References:

Bartlett, R. D., and Patricia Bartlett. *Turtles and Tortoises.* Hauppauge, NY: Barron's Educational Series, Inc., 1996.

Mediterranean Spur-thighed Tortoise

Trade Name(s): Greek Tortoise.

Family & Scientific Name: Testudinidae; *Testudo graeca.*

Identifying Features: These tortoises have a high-domed carapace with a ground color of horn-tan and some degree of black smudging on the anterior of each carapacial scute. The plastron is weakly hinged posteriorly (between the abdominal and the femoral scutes) There are enlarged conical spurs on each thigh and no enlarged horny spine on the tailtip.

Similar Species: Hermann's tortoise lacks thigh-spurs and has an enlarged horny tailtip scale. Central Asian tortoise has only four claws on forefeet.

Range & Origin: Southern Europe, south-central Asia, northern Africa. Some pet trade specimens are wild collected; most are captive-bred and hatched by American and European hobbyists.

Adult Size: 6–8 inches. Rarely to 11 inches.

Life Span: 50–80 years. Record is 127 years.

Terrarium Size: From one to several hatchlings can be maintained in a 15–20-gallon capacity terrarium. A pair of adults should have at least the floor space provided by a 75-gallon capacity (2 × 4 feet) terrarium.

Terrarium Type: Dry savanna or semiaridland terrarium or cage.

Social Structure: Communal, but breeding males may be aggressive.

Diet: Primarily vegetarian, with healthy greens being the preferred food. Some fruit, and very little animal protein (prepared tortoise food or low fat dog food) is also eaten. Food should be dusted biweekly (most adults) or once or twice weekly (hatchlings and ovulating females) with a good quality vitamin-mineral powder.

Potential Problems: Wild collected specimens may harbor heavy loads of endoparasites or be dehydrated. This may require veterinary assessment and, possibly treatment. Captive-bred specimens usually are trouble-free.

References:

Bartlett, R. D., and Patricia Bartlett. *Turtles and Tortoises.* Hauppauge, NY: Barron's Educational Series, Inc., 1996.

Central Asian Tortoise

Trade Name(s): Russian Tortoise, Four-toed Tortoise.

Family & Scientific Name: Testudinidae; *Testudo horsfieldii.*

Identifying Features: These tortoises are straw colored, with or without dark carapacial smudging and a highly domed carapace, flattened centrally. There is no posterior plastral hinge and only four claws on each forefoot.

Similar Species: Both the Hermann's and Mediterranean spur-thighed tortoise have five claws on the forefeet.

Range & Origin: Central Asia. Most examples in the pet trade are still collected from the wild. A few captive-bred babies are occasionally available.

Adult Size: 5½–7 inches; rarely to 8 inches.

Life Span: 10 years recorded, but 30–50 should be possible.

Terrarium Size: From one to several hatchlings can be maintained in a 15–20-gallon capacity terrarium. A pair of adults should have at least the floor space provided by a 75-gallon capacity (2 × 4 feet) terrarium.

Terrarium Type: Dry savanna or semiaridland terrarium or cage.

Social Structure: Communal, but breeding males need to be watched for aggressive tendencies.

Diet: Primarily vegetarian, with healthy greens being the preferred food. Some fruit, and very little animal protein (prepared tortoise food or low fat dog food) is also eaten. Food should be dusted biweekly (most adults) or once or twice weekly (hatchlings and ovulating females) with a good quality vitamin-mineral powder.

Potential Problems: Wild collected specimens may harbor heavy loads of endoparasites or be dehydrated. This may require veterinary assessment and, possibly, treatment. Captive-bred specimens usually are trouble-free.

References:

Bartlett, R. D., and Patricia Bartlett. *Turtles and Tortoises.* Hauppauge, NY: Barron's Educational Series, Inc., 1996.

Red-footed Tortoise

Trade Name(s): Same.

Family & Scientific Name: Testudinidae; *Geochelone (Chelonoidis) carbonaria*.

Identifying Features: A highly domed, elongated carapace, yellow-orange to red facial markings, and yellow-red to orange-red scales on the forelimbs typifies adults. There are yellowish centers to all large carapacial scutes as well as at the bottom center of each marginal, and no serrate marginals. The sides of the carapace are often concave when viewed from above, but may be straight or slightly convex. Hatchlings have a yellowish carapace with dark growth areas and yellow-orange leg scales. Hobbyists differentiate several morphs. Among these are the Paraguayan dwarf with a cherry head (small and very bright red); the Bolivian giant (to 18 inches, but normal color), and the Colombian with very concave, almost dumbbell-shaped, carapace sides.

Similar Species: Yellow-footed tortoise has strongly convex carapace sides, yellow (not orange or red) leg scales, and serrate anterior and posterior marginals.

Range & Origin: Panama through northern South America. Wild collected imports are occasionally available, but farmed and domestically captive-bred babies and juveniles are the mainstay of the pet trade.

Adult Size: Variable. Cherry heads seldom attain a foot in length while others may reach nearly 20 inches.

Life Span: 25–35 years, possibly to more than 50 years.

Terrarium Size: From one to several hatchlings can be maintained in a 15–20-gallon capacity terrarium. A pair of adults should have a floor space of at least 4 × 8 feet.

Terrarium Type: Dry savanna or semiarid-land terrarium or cage.

Social Structure: Communal, but breeding males can be aggressive.

Diet: This species eats berries and other fruits, green leafy vegetables, and some animal protein (such as low fat dry dog and cat foods). Food should be dusted biweekly with a good quality vitamin-mineral powder.

Potential Problems: Imports may be dehydrated and poorly fed when received. Captive-bred babies are hardy and largely trouble-free. Ample water should always be available, both for drinking and for soaking.

References:
Bartlett, R. D., and Patricia Bartlett. *Turtles and Tortoises.* Hauppauge, NY: Barron's Educational Series, Inc., 1996.

Yellow-footed Tortoise

Trade Name(s): Same.
Family & Scientific Name: Testudinidae; *Geochelone (Chelonoidis) denticulata*.
Identifying Features: These have cream to yellow highlights on head and yellow(ish) scales

on the anterior of the forelimbs. They have strongly convex carapace sides (when viewed from above), and serrate (denticulate) anterior and posterior marginals. Hatchlings are paler and with very serrate marginals.
Similar Species: Red-footed tortoise is more brightly colored (see account for red-footed tortoise), lacks serrate marginals, and tends to have straight or concave sides to its carapace.
Range & Origin: Northern South America. Most now available in the pet trade are captive-bred and hatched babies.
Adult Size: Often to 15 inches; rarely to 30 inches (some Amazon Basin populations).
Life Span: 10–20 years; 30–40 (or more) years should be attainable.
Terrarium Size: From one to several hatchlings can be maintained in a 15-20-gallon capacity terrarium. A pair of adults should have a floor space of at least 4 × 8 feet, and preferably larger.

Terrarium Type: This rain forest tortoise can tolerate more humidity and slightly damper conditions than most of its congenerics. However, as long as it has ample water to drink, moist cage conditions are not actually necessary for its well-being and may prove, over time, to be harmful.
Social Structure: Communal, but breeding males may show aggressive tendencies.
Diet: Primarily vegetarian, this species eats berries and other fruits, green leafy vegetables, and some animal protein (such as low fat dry dog and cat foods). Food should be dusted biweekly (most adults) or once or twice weekly (hatchlings and ovulating females) with a good quality vitamin-mineral powder.
Potential Problems: Imports may be dehydrated and poorly fed when received. These may require veterinary intervention to ascertain recovery. Captive-bred babies are hardy and largely trouble-free. Ample water should always be available, both for drinking and for soaking.
References:
Bartlett, R. D., and Patricia Bartlett. *Turtles and Tortoises.* Hauppauge, NY: Barron's Educational Series, Inc., 1996.

Serrated Hinge-backed Tortoise

Trade Name(s): Forest Hinge-backed Tortoise.

Family & Scientific Name: Testudinidae; *Kinixys erosa.*

Identifying Features: This tortoise is carapace hinged and flared anteriorly and posteriorly with serrate posterior marginals.

Social Structure: These tortoises are communal.

Diet: Somewhat omnivorous, this tortoise eats worms, caterpillars, low fat dog foods, and prepared tortoise chows, but prefers healthy greens, berries, and other fruits.

Similar Species: See account for Bell's hinge-backed tortoise.

Range & Origin: Collected from the wild in western central Africa.

Adult Size: Usually in the 7–10-inch size range, some may attain a 12-inch length.

Life Span: If successfully acclimated, this tortoise can live for several decades.

Terrarium Size: Minimum of 50 gallons (75 would be better) for one or two tortoises of moderate size. Low cage (15 inches high) with floor space of at least 2 × 4 feet (4 × 8 feet is suggested as a permanent cage for two or three tortoises) is also fine.

Terrarium Type: Unlike most tortoises, this species is associated with moist, bottom-land, habitats. A cage with a substrate of barely dampened mulch is suggested. A water dish large enough for the tortoise to lie in and soak is also needed.

Vitamin D_3 and calcium additives may be given once weekly.

Potential Problems: Until acclimated (this can take as long as a year!), these are shy and delicate tortoises with a very high mortality rate. Many imports are seriously dehydrated, harbor potentially lethal levels of endoparasites, and have at least the start of respiratory ailments. Immediate veterinary assessment (and treatment when necessary) is suggested. The tortoises must be kept humid and warm, provided a healthy diet, and have continual access to clean water. UV-B will help with vitamin D_3-calcium synthesis and metabolizing. Once stabilized, they are reasonably hardy.

References:

Bartlett, R. D., and Patricia Bartlett. *Turtles and Tortoises.* Hauppauge, NY: Barron's Educational Series, Inc., 1996.

Bell's Hinge-backed Tortoise

Trade Name(s): Hinge-backed Tortoise, African Hinge-backed Tortoise.

Family & Scientific Name: Testudinidae; *Kinixys belliana.*

Identifying Features: On this tortoise, the central carapacial area is flattened, and

anterior and posterior marginals are not flared. Rear marginals are not strongly serrate and there are large scales on anterior of forelimbs. There is a carapacial hinge between the fourth and fifth costal scute.

Similar Species: Other hinge-backed tortoises have broad flaring of anterior and posterior marginals and/or strongly serrate rear marginals.

Range & Origin: Collected from the wild in Africa, from Somalia westward.

Adult Size: Usually in the 6–8-inch size range, some may attain a 10-inch length.

Life Span: If successfully acclimated, this tortoise can live for several decades.

Terrarium Size: Minimum of 50 gallons (75 would be better) for one or two tortoises of moderate size. Low cage (15 inches high) with floor space of at least 2 × 4 feet (4 × 8 feet is suggested as a permanent cage for two or three tortoises) is also fine.

Terrarium Type: A dry savanna terrarium or a plain dry cage with a shallow water bowl

in normally arid and semiarid regions is fine. An outside cage (offer protection from the sun) is ideal when temperatures are in the 85–100°F range.

Social Structure: These tortoises are communal.

Diet: Somewhat omnivorous, this tortoise eats worms, caterpillars, low fat dog foods, and prepared tortoise chows, but prefers healthy greens, berries, and other fruits. Vitamin D_3 and calcium additives may be given once weekly.

Potential Problems: Until acclimated (this can take as long as a year!), these are delicate tortoises with a very high mortality rate. Many imports are seriously dehydrated, harbor potentially lethal levels of endoparasites, and have at least the start of respiratory ailments. Immediate veterinary assessment (and treatment when necessary) of all imported specimens is suggested. The tortoises must be kept dry and warm, provided a healthy diet, and have continual access to clean water. UV-B will help with vitamin D_3-calcium synthesis and metabolizing. Once stabilized, they are reasonably hardy.

References:

Bartlett, R. D., and Patricia Bartlett. *Turtles and Tortoises.* Hauppauge, NY: Barron's Educational Series, Inc., 1996.

Painted Turtle

Trade Name(s): There are four subspecies sold. In declining availability, these are: Western Painted Turtle, *Chrysemys picta bellii;* Southern Painted Turtle, *C. p. dorsalis;* Midland Painted Turtle, *C. p marginata;* Eastern Painted Turtle, *C. p. picta* (shown).

Family & Scientific Name: Emydidae; the individual names are listed above.

Identifying Features: These turtles have black to olive smoothly domed carapace (hatchlings have a middorsal keel), brilliant red in the marginal scutes, yellow stripes and/or spots on the black head. Additionally, the western painted has light and dark carapacial reticulations and a reddish plastron containing a large dark figure. The southern painted has a yellow to orange vertebral stripe; the midland painted has yellow plastron with a dark oval figure; eastern painted has a yellow plastron, with or without a dark spot or two.

Similar Species: None.

Range & Origin: North America. Many are collected from the wild. Some are captive-bred and hatched.

Adult Size: 4½–6½ inches; the western race may rarely attain 9 inches.

Life Span: 10–25 (or more) years.

Terrarium Size: One to four hatchlings can be maintained in a filtered 10-gallon aquarium. One to four adults require a filtered 50-gallon tank.

Terrarium Type: Filtered aquarium or semi-aquatic terrarium with filtered water section. Adult painted turtles crush most plantings in the land section of a semi-aquatic terrarium, and eat most aquatic plants placed in the aquarium. These hardy turtles thrive in a fenced garden pond.

Social Structure: These turtles are communal.

Diet: Omnivorous. Painted turtles eat worms, caterpillars, minnows, insects, low fat dog and cat chows, pelleted trout chow, pelleted catfish chow, koi pellets, and prepared turtle foods. They also eat dark greens, berries, and other fruits. Vitamin D_3 and calcium additives may be given once weekly.

Potential Problems: These very hardy turtles usually pose no problems for their keepers. Bacteria-caused shell ulcers (shell rot) can occur unless the water is kept quite clean.

References:

Bartlett, R. D., and Patricia Bartlett. *Turtles and Tortoises.* Hauppauge, NY: Barron's Educational Series, Inc., 1996.

Florida Red-bellied Turtle

Trade Name(s): Red-bellied Slider.

Family & Scientific Name: Emydidae; *Pseudemys nelsoni.*

Identifying Features: On these turtles, a yellow interorbital stripe connects (or almost connects) with a

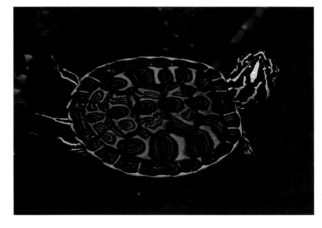

V on the snout to form an arrow. Carapace has a wide vertical bar in each scute. The belly (of hatchlings) tends to be red-orange in color. This may pale to yellow as the turtle grows.

Similar Species: None.

Range & Origin: Florida. A few are wild collected; most hatchlings available in the pet trade are captive-bred and hatched.

Adult Size: 8–11 inches long; rarely to 14 inches.

Life Span: Potentially, to several decades.

Terrarium Size: One to several babies can be kept in a filtered 10-gallon aquarium. Adults are very large. One requires a 50-gallon filtered aquarium and two need a tank of 75-gallon capacity.

Terrarium Type: These semiaquatic turtles are strong swimmers and persistent baskers. Deep, clean water for swimming and an above water basking site warmed and illuminated by a UV bulb are suggested. Water requires both filtration and frequent changing. A fenced garden pool is an excellent choice during the summer (or year round in very warm climates).

Social Structure: These turtles are communal

Diet: Omnivorous, but strongly vegetarian, especially when adult. This turtle eats dark greens, berries, and other fruits. Worms, minnows, insects, low fat dog and cat chows, pelleted trout chow, pelleted catfish chow, koi pellets, and prepared turtle foods are also eaten. Vitamin D_3 and calcium additives may be given once weekly.

Potential Problems: If provided with a good diet, this is a very hardy turtle. Providing sufficient space for the very large adults is usually the main concern.

References:
Bartlett, R. D., and Patricia Bartlett. *Turtles and Tortoises.* Hauppauge, NY: Barron's Educational Series, Inc., 1996.

Red-eared Slider

Trade Name(s): Red-eared Turtle, Green Turtle.

Family & Scientific Name: Emydidae; *Trachemys scripta elegans.*

Identifying Features: This turtle has a red post-orbital stripe.

Similar Species: None.

Range & Origin: North America. The vast majority of the hundreds of thousands of hatchlings sold annually are captive-bred and hatched.

Adult Size: 8–10 inches; some near a foot in length.

Life Span: More than a half century.

Terrarium Size: One to several babies can be kept in a filtered 10-gallon aquarium. Adults are very large. One requires a 50-gallon filtered aquarium and two need a tank of 75-gallon capacity.

Terrarium Type: These semiaquatic turtles are strong swimmers and persistent baskers. Deep, clean water for swimming and an above water basking site warmed and illuminated by a UV bulb are suggested. Water requires both filtration and frequent changing. A fenced garden pool is an excellent choice for much of the year for these very adaptable and hardy turtles.

Social Structure: These turtles are communal.

Diet: Omnivorous, but strongly vegetarian, especially when adult. This turtle eats healthy greens, berries, and other fruits. Worms, minnows, insects, low fat dog and cat chows, pelleted trout chow, pelleted catfish chow, koi pellets, and prepared turtle foods are also eaten. Vitamin D_3 and calcium additives may be given once weekly.

Potential Problems: If provided with a good diet, this is a very hardy turtle. Providing sufficient space for the very large adults is usually the main concern.

References:

Bartlett, R. D., and Patricia Bartlett. *Turtles and Tortoises.* Hauppauge, NY: Barron's Educational Series, Inc., 1996.

Yellow-bellied Slider

Trade Name(s):
Yellow-eared
Slider.
Family & Scientific Name:
Emydidae;
*Trachemys
scripta scripta.*
**Identifying
Features:** A
bright yellow
patch (not multiple stripes)
dominates each
cheek.

Water requires
both filtration
and frequent
changing. A
fenced garden
pool is an excellent choice for
much of the year
for these very
adaptable and
hardy turtles.
Social Structure: These
turtles are
communal.

Similar Species: None.
Range & Origin: Southeastern United
States. Many of those sold annually are
captive-bred and hatched; some are collected from the wild.
Adult Size: 8–10 inches; some near a foot
in length.
Life Span: More than 50 years.
Terrarium Size: One to several babies can
be kept in a filtered 10-gallon aquarium.
Adults are very large. One requires a 50-
gallon filtered aquarium and two need a tank
of 75-gallon capacity.
Terrarium Type: These semiaquatic turtles
are strong swimmers and persistent
baskers. Deep, clean water for swimming
and an above water basking site warmed
and illuminated by a UV bulb are suggested.

Diet: Omnivorous, but strongly vegetarian,
especially when adult. This turtle eats dark
greens, berries, and other fruits. It is most
comfortable swallowing while in the water.
Worms, minnows, insects, low fat dog and
cat chows, pelleted trout chow, pelleted
catfish chow, koi pellets, and prepared
turtle foods are also eaten. Vitamin D_3 and
calcium additives may be given once
weekly.
Potential Problems: If provided with a
good diet, this is a very hardy turtle. Providing sufficient space for the very large adults
is usually the main concern.
References:
Bartlett, R. D., and Patricia Bartlett. *Turtles
and Tortoises.* Hauppauge, NY: Barron's
Educational Series, Inc., 1996.

Mississippi Map Turtle

Trade Name(s):
Map Turtle,
False Map Turtle, Grayback.
Family & Scientific Name:
Emydidae;
Graptemys pseudogeographica kohni.
Identifying Features: A yellow post-orbital crescent and a grayish carapace with a strong vertebral keel are identifying characters. They have strongly serrate rear marginals.

Similar Species: This species resembles the Ouachita map turtle, but with different head markings.

Range & Origin: Southcentral United States. Almost all of the hatchlings offered in the pet trade are captive-bred and hatched on Louisiana turtle farms.

Adult Size: Males are adult at from 3½–4½ inches; females attain a length of 6½–8 inches (rarely to 10 inches).

Life Span: Several decades.

Terrarium Size: One to several babies can be kept in a filtered 10-gallon aquarium. Several adult males may be kept in a 29–40-gallon aquarium. Females are very large. One or two require an aquarium with a minimum of 50-gallons in capacity.

Terrarium Type: These semiaquatic turtles are strong swimmers and persistent baskers. Deep, clean water for swimming and an above water basking site warmed and illuminated by a UV bulb are suggested. Water requires both filtration and frequent changing. During the summer months, a fenced garden pool is an excellent choice for these very adaptable and hardy turtles.

Social Structure: These turtles are communal.

Diet: Omnivorous, but strongly oriented toward insects and gastropods. Worms, minnows, crickets, aquatic insects, low fat dog and cat chows, pelleted trout chow, pelleted catfish chow, koi pellets, and prepared turtle foods are eaten. Dark greens are also occasionally eaten. Vitamin D_3 and calcium additives may be given once weekly.

Potential Problems: Bacterial ulcerative shell disease (shell rot) quickly appears when the water is not kept scrupulously clean. If provided with clean water and a good diet, Mississippi map turtles may be considered a hardy species. Providing sufficient space for the very large adult females is usually the main concern.

References:
Bartlett, R. D., and Patricia Bartlett. *Turtles and Tortoises.* Hauppauge, NY: Barron's Educational Series, Inc., 1996.

Ornate Box Turtle; Western Box Turtle

Trade Name(s): Same.

Family & Scientific Name: Emydidae; *Terrapene ornata ornata*.

Identifying Features: These turtles have heavy yellow radiating markings on dark carapace. The colors are reversed on the prominently hinged plastron and the carapace is flattened in the vertebral region.

Similar Species: See accounts for eastern box turtle, three-toed box turtle, Chinese box turtle, and Malayan box turtle.

Range & Origin: Most are collected from the wild. This species ranges widely in the western United States.

Adult Size: 4½–6 inches.

Life Span: Once acclimated, this species lives for several decades. It can be difficult to keep in normally humid regions.

Terrarium Size: Minimum of 20-gallon, long for one or two specimens; larger is better. Backyard cage with suitable weather protection best where possible.

Terrarium Type: Desert, dry savanna, or plain cage with absorbent substrate. Prefers low humidity.

Social Structure: Adult males can be quarrelsome during the breeding season, but females and immatures can be kept communally.

Diet: Eats on land. Diet includes healthy fruits, vegetables, low fat dog foods, turtle chows, and insects. Food should be dusted with vitamin-mineral additives once (adults) or twice (juveniles and ovulating females) weekly.

Potential Problems: Easily stressed by high humidity, excessive moisture, and overcrowding.

References:

Bartlett, R. D., and Patricia Bartlett. *American and Asian Box Turtles.* Hauppauge, NY: Barron's Educational Series, Inc., (forthcoming).

Bartlett, R. D., and Patricia Bartlett. *Turtles.* Hauppauge, NY: Barron's Educational Series, Inc., 1996.

Eastern Box Turtle

Trade Name(s): Same.

Family & Scientific Name: Emydidae; *Terrapene carolina carolina.*

Identifying Features: This turtle has a dark carapace usually rounded and bearing light dots, spots, streaks, or radiating markings.

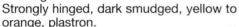

Strongly hinged, dark smudged, yellow to orange, plastron.

Similar Species: See accounts for ornate box turtle, three-toed box turtle, Chinese box turtle, and Malayan box turtle.

Range & Origin: Now protected over much of its eastern United States range, but some wild collected specimens still available. Captive-bred in small numbers.

Adult Size: 4½–6 inches.

Life Span: Once acclimated, to more than 50 years

Terrarium Size: Minimum of 20-gallon, long for one or two specimens; larger terrarium is much better. Where feasible, backyard cage with suitable weather protection is best.

Terrarium Type: Woodland or damp savanna terrarium or plain cage with absorbent substrate. Prefers relatively high humidity.

Social Structure: Males are quarrelsome during breeding season. With adequate space and visual barriers may be maintained communally.

Diet: Eats on land. Berries, fruits, healthy greens, insects, worms, low fat dog and cat chows, prepared land-turtle food, pelleted trout chow, pelleted catfish chow are all eaten. Multi-vitamin-calcium powder should be added to food weekly (adults) or twice weekly (ovulating females and juveniles).

Potential Problems: Must be kept humid in dry areas. Freshly collected specimens may refuse food. Tempt with large earthworms.

References:

Bartlett, R. D., and Patricia Bartlett. *American and Asian Box Turtles.* Hauppauge, NY: Barron's Educational Series, Inc., (forthcoming).

Bartlett, R. D., and Patricia Bartlett. *Turtles.* Hauppauge, NY: Barron's Educational Series, Inc., 1996.

Three-toed Box Turtle

Trade Name(s): Same.

Family & Scientific Name: Emydidae; *Terrapene carolina triunguis*.

Identifying Features: These turtles have olive brown carapace, with or without vague lighter markings. The face is marked with

white and orange or red. The plastron is hinged and olive yellow. There are usually three (rarely four) toes on the hind foot.

Similar Species: See accounts for ornate, eastern, Malayan, and Chinese box turtles.

Range & Origin: Wild collected in central United States.

Adult Size: 5–7 inches.

Life Span: Once acclimated, this turtle may live for more than 20 years in captivity.

Terrarium Size: Minimum of 20-gallon, long for one or two specimens; larger is better. Backyard cage with suitable weather protection best where possible.

Terrarium Type: Desert, dry savanna, or plain cage with absorbent substrate. Prefers low humidity.

Social Structure: Usually not overly aggressive, especially if in large cages with visual barriers.

Diet: Eats on land. Berries, fruits, healthy greens, insects, worms, low fat pelleted dog and cat foods, pelleted trout chow, pelleted catfish chow are accepted. This race of the eastern box turtle is especially fond of grasshoppers and crickets. Multivitamin-calcium powder should be added to food weekly (adults) or twice weekly (ovulating females and juveniles).

Potential Problems: The three-toed box turtle is reasonably hardy, but may be difficult to acclimate in humid or wet climates. Lowered humidity (such as in air conditioning) may help.

References:

Bartlett, R. D., and Patricia Bartlett. *American and Asian Box Turtles.* Hauppauge, NY: Barron's Educational Series, Inc., (forthcoming).

Bartlett, R. D., and Patricia Bartlett. *Turtles.* Hauppauge, NY: Barron's Educational Series, Inc., 1996.

Chinese Box Turtle

Trade Name(s): Chinese Box Turtle. Yellow-margined Box Turtle.

Family & Scientific Name: Emydidae; *Cuora (Cistoclemmys) flavomarginata.*

Identifying Features: This turtle has yellow submarginal scutes, highly domed carapace with broken yellow keel, and yellow edging to the black plastron. There is a single yellow green to lime green stripe on the face (above the eye), yellowish cheeks (sometimes suffused with pale orange), and a pinkish throat.

Similar Species: See accounts for other box turtle species.

Range & Origin: China; most specimens available in the pet trade are collected from the wild. A very few are bred in captivity.

Adult Size: Commonly attains 5½–6½ inches. inches in length; rarely may attain 7½–8 inches.

Life Span: Once acclimated, 10, 20, or more years.

Terrarium Size: Most Chinese box turtles available in the pet trade are subadults to adults. This is an active species that should be given as much room to roam as possible. While a 40-gallon capacity terrarium temporarily houses one or two box turtles, a terrarium at least twice that size would be better. Where temperatures are moderate a large, outdoor garden cage is best for these turtles.

Terrarium Type: A woodland or damp savanna-style terrarium, or an outside cage is the best for these pretty turtles.

Social Structure: Males can be aggressive, especially during the breeding season. However, if provided with a spacious cage and visual barriers, they generally coexist well in groups.

Diet: This turtle prefers to eat on land. Fruits, healthy greens, worms, insects, minnows, prepared turtle foods, pelleted trout chow, koi pellets, pelleted catfish chow, low fat dog and cat kibble are accepted. Dietary variety is best. Food should be vitamin-mineral dusted twice weekly for hatchlings and ovulating females, and once every week or two for all others.

Potential Problems: This is generally a hardy turtle species that, if adequately hydrated and fed, gives very few problems.

References:

Bartlett, R. D., and Patricia Bartlett. *American and Asian Box Turtles.* Hauppauge, NY: Barron's Educational Series, Inc., (forthcoming).

Bartlett, R. D., and Patricia Bartlett. *Turtles.* Hauppauge, NY: Barron's Educational Series, Inc., 1996.

Malayan Box Turtle

Trade Name(s): Asian Box Turtle, Amboina Box Turtle, Black Box Turtle, Malayan Box Turtle.

Family & Scientific Name: Emydidae; *Cuora amboinensis.*

Identifying Features: These turtles have highly domed black(ish) carapace, hinged all yellow plastron, and a head black with precise yellow facial stripes.

Similar Species: See accounts for other box turtle species.

Range & Origin: Wild collected; imported from Malaya.

Adult Size: 6–8 inches.

Life Span: Once acclimated, this turtle can be expected to live for 10 to 20 (or more) years.

Terrarium Size: Minimum of 40-gallon capacity for one or two adult specimens. If provided with a shallow pond, this turtle thrives in a warm, shaded outside cage.

Terrarium Type: This Asian turtle is much more aquatic than the American box turtles. It thrives in an aquarium holding several inches of water and a smooth, warmed and illuminated, easily accessible haulout, or in a semiaquatic setup.

Social Structure: Occasionally adult males are aggressive but this species is usually amenable to cagemates.

Diet: Although this turtle can eat on land, it usually prefers to eat in the water. Fruits, healthy greens, worms, insects, minnows, prepared turtle foods, pelleted trout chow, koi pellets, pelleted catfish chow, low fat dog and cat kibble are accepted. Dietary variety is best. Food should be vitamin-mineral dusted twice weekly for hatchlings and ovulating females, and once every week or two for all others.

Potential Problems: New imports may be seriously dehydrated and have a profusion of endoparasites. Prompt veterinary assessment and intervention may be necessary.

References:

Bartlett, R. D., and Patricia Bartlett. *American and Asian Box Turtles.* Hauppauge, NY: Barron's Educational Series, Inc., (forthcoming).

Bartlett, R. D., and Patricia Bartlett. *Turtles.* Hauppauge, NY: Barron's Educational Series, Inc., 1996.

Ornate Wood Turtle

Trade Name(s):
Painted Wood
Turtle.

Family & Scientific Name:
Emydidae;
Rhinoclemmys
pulcherrima
manni.

Identifying
Features: This
turtle has highly
domed olive
carapace patterned with
dark-edged
yellow to rose

markings. There is an olive head with bright
red lines on the snout and face. Carapacial
growth rings may not be well defined.

Similar Species: None.

Range & Origin: Central America. Most of
the specimens in the pet trade are collected
from the wild. A very few are captive-bred.

Adult Size: 5–6½ inches; rarely to 7½
inches.

Life Span: Once acclimated, this pretty
turtle may live for several decades.

Terrarium Size: Minimum terrarium size for
one or two adults is 40-gallon capacity;
larger is better.

Terrarium Type: This race is more aquatic
than the northerly forms. A pool deep
enough for it to
swim, as well as
a large land area,
should be provided. A semi-
aquatic terrarium
will suffice,
but like all turtles, this one
quickly tramples
and destroys all
but sturdy
plants.

Social Structure: These
turtles are
communal.

Diet: Prefers to feed in water, but can eat on
land. Fruits, tomatoes, and dark green vegetables are accepted, as are worms, minnows, insects, and many kinds of prepared
foods. Food should be vitamin-mineral
dusted twice weekly for hatchlings and
ovulating females, and once every week or
two for all others.

Potential Problems: This turtle is usually
trouble-free. Occasional specimens may
arrive from the wild in a dehydrated condition, but most rehydrate quickly and thrive.

References:

Bartlett, R. D., and Patricia Bartlett. *Turtles*
and Tortoises. Hauppauge, NY: Barron's
Educational Series, Inc., 1996.

South American Wood Turtle

Trade Name(s): Same.

Family & Scientific Name: Emydidae; *Rhinoclemmys punctularia punctularia.*

Identifying Features: They have dark brown to nearly black carapace. Scutes are usually sculptured with growth rings. The top of the head is black with broad red markings. Cheeks are striped with yellow and black, and the forelimbs are usually prominently spotted with cream to light yellow on black.

Similar Species: Painted wood turtle has thin red facial markings.

Range & Origin: Northern South America. Most of the specimens in the pet trade are collected from the wild. A very few are captive-bred.

Adult Size: Most are 6–7½ inches in length. Some attain a shell length of 10 inches.

Life Span: Once acclimated, this pretty turtle may live for several decades.

Terrarium Size: Minimum terrarium size for one or two adults is 75-gallon capacity; larger is better.

Terrarium Type: This race is more aquatic than the northerly forms. A pool deep enough for it to swim, as well as a large land area, should be provided. A semi-aquatic terrarium will suffice, but like all turtles, this one quickly tramples and destroys all but sturdy plants.

Social Structure: These turtles are communal.

Diet: Prefers to feed in water, but can eat on land. Fruits and healthy vegetables are accepted, as are worms, minnows, insects, and many kinds of prepared foods. Food should be vitamin-mineral dusted twice weekly for hatchlings and ovulating females, and once every week or two for all others.

Potential Problems: Some examples can be badly dehydrated when imported. These will seldom accept food, no matter how succulent. Immediately rehydrate in shallow, tepid water.

References:

Bartlett, R. D., and Patricia Bartlett. *Turtles and Tortoises.* Hauppauge, NY: Barron's Educational Series, Inc., 1996.

North American Wood Turtle

Trade Name(s): Same.

Family & Scientific Name: Emydidae; *Clemmys insculpta.*

Identifying Features: These turtles have brown, heavily sculptured carapace and a black head. The chin, neck, and apices of legs and tail are bright orange to olive yellow.

Similar Species: See accounts for all other wood turtles.

Range & Origin: Most specimens now entering the pet trade are captive-bred and reared hatchlings. Wild collected examples of this species are now protected by law from commercialization.

Adult Size: 7–8½ inches; occasionally to 10 inches.

Life Span: With good care, 30–50 years of age should be attainable.

Terrarium Size: Hatchlings can be housed in a 20-gallon, long tank. One or two adults would need a floor space of at least 4 × 8 feet.

Terrarium Type: This is a large, active, and hardy turtle. It does best if kept in an outside enclosure. A secure hibernaculum (a deep pond is best) that does not completely freeze must be provided.

Social Structure: Males can be aggressive to other males, especially during the breeding season. Providing the enclosure is large enough and provides visual barriers, this can usually be considered a communal turtle.

Diet: Can eat either in or out of the water. Omnivorous; eats some fruit and greens, but prefers insects, worms, minnows, trout chow, catfish chow, prepared turtle foods, low fat dry cat and dog foods. Food should be vitamin-mineral dusted twice weekly for hatchlings and ovulating females, and once every week or two for all others.

Potential Problems: This turtle is an excellent climber. It can escape from wood or wood and wire constructed pens unless covered, or a substantial overhang is provided.

References:

Bartlett, R. D., and Patricia Bartlett. *Turtles and Tortoises.* Hauppauge, NY: Barron's Educational Series, Inc., 1996.

Spotted Turtle

Trade Name(s):
Spotted Turtle,
Spotted Pond
Turtle.

Family & Scientific Name:
Emydidae;
Clemmys guttata.

Identifying Features:
These turtles
have black
heads with yellow spots (often
orange near the
neck), and carapace bearing one yellow spot (babies) to
several yellow spots (adults) per carapacial
scute. There is some orange on forelimbs.

Similar Species: None: the yellow spots are
distinctive.

Range & Origin: Most examples offered in
the pet trade have been collected from the
wild in eastern North America. A very few
are now being captive-bred.

Adult Size: 3½–4½ inches; rarely to 5½ inches.

Life Span: 20 or more years.

Terrarium Size: 20-gallon, long aquarium
can temporarily house one or two adults.
A larger terrarium or a garden pond is
better.

Terrarium Type: Semiaquatic terrarium or
aquarium with
adequate
haulout warmed
and illuminated
from above. This
turtle prefers
shallow, cool
water (68–74°F),
but thermoregulates by
basking.

Social Structure: These turtles are
communal.

Diet: May
accept food on
land, but takes it to the water to swallow.
Omnivorous; eats some fruit and greens, but
prefers insects, worms, minnows, trout
chow, catfish chow, and prepared turtle
foods. Food should be vitamin-mineral
dusted twice weekly for hatchlings and ovulating females, and once every week or two
for all others.

Potential Problems: Although an aquatic
species, this turtle is not a particularly
strong swimmer. It can drown in deep water,
especially in aquariums.

References:
Bartlett, R. D., and Patricia Bartlett. *Turtles
and Tortoises.* Hauppauge, NY: Barron's
Educational Series, Inc., 1996.

Reeve's Turtle

Trade Name(s): Same. Also, Japanese Coin Turtle.

Family & Scientific Name: Emydidae; *Chinemys reevesi.*

Identifying Features: These turtles have dark shells and skin, often with curved yellow lines on the side of the face, and three distinct carapacial keels.

Similar Species: None.

Range & Origin: Asia. Some pet trade specimens are wild collected, but a great many are now captive-bred and hatched in Europe and America.

Adult Size: Commonly 4–6 inches; occasionally to 8 inches.

Life Span: To 25 years. A greater longevity should be possible.

Terrarium Size: Several of the coin-sized babies can be housed in a well filtered 10-gallon tank. A pair or trio of adults should be given a tank with a minimum capacity of 40 gallons.

Terrarium Type: An aquarium with haulout areas illuminated and warmed from above is best. Water temperature can be in the 70s, but the basking area should be warmed to 95–100°F. Garden pools are ideal during the summer months.

Social Structure: These turtles are communal.

Diet: Although this turtle may accept its food on land, it will return to the water to swallow. Some fruits, some healthy greens, worms, insects, minnows, prepared turtle foods, pelleted trout chow, koi pellets, pelleted catfish chow, low fat dog and cat kibble are accepted. Dietary variety is best. Food should be vitamin-mineral dusted twice weekly for hatchlings and ovulating females, and once every week or two for all others.

Potential Problems: If insufficient calcium is given and metabolized, fast growing babies may develop a soft shell (MBD). UV-B helps all turtles metabolize calcium properly.

References:

Bartlett, R. D., and Patricia Bartlett. *Turtles.* Hauppauge, NY: Barron's Educational Series, Inc., 1996.

Eastern Mud Turtle

Trade Name(s): Same. Also, Common Mud Turtle.

Family & Scientific Name: Kinosternidae; *Kinosternon subrubrum* ssp.

Identifying Features: Although babies have a roughened carapace, the carapace of the adult is smoothly

domed. This turtle is dark brown to almost black in coloration, often with lighter (sometimes yellowish) markings on the cheeks. The large yellowish to brown plastron has two hinges and can be closed to partially protect the legs, tail, and head. There are small, but obvious, downward projecting barbels on the chin.

Similar Species: Other mud turtles are very similar in appearance. Compare the turtle with the above photo.

Range & Origin: Eastern United States. Although a few are bred by hobbyists, most available in the pet trade are collected from the wild.

Adult Size: 3–4 inches.

Life Span: To more than 18 years; 25+ years should be an attainable goal.

Terrarium Size: When babies, from one to several may be kept in a 5–10-gallon capacity aquarium. When adult, a single specimen or a pair may be maintained in a filtered 20-gallon aquarium.

Terrarium Type: A filtered aquarium with water temperature in the high 70s to low 80s, and a sloping ramp (driftwood, textured plastic, or other non-abrasive surface) leading from the bottom to an illuminated and warmed basking spot, should be provided.

Social Structure: These turtles are communal if not crowded.

Diet: The eastern mud turtle eats mostly animal matter. Snails, crayfish, minnows, worms, insects, and prepared foods such as pelleted trout chow, pelleted catfish chow, koi pellets, and turtle foods are all eaten.

Potential Problems: This is a very hardy turtle species that seldom presents any problems for its keepers.

References:

Bartlett, R. D., and Patricia Bartlett. *Turtles.* Hauppauge, NY: Barron's Educational Series, Inc., 1996.

Yellow Mud Turtle

Trade Name(s): Same.

Family & Scientific Name: Kinosternidae; *Kinosternon flavescens* ssp.

Identifying Features: Although babies have a somewhat roughened carapace, the carapace of the adult is smooth, domed, but flattened centrally. It is olive yellow, olive brown, or olive gray in coloration. The head and limbs are similarly colored but the throat is yellow. The ninth marginal is noticeably higher than the others. The large yellowish to brown plastron has two hinges and can be closed to partially protect the legs, tail, and head. There are small barbels on the chin.

Similar Species: Other mud turtles are very similar in appearance, but lack the yellow chin and the tall ninth marginal scute.

Range & Origin: Central United States and adjacent Mexico. Although a few are bred by hobbyists, most available in the pet trade are collected from the wild.

Adult Size: To 5½ inches.

Life Span: To more than 10 years. Double this should be an attainable goal.

Terrarium Size: When babies, from one to several may be kept in a 5–10-gallon capacity aquarium. When adult, a single specimen or a pair may be maintained in a filtered 20-gallon aquarium.

Terrarium Type: A filtered aquarium with water temperature in the high 70s to low 80s, and a sloping ramp (driftwood, textured plastic, or other non-abrasive surface) leading from the bottom to an illuminated and warmed basking spot, should be provided.

Social Structure: Communal, if not crowded.

Diet: The yellow mud turtle eats mostly animal matter. Snails, crayfish, minnows, worms, insects, and prepared foods such as pelleted trout chow, pelleted catfish chow, koi pellets, and turtle foods are all eaten.

Potential Problems: This is a very hardy turtle species that seldom presents any problems for its keepers.

References:
Bartlett, R. D., and Patricia Bartlett. *Turtles.* Hauppauge, NY: Barron's Educational Series, Inc., 1996.

Striped Mud Turtle

Trade Name(s): Same.

Family & Scientific Name: Kinosternidae; *Kinosternon bauri*.

Identifying Features: Although babies have a somewhat roughened carapace, the carapace of the adult is smooth and domed. It is black in coloration but is usually patterned with three yellowish lines. The head and limbs are dark, but the cheeks are usually strongly patterned with yellow lines. The large yellowish to brown plastron has two hinges and can be closed to partially protect the legs, tail, and head. There are small barbels on the chin.

Similar Species: Other mud turtles are very similar in appearance, but lack the carapacial stripes.

Range & Origin: Southeastern United States. Although a few are bred by hobbyists, most available in the pet trade are collected from the wild.

Adult Size: To 4½ inches.

Life Span: To more than 20 years.

Terrarium Size: When babies, from one to

several may be kept in a 5–10-gallon capacity aquarium. When adult, a single specimen or a pair may be maintained in a filtered 20-gallon aquarium.

Terrarium Type: A filtered aquarium, with water temperature in the high 70s to low 80s, and a sloping ramp (driftwood, textured plastic, or other non-abrasive surface) leading from the bottom to an illuminated and warmed basking spot, should be provided.

Social Structure: Communal, if not crowded.

Diet: Like other mud turtles, this one eats mostly animal matter. Snails, crayfish, minnows, worms, insects, and prepared foods such as pelleted trout chow, pelleted catfish chow, koi pellets, and turtle foods are all eaten.

Potential Problems: This is a very hardy turtle species that seldom presents any problems for its keepers.

References:
Bartlett, R. D., and Patricia Bartlett. *Turtles.* Hauppauge, NY: Barron's Educational Series, Inc., 1996.

Common & Razor-backed Musk Turtle

Trade Name(s): Same. Also, Stinkpot (Common Musk Turtle).

Family & Scientific Name: *Sternotherus odoratus* (common musk turtle) and *S. carinatus* (razor-backed musk turtle), shown here.

Identifying Features: Both species have small plastron with a single weak (anterior) hinge. Common musk has dark carapace (smooth when adult, rough when hatchling) and dark skin with yellow stripes on the face. Barbels occur on both the chin and the throat. Razor-backed musk has a steeply peaked, olive brown to brown carapace and a dark streaked and spotted olive head. There are barbels only on the chin.

Similar Species: Loggerhead musk looks much like a razorback in color but has three keels on the carapace.

Range & Origin: Common musk, eastern United States; razor-backed musk, southeastern United States. Both are bred in small numbers by hobbyists, but the pet trade remains largely dependent on wild collected specimens.

Adult Size: To 5 inches.

Life Span: Common musk to 54 years; razor-backed musk to 30 years.

Terrarium Size: When babies, from one to several may be kept in a 5–10 gallon capacity aquarium. When adult, a single specimen or a pair may be maintained in a filtered 20-gallon aquarium.

Terrarium Type: A filtered aquarium, with water temperature in the high 70s to low 80s, and a sloping ramp (driftwood, textured plastic, or other non-abrasive surface) leading from the bottom to an illuminated and warmed basking spot, will suffice.

Social Structure: Communal, if not crowded.

Diet: Like mud turtles, the musk turtles eat mostly animal matter. Snails, crayfish, minnows, worms, insects, and prepared foods such as pelleted trout chow, pelleted catfish chow, koi pellets, and turtle foods are all eaten.

Potential Problems: These are both very hardy turtle species that seldom present any problems for their keepers.

References:
Bartlett, R. D., and Patricia Bartlett. *Turtles.* Hauppauge, NY: Barron's Educational Series, Inc., 1996.

Red-bellied Side-necked Turtle

Trade Name(s):
Same. Also
D'Alberti's Side-
necked Turtle.
**Family & Scien-
tific Name:**
Chelidae; *Emy-
dura
subglobosa.*
Erroneously
called *E. alber-
tisii.*
**Identifying
Features:** A yel-
low (sometimes
a very pale pink)
postocular

Terrarium Type:
A filtered aquar-
ium, with water
temperature in
the high 70s to
low 80s, and a
sloping ramp
(driftwood, tex-
tured plastic,
or other non-
abrasive surface)
leading from
the bottom to
an above-water,
illuminated
and warmed
basking spot,

stripe, usually a similarly colored stripe
along the upper jaw, a brown carapace, a
red(dish) plastron and soft parts, and non-
serrate posterior marginals identify this
pretty turtle.
Similar Species: This is the only member of
this genus to appear regularly in the pet
trade.
Range & Origin: Southern New Guinea and
northern Australia. Captive-bred babies
account for most of the specimens now in
the pet trade.
Adult Size: To about 8 inches.
Life Span: To more than 10 years.
Terrarium Size: From one to several babies
may be kept in a 5–10-gallon capacity aquarium. When adult, a single specimen or a pair
requires a 50–75-gallon filtered aquarium.

should be provided.
Social Structure: Adults may be aggressive
toward each other. Watch groups carefully
and isolate aggressive individuals.
Diet: The red-bellied sideneck seems primarily carnivorous. Snails and other shell-
fish, minnows, worms, and insects are all
accepted. Captives can be acclimated to
eat prepared foods such as pelleted trout
chow, pelleted catfish chow, koi pellets, and
turtle foods.
Potential Problems: This is a very hardy
turtle. Seldom are problems encountered in
its captive maintenance.
References:
Bartlett, R. D., and Patricia Bartlett. *Turtles.*
  Hauppauge, NY: Barron's Educational
  Series, Inc., 1996.

Matamata

Trade Name(s): Same.

Family & Scientific Name: Chelidae; *Chelus fimbriatus*

Identifying Features: The very rough carapace, skin fringes on the neck and chin, very heavy and flattened neck, triangular head and snorkel-nose, make this is an unmistakable turtle.

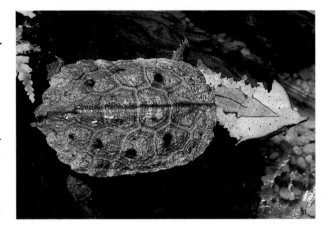

Similar Species: None.

Range & Origin: Northern South America. This species is seldom bred. The pet trade is dependent upon wild collected specimens.

Adult Size: 12–15 inches.

Life Span: To more than 30 years.

Terrarium Size: This turtle is a poor swimmer. If placed in water that is too deep, it will exhaust itself and drown. A baby or two can be kept in about 4 inches of water in a 20-gallon, long aquarium. An adult requires a 50–75-gallon terrarium, but should still have only shallow water.

Terrarium Type: A shallow water aquarium setup is fine. No basking area is needed.

Water temperature should be 78–86°F.

Social Structure: Not aggressive, but often does better when kept singly.

Diet: Fish and tadpoles. A diet exclusively of goldfish has been implicated in early deaths of matamatas; offer pond-seined minnows/shiners as well.

Potential Problems: Because the matamata is a weak swimmer, unless it can reach the surface of the water by extending its long neck, it will tire and drown. Babies that reach a 6-inch shell length often suddenly die for unknown reasons.

References:

Bartlett, R. D., and Patricia Bartlett. *Terrarium and Cage Construction and Care.* Hauppauge, NY: Barron's Educational Series, Inc., 1999.

Bartlett, R. D., and Patricia Bartlett. *Turtles.* Hauppauge, NY: Barron's Educational Series, Inc., 1996.

African Helmeted Turtle

Trade Name(s):
Same.
Family & Scientific Name:
Pelomedusidae;
*Pelomedusa
subrufa.*
**Identifying
Features:** The
brown carapace
is flattened on
top. The plastron is usually
yellow with dark
scute seams
and is unhinged.
The head is
olive brown dorsally and yellowish on the
sides and chin.

Similar Species: None. African mud turtles
have a hinged plastron.
Range & Origin: Much of Africa. Although
this species is occasionally captive-bred,
the pet trade depends almost entirely upon
wild collected specimens.
Adult Size: Commonly to 7 inches; rarely a
few inches larger.
Life Span: 20+ years.
Terrarium Size: From one to several babies
may be kept in a 5–10-gallon capacity
aquarium. When adult, a single specimen
or a pair requires a 40–75-gallon filtered
aquarium.

Terrarium Type:
A filtered aquarium, with water
temperature in
the high 70s to
low 80s, and a
sloping ramp
(driftwood, textured plastic, or
other non-abrasive surface)
leading from the
bottom to an illuminated and
warmed basking
spot, will suffice.
Social Structure: Adult males can be aggressive. It
may be necessary to keep this turtle species
singly.
Diet: This turtle is primarily carnivorous.
Snails, crayfish, minnows, worms, insects,
and prepared foods such as pelleted trout
chow, pelleted catfish chow, koi pellets, and
commercial turtle foods are all accepted.
Potential Problems: This is one of the
world's hardiest turtles. Seldom are problems encountered in its captive maintenance.
References:
Bartlett, R. D., and Patricia Bartlett. *Turtles.*
  Hauppauge, NY: Barron's Educational
  Series, Inc., 1996.

Indonesian Snake-necked Turtle

Trade Name(s):
Same. Also, Seibenrock's Snake-necked Turtle.

Family & Scientific Name:
Chelidae; *Chelodina seibenrockii.*

Identifying Features:
Teardrop-shaped carapace, very heavy and long neck, and a narrow unpatterned head identify this turtle.

Similar Species: This is the most common snakeneck now available. Most others have broader, less oval shells.

Range & Origin: New Guinea. This species is now captive-bred in fair numbers, but the pet trade is still dependent on the importation of wild collected specimens.

Adult Size: Carapace to about a foot in length.

Life Span: This species is so new to the hobby, that its potential lifespan is yet unknown. Other congeners have lived for 10–25 years in captivity. This should certainly be feasible with this robust turtle.

Terrarium Size: From one to several babies may be kept in a 5–10-gallon capacity aquarium. When adult, a single specimen or a pair requires a 100–150-gallon filtered aquarium.

Terrarium Type: A filtered aquarium, with water temperature in the high 70s to mid 80s, and a sloping ramp (driftwood, textured plastic, or other non-abrasive surface) leading upward from the bottom to an above-water, illuminated, and warmed, basking spot, is suggested.

Social Structure: These turtles seem reasonably compatible.

Diet: Our captives have fed upon minnows, worms, insects, and prepared foods such as pelleted trout chow, pelleted catfish chow, koi pellets, and turtle foods.

Potential Problems: Initial observations show this to be a hardy and trouble-free species.

References:
Bartlett, R. D., and Patricia Bartlett. *Turtles.* Hauppauge, NY: Barron's Educational Series, Inc., 1996.

Spiny Soft-shelled Turtle

Trade Name(s): Same.

Family & Scientific Name: Trionychidae; *Trionyx (Apalone) spiniferus* ssp.

Identifying Features: The underside of the carapace is light in color and does not contrast sharply with the plastral color. When viewed from above, the carapace is nearly round. Dark spots and small ocelli are present on some subspecies. Other subspecies have the carapace peppered with tiny white spots. All subspecies have small tubercles (spines) above and to each side of the neck.

Similar Species: Florida soft-shell is very dark in color and more oval in shape. Smooth soft-shell lacks the tubercles on the leading edge of the shell.

Range & Origin: Much of the eastern United States. Most pet trade babies are captive-hatched.

Adult Size: Females to more than 15 inches; males about half that size.

Life Span: To more than 25 years.

Terrarium Size: When babies, from one to several may be kept in a 10–15-gallon capacity aquarium. When adult, a single specimen or a pair may require a filtered 75–150-gallon aquarium.

Terrarium Type: Provide a filtered aquarium, with water temperature in the high 70s to low 80s, and a sloping ramp (driftwood, textured plastic, or other non-abrasive surface) leading from the bottom to an illuminated and warmed basking spot. Some hobbyists prefer water shallow enough to allow the turtle to extend its neck to breathe while resting on the bottom. If a substrate of several inches of clean, smooth (desert, not sharp silica play sand) is provided, the turtle often will be buried completely from sight or have only the head and neck visible.

Social Structure: Communal, if not crowded.

Diet: This soft-shell eats mostly animal matter. Minnows, worms, insects, and prepared foods such as pelleted trout chow, pelleted catfish chow, koi pellets, and turtle foods are all eaten.

Potential Problems: If water quality is maintained, and smooth sand is used for the substrate, this is a very hardy turtle species that seldom presents any problems for its keepers. Both sharp sand and poor water quality can cause skin and shell fungus, which must be addressed immediately.

References:
Bartlett, R. D., and Patricia Bartlett. *Turtles.* Hauppauge, NY: Barron's Educational Series, Inc., 1996.

Smooth Soft-shelled Turtle

Trade Name(s): Same.

Family & Scientific Name: Trionychidae; *Apalone (Trionyx) muticus* ssp.

Identifying Features: Babies: The carapace lacks well defined markings, and the underside of the carapace is brown. Adults: When seen from above, the pliable edged carapace is almost rounded. The snorkel-nose and the lack of conical tubercles on the leading edge of the carapace will identify this species.

Similar Species: Other softshells have short tubercles projecting forward from above, and to either side of the neck.

Range & Origin: Central and eastern United States, but not the Atlantic Coast. Most of the specimens in the pet trade are captive-hatched babies.

Adult Size: Females to about a foot in length; males about half that size.

Life Span: To more than 10 years. Double that, or longer, should be entirely possible.

Terrarium Size: When babies, from one to several may be kept in a 10–15-gallon capacity aquarium. When adult, a single specimen or a pair may be maintained in a filtered 50–150-gallon aquarium.

Terrarium Type: A filtered aquarium, with water temperature in the high 70s to low 80s, and a sloping ramp (driftwood, textured plastic, or other non-abrasive surface) leading from the bottom to an illuminated and warmed basking spot, should be provided. If a substrate of several inches of clean, smooth sand (desert, not sharp silica play sand) is provided, the turtle often will be buried completely from sight or have only the head and neck visible.

Social Structure: Communal, if not crowded.

Diet: This soft-shell eats mostly animal matter. Minnows, worms, insects, and prepared foods such as pelleted trout chow, pelleted catfish chow, koi pellets, and turtle foods are all eaten.

Potential Problems: If water quality is maintained, and smooth sand is used for the substrate, this is a very hardy turtle species that seldom presents any problems for its keepers. Both sharp sand and poor water quality can result in the appearance of a skin and shell fungus, which must be addressed immediately.

References:
Bartlett, R. D., and Patricia Bartlett. *Turtles.* Hauppauge, NY: Barron's Educational Series, Inc., 1996.

Crocodilians

Almost everyone can recognize the basic crocodilian shape. Individuals living in the subtropics or tropics may be able to claim a few live sightings.

Crocodilians are essentially lizard-like in basic shape and are adapted to a largely aquatic life. In water, they hunt and eat their prey and advertise their size and location by bellowing. They also utilize water as an escape route. With their legs pressed against their body, they swim in side-to-side undulations that appear effortless. On land, they are capable of impressive short bursts of speed.

Crocodilians occupy their own reptilian niche, a complete class unto themselves. There are about 38 kinds of crocodilians in the world today, only about four ever appearing in the pet trade.

This is due to several reasons. Most crocodilians are now considered threatened or endangered, and so are protected. A few types are farmed for meat and skin. In the United States, alligator meat is rather in vogue for fancy canapés and festival food booths.

Secondly, most crocodilians grow too large to remain pets, and they grow quickly. Newly hatched babies are almost absurdly cute, being some variation of an 8-inch long crocodilian with a yellow on black or olive color scheme. They even sound cute, honking like tiny geese with head colds when feeling threatened.

Even the smallest crocodilian, the dwarf caiman, may reach 7 feet. Caging quickly becomes a challenge. A crocodilian needs a cage at least twice the animal's length and $1^1/2$ times the animal's length in width. Add in the need for a swimming pool, and the realization that crocodilians feed, lounge, and defecate in their pool. Crocodilians need food, at least every other day, and those larger than four feet will need food bigger than rats. Add in the factor that any crocodilian has teeth and doesn't tame too well, and the attraction meter—for most people—disappears.

Nonetheless there are those who genuinely like crocodilians, who find them a challenge, and can provide them with good caging, temperature control, and diet. These people think ahead and have a disposal plan for where the crocodilian will go when it gets too big to be handled, or when the current owner is no longer able to keep the animal. This section is for them, and for those who think they *might* like to get a spectacled caiman baby to raise.

Spectacled Caiman

Trade Name(s): Same.

Family & Scientific Name: Alligatoridae; *Caiman crocodilus* complex.

Identifying Features: This is an olive to olive brown crocodilian with black crossbars. The ridge (spectacle bridge) across the base of the snout is diagnostic.

Similar Species: No other crocodilians have the spectacle bridge across the snout.

Range & Origin: Much of Latin America. Farmed and captive-bred and hatched babies supply the American pet trade.

Adult Size: To 7+ feet.

Life Span: To more than 20 years.

Terrarium Size: Although a 9-inch long hatchling can be maintained for a short time in a 20-gallon, long, or larger aquarium with a haulout space and a hotspot, it soon outgrows it. This crocodilian is untrustworthy as a pet.

Terrarium Type: These reptiles need both a heated land area onto which they can emerge to dry, and a constant supply of clean water in which to lie and hunt. **These are not satisfactory personal pets!**

Social Structure: As babies, these are communal.

Diet: This is a carnivorous species that eats insects, worms, and vertebrates.

Potential Problems: Healthwise, if kept warm, the spectacled caiman is mostly a trouble-free species. It quickly outgrows most hobbyist facilities, and may be difficult to dispose of legally.

References:

Bartlett, R. D., and Patricia Bartlett. *Terrarium and Cage Construction and Care.* Hauppauge, NY: Barron's Educational Series, Inc., 1999.

Smooth-fronted Caiman

Trade Name(s): Same.

Family & Scientific Name: Alligatoridae; *Paleosuchus trigonotus.*

Identifying Features: This reptile is brown with black crossbars and very rough scales on the nape and the tail. There are two rows of large scales over the pelvis.

Similar Species: The dwarf caiman has a different neck and four rows of very large scales over the pelvis.

Range & Origin: Tropical South America. A small number of captive-bred and farmed babies enter the pet trade each year.

Adult Size: 4½ feet.

Life Span: To more than 24 years.

Terrarium Size: Although a 9-inch long hatchling dwarf caiman can be maintained for a short time in a 20-gallon, long or larger aquarium, it will need a much larger environment within a year. A single subadult to adult can be kept in a 220-gallon terrarium or a 7-foot diameter stock watering tank, with a dry heated and illumed haulout space.

Terrarium Type: These reptiles need both a heated land area onto which they can emerge to dry, and a constant supply of clean water in which to lie and hunt. Having a closable drain drilled into the bottom of your terrarium simplifies cleaning the facility.

These are not satisfactory personal pets!

Social Structure: Males fight with other males, but if the facility is large enough, a pair will usually coexist nicely.

Diet: This is a carnivorous species that eats insects, worms, and vertebrates.

Potential Problems: Healthwise, if kept at a suitable temperature, the dwarf caiman is mostly a trouble-free species. It quickly outgrows most hobbyist facilities, and may be difficult to dispose of legally.

References:

Bartlett, R. D., and Patricia Bartlett. *Terrarium and Cage Construction and Care.* Hauppauge, NY: Barron's Educational Series, Inc., 1999.

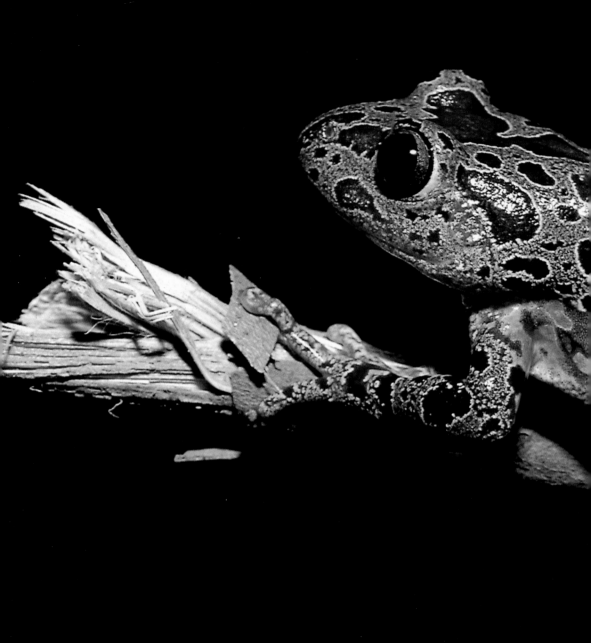

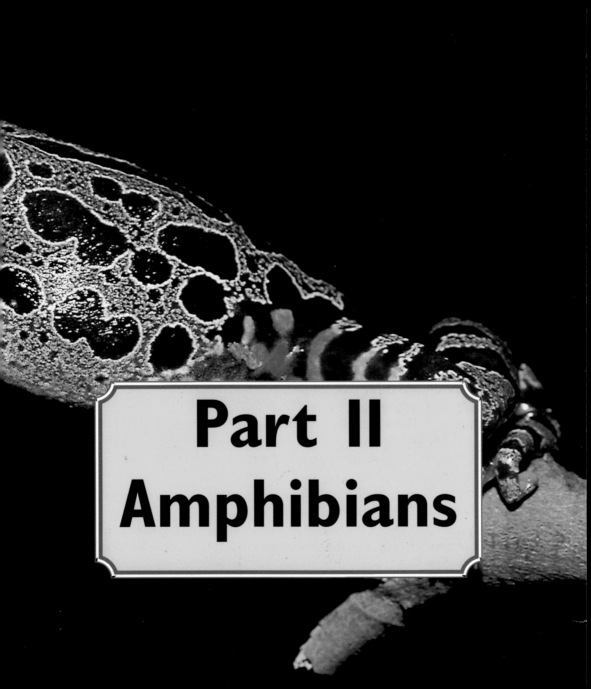

Part II
Amphibians

Frogs, Toads, and Treefrogs

Of the three groupings of amphibians—the tailless amphibians, the tailed amphibians, and the caecilians, only the former has gained a great deal of popularity among hobbyists. And of these, comparatively few species are seen with regularity. Not surprisingly, those seen most readily catch the attention of hobbyists—predaceous forms, beautiful species or colorations, or those with an unusual lifestyle.

Despite an overlying similarity, the frogs, toads, and treefrogs, are contained in a number of families. Of these, we discuss representatives of eleven families herein.

These vary from the voracious "hopping mouths" we know as horned (or PacMan) frogs (some females of which attain the size of a saucer), to the intricately beautiful, inch-long, poison (formerly poison-arrow) frogs, to the bizarre, 5-inch-long, Suriname toad, an aquatic species that looks as if it lost a battle with a steam-roller!

A few toads—those warty, garden, insect eaters, have gained favor, and albino morphs of the big, bass-voiced, American bullfrog are also seen in the pet industry.

Although most frogs breed and lay gelatinous covered eggs in water, a few (poison frogs among them) lay their eggs on land or, in the case of the red-eyed and Old World treefrogs, on leaves above the water. Some large species may lay many thousands of eggs, while others may produce only a dozen or so. Poison frogs provide parental care, a parent carrying the tadpoles pick-a-back to a quiet water source, and in some cases, even providing the tadpoles' food (in the form of infertile eggs).

According to species, tailless amphibians may be extensively arboreal, fully aquatic, entirely terrestrial, or combinations of these.

Large species often eat a hodgepodge of prey (including smaller frogs), and smaller forms may need insect prey the size of fruitflies or termites. Consider food availability and caging carefully.

Because they rapidly absorb impurities through their permeable skin, all frogs, toads, and treefrogs must be kept in immaculately clean quarters, and that you wash your hands before handling them. Conversely, since many of these creatures produce noxious to toxic skin secretions, you must also wash your hands after handling them.

Oriental Fire-bellied Toad

Trade Name(s):
Same. Chinese Fire-bellied Toad.

Family & Scientific Name:
Discoglossidae; *Bombina orientalis.*

Identifying Features: This is the only species of fire-bellied toad currently available in the pet trade.

Similar Species: None.

Range & Origin: Asia. These toads are both collected from the wild and captive-bred for the pet trade.

Adult Size: 1½–2 inches.

Life Span: To more than 14 years.

Terrarium Size: 10–20-gallon capacity.

Terrarium Type: Either a semi-aquatic terrarium or an aquarium. The latter should have planted and floating plants and a floating piece of driftwood or plastic lilypad to allow the frogs complete emergence from the water.

Social Structure: These toads are communal.

Diet: Consists most of insects and worms, but some will learn to accept pieces of koi chow that float in front of them. Food should be dusted with a vitamin/supplement once a week for adults, twice a week for juveniles.

Potential Problems: This is a very hardy anuran with which, providing its water is kept clean and cool, keepers experience few problems.

References:
Bartlett, R. D., and Patricia Bartlett. *Terrarium and Cage Construction and Care.* Hauppauge, NY: Barron's Educational Series, Inc., 1999.

Bartlett, R. D., and Patricia Bartlett. *Frogs, Toads, and Treefrogs.* Hauppauge, NY: Barron's Educational Series, Inc., 1996.

Giant Toad

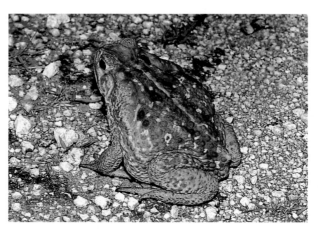

Trade Name(s): Same. Also Marine Toad.

Family & Scientific Name: Bufonidae; *Bufo marinus.*

Identifying Features: Adults can be identified by their huge size and equally huge, outwardly diverging, parotoid glands that extend downward onto the sides, and very tubercular (sometimes spinose) skin. Subadults can be very difficult to identify.

Similar Species: The Colorado River toad and the Rococo toad have large glands on the hind legs.

Range & Origin: Much of Latin America. Introduced elsewhere, including Florida. Pet trade specimens are collected from the wild.

Adult Size: 4–8+ inches.

Life Span: 24 years.

Terrarium Size: From one to several babies may be kept in a 10–20-gallon capacity terrarium. One or two adults require a 20-gallon, long to 40-gallon tank.

Terrarium Type: These large, active toads quickly destroy most plantings. A paper towel, or barely moist nonaromatic mulch substrate in a dry tank with a large water bowl in which the toad may sit, will suffice.

Social Structure: These toads are communal.

Diet: Consists mainly of insects and small rodents. This toad occasionally eats canned dog food from a dish.

Potential Problems: If kept dry to barely damp with a sizable accessible bowl of very clean water nearby, these are trouble-free pets. If quarters get dirty, a potentially fatal bacterial disease called redleg may strike. Consult a veterinarian.

References:

Bartlett, R. D., and Patricia Bartlett. *Frogs, Toads, and Treefrogs.* Hauppauge, NY: Barron's Educational Series, Inc., 1996.

Bartlett, R. D., and Patricia Bartlett. *Terrarium and Cage Construction and Care.* Hauppauge, NY: Barron's Educational Series, Inc., 1999.

American Toad

Trade Name(s): Same. Also Common Toad.

Family & Scientific Name: Bufonidae; *Bufo americanus.*

Identifying Features: This toad has tubercular skin, low cranial crests, and parotoid glands often not touching cranial crests. Rely on your dealer's skills for this difficult-to-identify toad.

Similar Species: Most other moderately-sized toads.

Range & Origin: Northeastern North America. Pet trade specimens are collected from the wild.

Adult Size: 2½–4 inches.

Life Span: 10+ years.

Terrarium Size: Several specimens can be kept in a 15–20-gallon terrarium.

Terrarium Type: Either a savanna setup, or a simple tank with a substrate of nonaromatic mulch and a sizable bowl of clean water, will suffice.

Social Structure: These toads are communal.

Diet: Consists mainly of insects and worms.

Potential Problems: If kept clean, this is a very hardy species.

References:

Bartlett, R. D., and Patricia Bartlett. *Frogs, Toads, and Treefrogs.* Hauppauge, NY: Barron's Educational Series, Inc., 1996.

Bartlett, R. D., and Patricia Bartlett. *Terrarium and Cage Construction and Care.* Hauppauge, NY: Barron's Educational Series, Inc., 1999.

Southern Toad

Trade Name(s): Same.

Family & Scientific Name: Bufonidae; *Bufo terrestris.*

Identifying Features: Tubercular skin, high cranial crest with prominent knob on the rear, and parotoid glands connected to

cranial crest by short projection characterize this toad. Rely on your dealer's skills for this difficult-to-identify toad.

Similar Species: The very high cranial knobs separate this species from other moderately sized toads.

Range & Origin: Southeastern North America. Pet trade specimens are collected from the wild.

Adult Size: 2½–4 inches.

Life Span: 10+ years.

Terrarium Size: Several specimens can be kept in a 15–20-gallon terrarium.

Terrarium Type: Either a savanna setup, or a simple tank with a substrate of nonaromatic mulch and a sizable bowl of clean water, will suffice.

Social Structure: These toads are communal.

Diet: Consists mainly of insects and worms.

Potential Problems: If kept clean, this is a very hardy species.

References:

Bartlett, R. D., and Patricia Bartlett. *Frogs, Toads, and Treefrogs.* Hauppauge, NY: Barron's Educational Series, Inc., 1996.

Bartlett, R. D., and Patricia Bartlett. *Terrarium and Cage Construction and Care.* Hauppauge, NY: Barron's Educational Series, Inc., 1999.

Great Plains Toad

Trade Name(s): Same.

Family & Scientific Name: Bufonidae; *Bufo cognatus.*

Identifying Features: This toad has tubercular skin, low cranial crests thta converge and touch anteriorly, and parotoid glands

often in direct contact with rear of cranial crests. Large, dark, dorsal blotches have a light edging. Rely on your dealer's skill for this difficult-to-identify toad.

Similar Species: Most other moderately sized toads.

Range & Origin: Central and western North America. Pet trade specimens are collected from the wild.

Adult Size: 2½–4 inches.

Life Span: To 10+ years.

Terrarium Size: Several specimens can be kept in a 15–20-gallon terrarium.

Terrarium Type: Either a savanna setup, or a simple tank with a substrate of nonaromatic mulch and a sizable bowl of clean water, will suffice.

Social Structure: These toads are communal.

Diet: Consists mainly of insects and worms.

Potential Problems: If kept clean, this is a very hardy species.

References:

Bartlett, R. D., and Patricia Bartlett. *Frogs, Toads, and Treefrogs.* Hauppauge, NY: Barron's Educational Series, Inc., 1996.

Bartlett, R. D., and Patricia Bartlett. *Terrarium and Cage Construction and Care.* Hauppauge, NY: Barron's Educational Series, Inc., 1999.

American Green Toad

Trade Name(s): Same. Also Eastern or Western Green Toad.

Family & Scientific Name: Bufonidae; *Bufo debilis* ssp.

Identifying Features: Distinctly green ground color with black flecks.

Similar Species: None in the pet trade.

Range & Origin: Central and western North America. Pet trade specimens are collected from the wild.

Adult Size: 1½–2 inches.

Life Span: 5–8+ years.

Terrarium Size: Several specimens can be kept in a 15–20-gallon terrarium.

Terrarium Type: Either a savanna setup, or a simple tank with a substrate of nonaro-matic mulch and a sizable bowl of clean water, will suffice.

Social Structure: These toads are communal.

Diet: Consists mostly of small insects, sometimes worms.

Potential Problems: If kept clean, this is a very hardy species.

References:

Bartlett, R. D., and Patricia Bartlett. *Frogs, Toads, and Treefrogs.* Hauppauge, NY: Barron's Educational Series, Inc., 1996.

Bartlett, R. D., and Patricia Bartlett. *Terrarium and Cage Construction and Care.* Hauppauge, NY: Barron's Educational Series, Inc., 1999.

Malayan Black-spined Toad

Trade Name(s): Same.

Family & Scientific Name: Bufonidae; *Bufo melanostictus*.

Identifying Features: Black spines on dorsal tubercles.

Similar Species: This species should not be difficult to identify.

Range & Origin: Malaya. Pet trade specimens are collected from the wild.

Adult Size: 2½–4 inches.

Life Span: 4–10+ years.

Terrarium Size: Several specimens can be kept in a 15–20-gallon terrarium.

Terrarium Type: Either a savanna setup, or a simple tank with a substrate of nonaromatic mulch and a sizable bowl of clean water, will suffice.

Social Structure: These toads are communal.

Diet: Consists mainly of insects and worms.

Potential Problems: If kept clean, this is a very hardy species.

References:

Bartlett, R. D., and Patricia Bartlett. *Frogs, Toads, and Treefrogs.* Hauppauge, NY: Barron's Educational Series, Inc., 1996.

Bartlett, R. D., and Patricia Bartlett. *Terrarium and Cage Construction and Care.* Hauppauge, NY: Barron's Educational Series, Inc., 1999.

Yellow-spotted (Argentine) Walking Toad

Trade Name(s): Same.

Family & Scientific Name: Bufonidae; *Melanophryniscus stelzneri*

Identifying Features: Unmistakable because of its tiny size, yellow spotted black back, and black spotted red belly.

Similar Species: None.

Range & Origin: Southern South America. Pet trade specimens are collected from the wild.

Adult Size: ¾–1¼ inches.

Life Span: 2+ years.

Terrarium Size: Several specimens can be kept in a 15–20-gallon terrarium.

Terrarium Type: Either a savanna setup, or a simple tank with a substrate of nonaro-matic mulch or barely dampened unmilled sphagnum moss, and a sizable but shallow bowl of clean water, will suffice.

Social Structure: These toads are communal.

Diet: Consists mostly of tiny insects such as termites and aphids.

Potential Problems: If kept clean and fed liberally, this seems to be a hardy species.

References:

Bartlett, R. D., and Patricia Bartlett. *Frogs, Toads, and Treefrogs.* Hauppauge, NY: Barron's Educational Series, Inc., 1996.

Bartlett, R. D., and Patricia Bartlett. *Terrarium and Cage Construction and Care.* Hauppauge, NY: Barron's Educational Series, Inc., 1999.

Malayan Horned Frog

Trade Name(s): Same.

Family & Scientific Name: *Megophrys montana nasuta.*

Identifying Features: Upper eyelids extended into broad, fleshy horns. Brownish dorsum, relatively long legs.

Similar Species: None at present in the pet trade.

Range & Origin: Malaya. Pet trade specimens are wild collected.

Adult Size: 2½–4 inches.

Life Span: 6–10 years.

Terrarium Size: Several similarly sized specimens can be kept in a 15–20-gallon terrarium.

Terrarium Type: This montane species needs clean, cool surroundings. Either a damp savanna setup, or a simple tank with a substrate of nonaromatic mulch or damp-ened unmilled sphagnum moss, and a sizable but shallow bowl of clean water, or a semiaquatic terrarium, will suffice.

Social Structure: These frogs are communal.

Diet: Includes insects of many varieties. Some specimens eat worms. Can be cannibalistic. Keep sizes segregated.

Potential Problems: If kept clean and cool this seems to be a hardy species.

References:

Bartlett, R. D., and Patricia Bartlett. *Frogs, Toads, and Treefrogs.* Hauppauge, NY: Barron's Educational Series, Inc., 1996.

Bartlett, R. D., and Patricia Bartlett. *Terrarium and Cage Construction and Care.* Hauppauge, NY: Barron's Educational Series, Inc., 1999.

African Green Running Frog

Trade Name(s): Same.

Family & Scientific Name: Hyperoliidae; *Kassina senegalensis.*

Identifying Features: This green frog is longitudinally striped with wide areas of black. It generally runs rather than hops.

Similar Species: Seldom do other green and black species appear in the pet trade. Rely on your dealer's identifications.

Range & Origin: Eastern and southern Africa. All currently in the pet trade are collected from the wild.

Adult Size: 2 inches.

Life Span: To 6 years; possibly considerably more.

Terrarium Size: Several specimens can be kept in a 15–20-gallon terrarium.

Terrarium Type: As with all frogs this species needs clean, somewhat cool, surroundings. Either a damp savanna setup, or a simple tank with a substrate of nonaromatic mulch or dampened unmilled sphagnum moss, and a sizable but shallow bowl of clean water, or a semiaquatic terrarium, will suffice.

Social Structure: These frogs are communal.

Diet: Includes insects of many varieties. Some specimens eat small worms.

Potential Problems: If kept clean and cool, this seems to be a hardy species.

References:

Bartlett, R. D., and Patricia Bartlett. *Frogs, Toads, and Treefrogs.* Hauppauge, NY: Barron's Educational Series, Inc., 1996.

Bartlett, R. D., and Patricia Bartlett. *Terrarium and Cage Construction and Care.* Hauppauge, NY: Barron's Educational Series, Inc., 1999.

Red-legged Running Frog

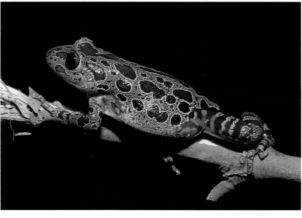

Trade Name(s): Same. Also Red-legged Treefrog.

Family & Scientific Name: Hyperoliidae; *Kassina maculata.*

Identifying Features: This frog has grayish to tan dorsum and sides patterned with large brown spots. A great deal of red appears in the groin beneath the hind legs.

Similar Species: None.

Range & Origin: Eastern and southern Africa. Pet trade specimens are wild collected.

Adult Size: To about 2 inches.

Life Span: Probably to 5+ years.

Terrarium Size: Several specimens can be kept in a 15–20-gallon terrarium.

Terrarium Type: This arboreal species needs clean surroundings and climbing perches. Either a damp savanna setup, or a simple tank with a substrate of nonaromatic mulch or dampened unmilled sphagnum moss, and a sizable but shallow bowl of clean water, are suitable.

Social Structure: These frogs are communal.

Diet: Includes insects of many varieties. Some specimens eat small worms.

Potential Problems: If kept clean and cool this seems to be a hardy species.

References:

Bartlett, R. D., and Patricia Bartlett. *Frogs, Toads, and Treefrogs.* Hauppauge, NY: Barron's Educational Series, Inc., 1996.

Bartlett, R. D., and Patricia Bartlett. *Terrarium and Cage Construction and Care.* Hauppauge, NY: Barron's Educational Series, Inc., 1999.

Variable Reed Frog

Trade Name(s): Same. Also Marbled Reed Frog, Striped Reed Frog, Red-legged Reed Frog.

Family & Scientific Name: Hyperoliidae; *Hyperolius marmoratus.*

Identifying Features: Small size, red in groin and under hind legs, and tan ground color with very variable (lines, stripes, spots) red-brown markings identify this frog.

Similar Species: Many of the reed frogs can be similar. Rely on your dealer for identification.

Range & Origin: Tropical Africa. Specimens from the wild supply the pet trade.

Adult Size: ¾–1 inch.

Life Span: 4–5+ years.

Terrarium Size: Several specimens can be kept in a 10–15-gallon terrarium.

Terrarium Type: This species needs clean surroundings. Either a damp savanna setup, or a simple tank with a substrate of nonaromatic mulch or dampened unmilled sphagnum moss, and a sizable but shallow bowl of clean water, are suitable.

Social Structure: These frogs are communal.

Diet: Tiny insects of many varieties, including pinhead crickets, termites, and aphids are accepted.

Potential Problems: Tank must be tightly covered. If kept clean and cool, this seems to be a hardy species.

References:

Bartlett, R. D., and Patricia Bartlett. *Frogs, Toads, and Treefrogs.* Hauppauge, NY: Barron's Educational Series, Inc., 1996.

Bartlett, R. D., and Patricia Bartlett. *Terrarium and Cage Construction and Care.* Hauppauge, NY: Barron's Educational Series, Inc., 1999.

African Green Treefrog

Trade Name(s):
Same. Green Big-eyed Treefrog.

Family & Scientific Name:
Hyperoliidae; *Leptopelis vermiculatus.*

Identifying Features: This frog is identified by bright green coloring with at least vestiges of

dark vermiculations; proportionately large, veined, golden eyes, and well-developed toepads.

Similar Species: Many confusing species. Rely on your dealer for identifications.

Range & Origin: Southeastern Africa. The pet trade is dependent on wild collected specimens.

Adult Size: 1¼–1¾ inches.

Life Span: To 6 years; possibly considerably more.

Terrarium Size: Several specimens can be kept in a 15–20-gallon terrarium.

Terrarium Type: As with all frogs, this species needs clean, somewhat cool surroundings. Either a damp savanna setup, or a simple tank with a substrate of nonaromatic mulch or dampened unmilled sphagnum moss, and a sizable but shallow bowl of clean water, or a semiaquatic terrarium, will suffice.

Social Structure: These frogs are communal.

Diet: Includes insects of many varieties.

Potential Problems: If kept clean and cool, this seems to be a hardy species.

References:

Bartlett, R. D., and Patricia Bartlett. *Frogs, Toads, and Treefrogs.* Hauppauge, NY: Barron's Educational Series, Inc., 1996.

Bartlett, R. D., and Patricia Bartlett. *Terrarium and Cage Construction and Care.* Hauppauge, NY: Barron's Educational Series, Inc., 1999.

Chinese Foam-nest Treefrog

Trade Name(s):
Same. Also
Denny's
Treefrog,
Chinese Green
Treefrog.
Family & Scientific Name:
Rhacophoridae;
*Polypedates
dennysi.*
***Identifying
Features:*** This
frog is primarily
green with some

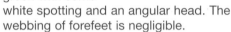

white spotting and an angular head. The
webbing of forefeet is negligible.
Similar Species: None.
Range & Origin: China. Specimens collected from the wild supply the pet trade.
Adult Size: 1½–3 inches.
Life Span: 2–10 years.
Terrarium Size: Several specimens of this
moderately active species can be kept in a
15–20-gallon terrarium, but a larger tank
would be better.
Terrarium Type: As with all frogs, this
species needs clean, somewhat cool, surroundings. Either a damp savanna setup, or

a simple tank
with a substrate
of nonaromatic
mulch or dampened unmilled
sphagnum moss,
and a sizable but
shallow bowl of
clean water, or a
semiaquatic terrarium, will suffice. Provide
horizontal
perches of at
least the diameter of the frog's body.
Social Structure: These frogs are
communal.
Diet: Includes insects of many varieties.
Potential Problems: If kept clean and cool,
this seems to be a hardy species.
References:
Bartlett, R. D., and Patricia Bartlett. *Frogs,
Toads, and Treefrogs.* Hauppauge, NY:
Barron's Educational Series, Inc., 1996.
Bartlett, R. D., and Patricia Bartlett. *Terrarium and Cage Construction and Care.*
Hauppauge, NY: Barron's Educational
Series, Inc., 1999.

Borneo Eared Treefrog

Trade Name(s): Same.

Family & Scientific Name: Rhacophoridae; *Polypedates otilophus.*

Identifying Features: This frog has tan coloration, is a moderately large size, and has bony flanges above tympani.

Similar Species: None.

Range & Origin: Borneo. Pet trade specimens are collected from the wild.

Adult Size: 2½–3 inches.

Life Span: Unknown, but congenerics have lived for more than six years.

Terrarium Size: This is an active frog that utilizes all of the space it is given. One to four specimens should have a 40-gallon, vertically oriented, terrarium.

Terrarium Type: As with all frogs, this species needs clean, somewhat cool, surroundings. Either a damp savanna setup, or a simple tank with a substrate of nonaromatic mulch or dampened unmilled sphagnum moss, and a sizable but shallow bowl of clean water, or a semiaquatic terrarium, will suffice. Provide horizontal perches of at least the diameter of the frog's body.

Social Structure: These frogs are communal.

Diet: Consists of many species of insects. Worms are accepted from forceps.

Potential Problems: Hardy, apparently largely trouble-free if kept clean.

References:

Bartlett, R. D., and Patricia Bartlett. *Frogs, Toads, and Treefrogs.* Hauppauge, NY: Barron's Educational Series, Inc., 1996.

Bartlett, R. D., and Patricia Bartlett. *Terrarium and Cage Construction and Care.* Hauppauge, NY: Barron's Educational Series, Inc., 1999.

Black-webbed Gliding Frog

Trade Name(s):
Same.
Family & Scientific Name:
Rhacophoridae;
Polypedates nigropalmatus.
Identifying Features: Bright green back, usually yellowish sides, moderately large size, fully webbed hands

and feet, black to dark blue interdigital webbing, and yellowish toes identify this frog.
Similar Species: Javan (Reinwardt's) gliding frog is very similar, but often is a duller green and may have dark sides and toes.
Range & Origin: Malaysia. Pet trade specimens are collected from the wild.
Adult Size: 2½–3 inches.
Life Span: To about six years; longer durations seem possible.
Terrarium Size: This is an active frog that utilizes all of the space it is given. One to four specimens should have a 40-gallon, vertically oriented, terrarium. Cover the sides of the tank so the frog won't damage its nose as it tries to jump "through" the glass (and it will).
Terrarium Type: As with all frogs, this species needs clean, somewhat cool, surroundings. Either a damp savanna setup, or a simple tank with a substrate of nonaro-

matic mulch or dampened unmilled sphagnum moss, and a sizable but shallow bowl of clean water, or a semiaquatic terrarium, will suffice. Provide horizontal perches of at least the diameter of the frog's body.
Social Structure: These frogs are communal.
Diet: Includes many species of insects. Worms are accepted from forceps.
Potential Problems: Some specimens injure their noses by jumping into the glass side of the terrarium. Bathe this daily with a sulfa-drug and render glass opaque with paper or cloth. Other than this, if in good condition when received, this is a hardy, apparently largely trouble-free frog, if its facilities are kept clean.
References:
Bartlett, R. D., and Patricia Bartlett.
   Frogs, Toads, and Treefrogs. Hauppauge,
   NY: Barron's Educational Series, Inc.,
   1996.
Bartlett, R. D., and Patricia Bartlett. *Terrarium and Cage Construction and Care.*
   Hauppauge, NY: Barron's Educational
   Series, Inc., 1999.

Tomato Frog

Trade Name(s): Same.

Family & Scientific Name: Microhylidae; *Dyscophus guineti.*

Identifying Features: This frog is a bright tomato to brownish-red color. Darker stripes of variable width are present on the sides.

Similar Species: None currently in the pet trade.

Range & Origin: Madagascar. Although this species is now being captive-bred in small numbers, the pet trade is still largely dependent on wild collected specimens.

Adult Size: 2–3 inches.

Life Span: 2–8 years.

Terrarium Size: Several specimens can be kept in a 15–20-gallon, long terrarium.

Terrarium Type: This species needs clean surroundings. Either a damp savanna setup, or a simple tank with a substrate of nonaromatic mulch or dampened unmilled sphagnum moss, and a sizable but shallow bowl of clean water, are suitable.

Social Structure: These frogs are communal.

Diet: Tiny insects of many varieties, including pinhead crickets, termites, and aphids are accepted.

Potential Problems: Tank must be tightly covered. If kept clean and cool, this seems to be a hardy species.

References:

Bartlett, R. D., and Patricia Bartlett. *Frogs, Toads, and Treefrogs.* Hauppauge, NY: Barron's Educational Series, Inc., 1996.

Bartlett, R. D., and Patricia Bartlett. *Terrarium and Cage Construction and Care.* Hauppauge, NY: Barron's Educational Series, Inc., 1999.

Malayan Painted Bullfrog

Trade Name(s): Same.

Family & Scientific Name: Microhylidae; *Kaloula pulchra*.

Identifying Features: Small rounded head, variable toepads, purplish-brown back and lower sides, tan crown, and dorsolateral stripes identify this frog.

Similar Species: None.

Range & Origin: Malaya, southeast Asia. The pet trade is dependent on wild collected specimens.

Adult Size: This microhylid is called a bullfrog for its call, not its size. Attains 2–3 inches.

Life Span: 10–12 years; perhaps longer.

Terrarium Size: Several specimens can be kept in a 15–20-gallon, long terrarium.

Terrarium Type: This species needs clean surroundings. Either a damp savanna setup, or a simple tank with a substrate of nonaromatic mulch or dampened unmilled sphagnum moss, and a sizable but shallow bowl of clean water, are suitable.

Social Structure: These frogs are communal.

Diet: Tiny insects of many varieties, including pinhead crickets, termites, and aphids are accepted.

Potential Problems: Tank must be tightly covered. If kept clean and cool, this seems to be a hardy species.

References:

Bartlett, R. D., and Patricia Bartlett. *Frogs, Toads, and Treefrogs.* Hauppauge, NY: Barron's Educational Series, Inc., 1996.

Bartlett, R. D., and Patricia Bartlett. *Terrarium and Cage Construction and Care.* Hauppauge, NY: Barron's Educational Series, Inc., 1999.

Painted Pudge Frog

Trade Name(s):
Same. Also
Rose-backed
Pudge Frog.
Family & Scientific Name:
Microhylidae;
Scaphiophryne
gottlebei.
Identifying
Features: Small
size, marbled
black and green
sides, and a
strawberry back
identify this frog.

matic mulch or
dampened
unmilled sphagnum moss, and
a sizable but
shallow bowl of
clean water, are
suitable.
Social Structure: These
frogs are communal.
Diet: Tiny
insects of many
varieties, including pinhead crickets, termites, and aphids
are accepted.

Similar Species: None.

Range & Origin: Madagascar. Pet trade
is entirely dependent on wild collected
specimens.

Adult Size: 1¼ inches.

Life Span: Unknown, but probably to several years.

Terrarium Size: Several specimens can be
kept in a 10–15-gallon terrarium.

Terrarium Type: This species needs clean
surroundings. Either a damp savanna setup,
or a simple tank with a substrate of nonaro-

Potential Problems: Tank must be tightly
covered. If kept clean and cool, this seems
to be a hardy species.

References:
Bartlett, R. D., and Patricia Bartlett. *Frogs,*
Toads, and Treefrogs. Hauppauge, NY:
Barron's Educational Series, Inc., 1996.
Bartlett, R. D., and Patricia Bartlett. *Terrar-*
ium and Cage Construction and Care.
Hauppauge, NY: Barron's Educational
Series, Inc., 1999.

Giant African Bullfrog

Trade Name(s): Same. Also Pyxie.

Family & Scientific Name: Ranidae; *Pyxicephalus adspersus.*

Identifying Features: This frog has elongate rugosities on the skin and an olive-green color. Adult

Diet: Insects, fish, nightcrawlers, and other low fat foods should make up the majority of the diet. An occasional mouse is acceptable.

Potential Problems: Because of the prodigious amount of body waste these

males have a yellow throat. These have a compact, toad-like build, a huge head and large size. Adults can bite painfully.

Similar Species: The African bullfrog, *P. edulis*, is smaller and darker.

Range & Origin: Central and southern Africa. Specimens in the pet trade are mostly captive-bred.

Adult Size: Males to 8 inches; females to about half that size.

Life Span: 15–20 years.

Terrarium Size: These are huge, but not overly active frogs. One may be kept in a 20-gallon, long terrarium, but it require frequent cleaning.

Terrarium Type: A dry savanna terrarium with several inches of sandy soil for burrowing, or a bare tank with an inch or two of *clean* water and a styro platform for complete emergence.

Social Structure: Babies are cannibalistic, but similarly sized adults can be kept together providing the tank is large enough.

frogs produce, their cages need to be cleaned frequently to prevent bacterial produced maladies such as redleg. Cannibalism can be a problem if disparate sizes are housed together. Blindness-causing corneal lipid deposits may occur if this frog is fed a predominantly high fat diet (i.e., mice and baby rats).

References:

Bartlett, R. D., and Patricia Bartlett. *Frogs, Toads, and Treefrogs.* Hauppauge, NY: Barron's Educational Series, Inc., 1996.

Bartlett, R. D., and Patricia Bartlett. *Horned Frogs and African Bullfrogs.* Hauppauge, NY: Barron's Educational Series, Inc., 1999.

Bartlett, R. D., and Patricia Bartlett. *Terrarium and Cage Construction and Care.* Hauppauge, NY: Barron's Educational Series, Inc., 1999.

Lowveld Bullfrog

Trade Name(s): Same. Also Pyxie.

Family & Scientific Name: Ranidae; *Pyxicephalus edulis.*

Identifying Features: Smooth skin and olive-tan coloring with dark olive green mottlings identify this frog.

Adult males have a yellow throat. They have a compact, toad-like build, a huge head, and medium size. Adults may bite.

Similar Species: The giant African bullfrog, *P. adspersus*, is larger and greener.

Range & Origin: Tropical Africa. Specimens in the pet trade may be either captive-bred or wild caught.

Adult Size: Males to 5 inches; females smaller.

Life Span: 8–15 years.

Terrarium Size: These are large, heavy, but not overly active frogs. One may be kept in a 15-gallon, long terrarium, but it require frequent cleaning.

Terrarium Type: A dry savanna terrarium with several inches of sandy soil for burrowing, or a bare tank with an inch or two of clean water and a styro platform for complete emergence.

Social Structure: Babies are cannibalistic, but similarly sized adults can be kept together providing the tank is large enough.

Diet: Insects, nightcrawlers, fish, and other low fat foods should make up the majority of the diet. An occasional mouse is acceptable.

Potential Problems: The cage of any African bullfrog needs to be cleaned frequently to prevent bacterial caused maladies such as redleg. Cannibalism can be a problem if disparate sizes are housed together. Blindness-causing corneal lipid deposits may occur if this frog is fed a predominantly high fat diet (i.e., mice).

References:

Bartlett, R. D., and Patricia Bartlett. *Frogs, Toads, and Treefrogs.* Hauppauge, NY: Barron's Educational Series, Inc., 1996.

Bartlett, R. D., and Patricia Bartlett. *Horned Frogs and African Bullfrogs.* Hauppauge, NY: Barron's Educational Series, Inc., 1999.

Bartlett, R. D., and Patricia Bartlett. *Terrarium and Cage Construction and Care.* Hauppauge, NY: Barron's Educational Series, Inc., 1999.

American Bullfrog

Trade Name(s): Same.

Family & Scientific Name: Ranidae; *Rana catesbeiana.*

Identifying Features: Adults are the largest American frog. They are green to brownish-green, with smooth skin, fully

webbed hind feet, and no dorsolateral ridges. Adult males have a yellow throat and eardrum (tympanum) larger than the diameter of the eye.

Similar Species: When adult, none. Green frogs have dorsolateral ridges.

Range & Origin: Much of North America. Wild collected specimens supply most of the pet trade demand. This species is occasionally farmed.

Adult Size: 4–7½ inches.

Life Span: 12–20 years.

Terrarium Size: This is an active frog. One to several babies may be kept in a 15–20-gallon, long terrarium. A pair of adults should be given a 29–40-gallon tank.

Terrarium Type: Most easily kept in a bare tank with an inch or two of clean water and a styrofoam platform to allow the frog(s) to emerge fully from the water.

Social Structure: Cannibalism is well documented. Do not mix sizes.

Diet: Insects, worms, and fish should predominate in the diet. An *occasional* mouse is relished.

Potential Problems: Bacterial redleg can occur if water becomes dirty. Do not overfeed high fat diets.

References:

Bartlett, R. D., and Patricia Bartlett. *Frogs, Toads, and Treefrogs.* Hauppauge, NY: Barron's Educational Series, Inc., 1996.

Bartlett, R. D., and Patricia Bartlett. *Terrarium and Cage Construction and Care.* Hauppauge, NY: Barron's Educational Series, Inc., 1999.

Malayan Green-striped Frog

Trade Name(s): Same.

Family & Scientific Name: Ranidae; *Rana erythraea.*

Identifying Features: The typical frog-like appearance and broad tan and green stripes on body make this frog identifiable.

Similar Species: None.

Range & Origin: Malaya, southeast Asia.

Adult Size: 2–3 inches.

Life Span: 3–5 years; 10 years should be an attainable goal.

Terrarium Size: From one to several may be kept in a 15–20-gallon, long terrarium. This must be kept clean.

Terrarium Type: Most easily kept in a bare tank with an inch or two of clean water and a styrofoam platform to allow the frog(s) to emerge fully from the water. Floating water plants can be added for aesthetic purposes.

Social Structure: These frogs are communal.

Diet: Insects, nightcrawlers, fish, and other low fat foods should be offered.

Potential Problems: The aquarium requires frequent cleaning to prevent bacterial produced maladies such as redleg.

References:

Bartlett, R. D., and Patricia Bartlett. *Frogs, Toads, and Treefrogs.* Hauppauge, NY: Barron's Educational Series, Inc., 1996.

Bartlett, R. D., and Patricia Bartlett. *Terrarium and Cage Construction and Care.* Hauppauge, NY: Barron's Educational Series, Inc., 1999.

Rice Paddy Frog

Trade Name(s): Same. Also Floating Frog.

Family & Scientific Name: Ranidae; *Occidozyga lima.*

Identifying Features: The small size, typical frog-like appearance, and robust build identify this frog. Eyes

somewhat dorsal in aspect, and they have fully webbed hind feet. They are grayish color, with or without darker markings.

Similar Species: None.

Range & Origin: Southeast Asia. Wild collected specimens supply the pet trade.

Adult Size: About 1¼ inches.

Life Span: 1½–5 years.

Terrarium Size: From 1–10 of these small frogs may be kept in a 10–20-gallon tank.

Terrarium Type: Filtered aquarium, with or without gravel substrate. Dense floating plants are used as both a hide and a haulout by rice paddy frogs.

Social Structure: These frogs are communal.

Diet: Consists mainly of tiny insects like fruit flies and small crickets. Pieces of earthworm offered while impaled on a broomstraw are eagerly accepted.

Potential Problems: If the water is kept clean, these frogs offer no problems to their keepers.

References:

Bartlett, R. D., and Patricia Bartlett. *Frogs, Toads, and Treefrogs.* Hauppauge, NY: Barron's Educational Series, Inc., 1996.

Bartlett, R. D., and Patricia Bartlett. *Terrarium and Cage Construction and Care.* Hauppauge, NY: Barron's Educational Series, Inc., 1999.

Golden Mantella

Trade Name(s): Same. Also Red Mantella, Black-eared Mantella.

Family & Scientific Name: Ranidae; *Mantella aurantiaca.*

Identifying Features: These frogs have gold to red coloration, sometimes with a dark ear streak.

Similar Species: None.

Range & Origin: Madagascar. Specimens collected from the wild supply the pet trade. A very few are now being captive-bred.

Adult Size: ¾–1 inch.

Life Span: 3–10 years.

Terrarium Size: Several specimens can be kept in a 10–15-gallon terrarium.

Terrarium Type: This minuscule frog does best when given a simple tank with a substrate of nonaromatic mulch or dampened unmilled sphagnum moss, a sizable but shallow bowl of clean water, and a potted vining plant or two.

Social Structure: These frogs are communal.

Diet: These active frogs need daily feedings. Offer tiny insects of many varieties, pinhead crickets, termites, and aphids.

Potential Problems: Tank must be tightly covered. If kept clean and cool this seems to be a hardy species.

References:

Bartlett, R. D., and Patricia Bartlett. *Frogs, Toads, and Treefrogs.* Hauppauge, NY: Barron's Educational Series, Inc., 1996.

Bartlett, R. D., and Patricia Bartlett. *Terrarium and Cage Construction and Care.* Hauppauge, NY: Barron's Educational Series, Inc., 1999.

Painted Mantella

Trade Name(s): Same.

Family & Scientific Name: Ranidae; *Mantella baroni* (=*madagascariensis*).

Identifying Features: Rainbow colors, tiny size; compare with photo.

Similar Species: Other multi-colored species have less precise delineation of colors.

Range & Origin: Madagascar. Specimens collected from the wild supply the pet trade. A very few are now being captive-bred.

Adult Size: ¾–1 inch.

Life Span: 3–10 years.

Terrarium Size: Several specimens can be kept in a 10–15-gallon terrarium.

Terrarium Type: This minuscule frog does best when given a simple tank with a substrate of nonaromatic mulch or dampened unmilled sphagnum moss, a sizable but shallow bowl of clean water, and a potted vining plant or two.

Social Structure: These frogs are communal.

Diet: Feed daily. Offer tiny insects of many varieties, such as pinhead crickets, termites, and aphids.

Potential Problems: Tank must be tightly covered. If kept clean and cool, this seems to be a hardy species.

References:

Bartlett, R. D., and Patricia Bartlett. *Frogs, Toads, and Treefrogs.* Hauppauge, NY: Barron's Educational Series, Inc., 1996.

Bartlett, R. D., and Patricia Bartlett. *Terrarium and Cage Construction and Care.* Hauppauge, NY: Barron's Educational Series, Inc., 1999.

Ornate Horned Frog

Trade Name(s): Same. Also Pac-Man Frog.

Family & Scientific Name: Leptodactylidae; *Ceratophrys ornata.*

Identifying Features: Large size, squat body, large head, short supraocular appendages, brown or green color, and readiness to bite identify this frog.

Similar Species: The Chaco horned frog has a proportionately larger head, longer horns, and is often a rusty brown or albino.

Range & Origin: Southern South America. Captive-bred babies supply the pet industry.

Adult Size: 3–6 inches, and often as wide as long.

Life Span: To 16+ years.

Terrarium Size: This is an inactive frog. A single adult thrives in a 10-gallon terrarium.

Terrarium Type: Substrate of clean unmilled sphagnum, nonaromatic mulch, or a bare tank containing a half inch of water cleaned daily or more often.

Social Structure: Absolutely not communal.

Diet: Should consist primarily of insects, minnows, goldfish, or other low fat foods. High fat rodents should be fed sparingly if at all. Add vitamin-mineral supplements.

Potential Problems: Cage, water, and substrate cleanliness is very important to avoid redleg. MBD can afflict fast growing babies receiving insufficient vitamin D_3 and calcium. Blindness-causing corneal lipid deposits may occur if frogs are fed a primary diet of rodents or other high fat items.

References:

Bartlett, R. D., and Patricia Bartlett. *Frogs, Toads, and Treefrogs.* Hauppauge, NY: Barron's Educational Series, Inc., 1996.

Bartlett, R. D., and Patricia Bartlett. *Horned Frogs and African Bullfrogs.* Hauppauge, NY: Barron's Educational Series, Inc., 1999.

Bartlett, R. D., and Patricia Bartlett. *Terrarium and Cage Construction and Care.* Hauppauge, NY: Barron's Educational Series, Inc., 1999.

Chaco Horned Frog

Trade Name(s): Same. Also Cranwell's Horned Frog, Pac Man Frog.

Family & Scientific Name: Leptodactylidae; *Ceratophrys cranwelli.*

Identifying Features: Large size, squat body, large head, long supraocular appendages, brown or white (albino) in color, and readiness to bite characterize this frog.

Similar Species: The Ornate horned frog has a proportionately smaller head, shorter horns, and is often a bright green in ground color.

Range & Origin: Southern South America. Captive-bred babies supply the pet industry.

Adult Size: 3–5 inches, and often as wide as long.

Life Span: 4–10 years, perhaps longer.

Terrarium Size: This is an inactive frog. A single adult thrives in a 10-gallon terrarium.

Terrarium Type: Substrate of clean unmilled sphagnum, nonaromatic mulch, or a bare tank containing a half inch of water cleaned daily or more often.

Social Structure: Very cannibalistic. Keep singly.

Diet: Should consist primarily of insects, minnows, goldfish, or other low fat foods. High fat rodents should be fed sparingly, if at all. Add vitamin-mineral supplements.

Potential Problems: Must be kept immaculately clean to avoid redleg. MBD can afflict fast growing babies receiving insufficient vitamin D_3 and calcium. Blindness-causing corneal lipid deposits may occur if frogs are fed a primary diet of rodents or other high fat items.

References:

Bartlett, R. D., and Patricia Bartlett. *Frogs, Toads, and Treefrogs.* Hauppauge, NY: Barron's Educational Series, Inc., 1996.

Bartlett, R. D., and Patricia Bartlett. *Horned Frogs and African Bullfrogs.* Hauppauge, NY: Barron's Educational Series, Inc., 1999.

Bartlett, R. D., and Patricia Bartlett. *Terrarium and Cage Construction and Care.* Hauppauge, NY: Barron's Educational Series, Inc., 1999.

Fantasy Frog

Trade Name(s): Same.

Family & Scientific Name: Leptodactylidae; *Ceratophrys* sp. (hybrid).

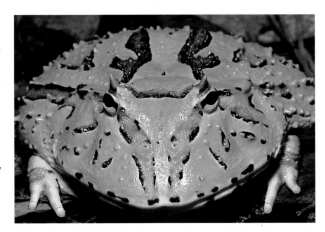

Identifying Features: These frogs are characterized by medium size, squat body, large head, tall supraocular appendages, comparatively smooth skin, brown or green color, and readiness to bite. This is a captive breeding derived frog, a hybrid between the Suriname and the Chaco horned frogs.

Similar Species: The Chaco and the ornate horned frogs are larger, squattier, and have rougher skin.

Range & Origin: Southern South America. Captive-bred babies supply the pet industry.

Adult Size: 2½–4 inches.

Life Span: Unknown, but will probably regularly exceed 10 years.

Terrarium Size: This is an inactive frog. A single adult thrives in a 10-gallon terrarium.

Terrarium Type: Substrate of clean unmilled sphagnum, nonaromatic mulch, or a bare tank containing a half inch of water cleaned daily or more often.

Social Structure: Not communal, especially when young.

Diet: Diet should consist primarily of insects, minnows, goldfish, or other low fat foods. High fat rodents should be fed sparingly, if at all. Add vitamin-mineral supplements.

Potential Problems: Keep cage immaculately clean to avoid redleg. MBD can afflict fast growing babies receiving insufficient vitamin D_3 and calcium. Blindness-causing corneal lipid deposits may occur if frogs are fed a primary diet of rodents or other high fat items.

References:

Bartlett, R. D., and Patricia Bartlett. *Frogs, Toads, and Treefrogs.* Hauppauge, NY: Barron's Educational Series, Inc., 1996.

Bartlett, R. D., and Patricia Bartlett. *Horned Frogs and African Bullfrogs.* Hauppauge, NY: Barron's Educational Series, Inc., 1999.

Budgett's Frog

Trade Name(s): Same. Also Freddie Krueger Frog.

Family & Scientific Name: Leptodactylidae; *Lepidobatrachus laevis.*

Identifying Features: These frogs are aquatic and have very short hind legs. The

eyes oriented dorsally with round pupils. There is mottled green coloration and an immense head. There is no reluctance to bite.

Similar Species: Other species in the genus have differently shaped pupils.

Range & Origin: Chaco, or seasonally flooded parts of interior southern South America. Captive-bred babies largely supply the pet industry.

Adult Size: 3–4½ inches.

Life Span: To 10+ years.

Terrarium Size: This is an inactive frog. A single adult thrives in a 5-gallon aquarium.

Terrarium Type: No substrate necessary. Water should be well, but gently, filtered. Floating plants provide security of visual barriers.

Social Structure: Very cannibalistic. Keep singly.

Diet: Should consist of insects, worms, minnows, goldfish, or other low fat foods. Add vitamin-mineral supplements.

Potential Problems: MBD can afflict fast growing babies receiving insufficient vitamin D_3 and calcium. Water must be kept scrupulously clean.

References:

Bartlett, R. D., and Patricia Bartlett. *Horned Frogs and African Bullfrogs.* Hauppauge, NY: Barron's Educational Series, Inc., 1999.

African Underwater Frog

Trade Name(s): Same. Also Clawed Frog.

Family & Scientific Name: Pipidae; *Xenopus laevis.*

Identifying Features: These frogs have a flattened body and webless fingers. They have fully webbed toes

with black claws on many digits. Also, small, dorsally oriented lidless eyes, and lateral line organs that look like lines of stitching.

Similar Species: Laevis is usually the only species in the pet trade, but Xenopus tropicalis, a species about half the size of laevis, has been readily available in New York.

Range & Origin: Eastern and southern Africa. Those present in the pet trade are captive-bred.

Adult Size: 2½–5 inches.

Life Span: 30+ years.

Terrarium Size: One or two adults live in a well-filtered 10-gallon aquarium. A larger tank should be used for greater numbers.

Terrarium Type: Filtered aquarium, either with or without a gravel substrate, and aquatic plants. Use gravel too large to be ingested while feeding.

Social Structure: These frogs are communal.

Diet: Will eat many kinds of prepared tropical fish foods as well as the normal frog fare of worms, small fish, and insects.

Potential Problems: Aquatic bacteria can quickly cause redleg in unsatisfactory water conditions. Other than that, these are very hardy, long-lived frogs.

References:

Bartlett, R. D., and Patricia Bartlett. *Frogs, Toads, and Treefrogs.* Hauppauge, NY: Barron's Educational Series, Inc., 1996.

Bartlett, R. D., and Patricia Bartlett. *Terrarium and Cage Construction and Care.* Hauppauge, NY: Barron's Educational Series, Inc., 1999.

Dwarf Underwater Frog

Trade Name(s):
Same.
Family & Scientific Name:
Pipidae;
*Hymenochirus
curtipes.*
**Identifying
Features:**
These frogs are
identified by laterally oriented
eyes, small size,
webs on all four
feet, and a flat-

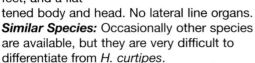

tened body and head. No lateral line organs.
Similar Species: Occasionally other species
are available, but they are very difficult to
differentiate from *H. curtipes.*
Range & Origin: Tropical Africa. Pet trade
specimens are captive-bred.
Adult Size: 1–1½ inches.
Life Span: 3–5 years.
Terrarium Size: 4–5 of these tiny frogs can
be kept in a filtered 5-gallon aquarium.

Terrarium Type:
Gently but efficiently filtered
aquarium, either
with or without
gravel substrate
and aquatic
plants.
Social Structure: These
frogs are
communal.
Diet: Live blackworms, guppy
fry, brine shrimp,
or bloodworms are accepted. Some freeze-
dried forms or prepared fish foods may be
accepted.
Potential Problems: Very hardy. Providing
water quality is maintained, no problems
should be expected.
References:
Bartlett, R. D., and Patricia Bartlett. *Frogs,
Toads, and Treefrogs.* Hauppauge, NY:
Barron's Educational Series, Inc., 1996.

Suriname Toad

Trade Name(s): Same. Also Pipa Toad.

Family & Scientific Name: Pipidae; *Pipa pipa*.

Identifying Features: This frog is almost unmistakable with a very flattened mud-brown body and head, tiny, lidless, dorsally oriented eyes, fleshy lobes on the fingers, and fully webbed hind feet. There are skin flaps at corners of the jaws and on the chin.

Similar Species: This is the only large species of Suriname toad in the trade at present.

Range & Origin: Tropical South America. Wild collected imports are sold in the pet trade.

Adult Size: 3½–6 inches.

Life Span: 7–10 years; possibly considerably longer.

Terrarium Size: 20-gallon, long for one or two Suriname toads; 40 to 50 gallons for up to five toads.

Terrarium Type: Large, well but gently filtered, aquarium with or without a substrate and floating aquatic plants. Use gravel too large to be ingested while feeding.

Social Structure: These frogs are communal.

Diet: Worms, small fish, some pelleted fish foods.

Potential Problems: When water quality is maintained, no problems should be expected.

References:

Bartlett, R. D., and Patricia Bartlett. *Frogs, Toads, and Treefrogs.* Hauppauge, NY: Barron's Educational Series, Inc., 1996.

White's Treefrog

Trade Name(s): Same. Also Australian Giant Green Treefrog, Dumpy Treefrog.

Family & Scientific Name: Hylidae; *Litoria (=Pelodryas) caerulea.*

Identifying Features: Medium to large size, jade green to olive brown dorsum, folds above the eyes, relatively smooth skin, and green(ish) lips identify these frogs.

Similar Species: The white-lipped treefrog has white lips and granular skin.

Range & Origin: Australia and Indonesia. Although captive-bred in large numbers, some wild collected examples still bolster the pet trade.

Adult Size: 2–4½ inches.

Life Span: 20+ years.

Terrarium Size: Although often large, this is a quiet treefrog that does not require much room. One to three individuals thrive in a 15-gallon terrarium. If a greater number is to be kept, go to a larger tank.

Terrarium Type: For these beautiful treefrogs, simple is best. Dry paper towels for the substrate and a sizable, but shallow dish of clean water suffices. Add a large limb, at least the diameter of the frog's body, or a clay flowerpot on its side, for a perching spot for this big-bodied frog.

Social Structure: These frogs are communal.

Diet: A variety of insects is best for dumpy treefrogs. If fed high fat diets (such as pinky mice) the treefrogs soon become obese and experience a shortened lifespan. Vitamin-mineral (D_3-calcium) supplements should be given to fast growing babies twice weekly and to adults about once a week.

Potential Problems: Provided it is not kept too wet or fed a high fat diet, this is a very hardy and easily kept treefrog.

References:

Bartlett, R. D., and Patricia Bartlett. *Frogs, Toads, and Treefrogs.* Hauppauge, NY: Barron's Educational Series, Inc., 1996.

Bartlett, R. D., and Patricia Bartlett. *Terrarium and Cage Construction and Care.* Hauppauge, NY: Barron's Educational Series, Inc., 1999.

White-lipped Treefrog

Trade Name(s): Same.

Family & Scientific Name: Hylidae; *Litoria infrafrenata*

Identifying Features: These frogs are identified by large size, bright green to olive brown dorsum, white lips, and granular skin.

Similar Species: Dumpy treefrog lacks white lips and has a smoother dorsal skin.

Range & Origin: Australia and New Guinea. Wild collected examples still supply the pet trade.

Adult Size: 2–4½ inches.

Life Span: 10+ years.

Terrarium Size: Although large, this is not a particularly excitable treefrog. From one to three or four individuals thrive in a 29-gallon terrarium. If a greater number is to be kept, go to a larger tank.

Terrarium Type: For these beautiful treefrogs, simple is best. Dry paper towels for the substrate and a sizable, but shallow dish of clean water suffices. Add a clay flowerpot on its side and big diameter branch sections for perching/seclusion areas.

Social Structure: These frogs are communal.

Diet: A variety of insects is best for white-lipped treefrogs. If fed high fat diets (such as pinky mice) the treefrogs soon become obese and experience a shortened lifespan. Vitamin-mineral (D_3-calcium) supplements should be given to fast growing babies twice weekly and to adults about once a week.

Potential Problems: Provided it is not kept too wet or fed a high fat diet, this is a very hardy and easily kept treefrog.

References:

Bartlett, R. D., and Patricia Bartlett. *Frogs, Toads, and Treefrogs.* Hauppauge, NY: Barron's Educational Series, Inc., 1996.

Green Treefrog

Trade Name(s):
Same.
Family & Scientific Name:
Hylidae; *Hyla cinerea.*
Identifying Features:
These frogs have smooth green to brown dorsum, often with enamel-white lateral stripes.

mulch or unmilled sphagnum substrate. Plants preferable. Horizontal or diagonal perches at least twice the diameter of the treefrog's girth. Shallow bowl of clean water should be provided.
Social Structure: These frogs are communal.

Similar Species: Squirrel treefrog is smaller and lacks well-defined lateral stripes.

Range & Origin: Southeastern North America. The pet trade depends on wild collected examples.

Adult Size: About 2 inches.

Life Span: To 6+ years.

Terrarium Size: From one to several may be maintained in a 10–15-gallon capacity terrarium.

Terrarium Type: Woodland terrarium or simple terrarium with damp nonaromatic

Diet: A variety of insects should be offered. Add vitamin-mineral (D_3-calcium) supplement twice weekly for growing baby treefrogs, once weekly otherwise.

Potential Problems: Providing the terrarium and the water are kept clean, this is a hardy and trouble-free species.

References:

Bartlett, R. D., and Patricia Bartlett. *Frogs, Toads, and Treefrogs.* Hauppauge, NY: Barron's Educational Series, Inc., 1996.

Barking Treefrog

Trade Name(s):
Same.
Family & Scientific Name:
Hylidae; *Hyla gratiosa.*
Identifying Features: This frog has rough green to brown dorsum, often with darker spots or ocelli, and irregular lateral stripes. It is capable of chameleon-like color and pattern changes.

Similar Species: Green treefrog has smooth dorsal skin and even-edged lateral stripes.
Range & Origin: Eastern North America. The pet trade depends on wild collected examples.
Adult Size: 2–2½ inches.
Life Span: 7–10+ years.
Terrarium Size: These are not overly active treefrogs. From one to several may be maintained in a 10–15-gallon capacity terrarium.
Terrarium Type: Damp savanna terrarium, or simple terrarium with damp nonaromatic mulch, or unmilled sphagnum substrate. Plants preferable. Horizontal or diagonal perches at least twice the diameter of the treefrog's girth. Shallow bowl of clean water should be provided.
Social Structure: These frogs are communal.
Diet: A variety of insects are accepted. Add vitamin-mineral (D_3-calcium) supplement twice weekly for growing baby treefrogs, once weekly otherwise.
Potential Problems: If the terrarium and the water are kept clean, this is a hardy and trouble-free species.
References:
Bartlett, R. D., and Patricia Bartlett. *Frogs, Toads, and Treefrogs.* Hauppauge, NY: Barron's Educational Series, Inc., 1996.

Clown Treefrog

Trade Name(s): Reticulated phase is called the Giraffe Treefrog.

Family & Scientific Name: Hylidae; *Hyla leucophyllata.*

Identifying Features: The giraffe phase has a busy reticulum of light pigment separating odd shaped (not rounded) spots. Normal phase has dark body with light nose and dorsolateral stripes, spots on thigh, and orange fingers and toes.

Similar Species: *Hyla sarayacuensis* has hazy edges to its light markings. *Hyla ebraccata* is very similar, but tends to lack orange on the toes and fingers. *Hyla bifurca* lacks light bars on thigh. *Hyla triangulum* (spotted phase) tends to have rounded discrete spots and has red webbing.

Range & Origin: Tropical Latin America. Those available in the pet trade are collected from the wild.

Adult Size: 1 inch.

Life Span: Unknown, but should be upwards of two years.

Terrarium Size: From one to several of these tiny, beautiful treefrogs may be maintained in a 10–15-gallon capacity terrarium.

Terrarium Type: Damp savanna terrarium, or simple terrarium with damp nonaromatic mulch, or unmilled sphagnum substrate. Vining plant (pothos) preferable. Include horizontal or diagonal perches at least twice the diameter of the treefrog's girth. Shallow bowl of clean water should be provided.

Social Structure: These frogs are communal.

Diet: A variety of tiny insects are accepted. Add vitamin-mineral (D_3-calcium) supplement twice weekly for baby treefrogs, once weekly otherwise.

Potential Problems: If the terrarium and the water are kept clean, this is a hardy and trouble-free species.

References:

Bartlett, R. D, and Patricia Bartlett. *Frogs, Toads, and Treefrogs.* Hauppauge, NY: Barron's Educational Series, Inc., 1996.

Red-eyed Treefrog

Trade Name(s): Same.

Family & Scientific Name: Hylidae; *Agalychnis callidryas*

Identifying Features: This frog usually has a bright green dorsum. Blue flanks, often with vertical bars, and large, bright red eyes help identify it.

Similar Species: None in the pet trade.

Range & Origin: Southern Mexico through Central America. Although some wild collected specimens still enter the pet trade, a great number are captive-bred each year.

Adult Size: 2–2½ inches.

Life Span: 4–10 years.

Terrarium Size: From one to three or four individuals thrive in a 20-gallon terrarium. If a greater number is to be kept, go to a larger tank.

Terrarium Type: A woodland terrarium is an ideal setup for this species, but a bare terrarium with damp paper towels or unmilled sphagnum moss substrate, a potted plant, diagonal limbs, and a sizable, but shallow, dish of clean water will also suffice.

Social Structure: These frogs are communal.

Diet: Feed these a variety of insects. Vitamin-mineral (D₃-calcium) supplements should be given to fast growing babies twice weekly and to adults about once a week.

Potential Problems: Provided it is not kept too wet or too cold, this is a very hardy and easily kept treefrog.

References:

Bartlett, R. D., and Patricia Bartlett. *Frogs, Toads, and Treefrogs.* Hauppauge, NY: Barron's Educational Series, Inc., 1996.

Bartlett, R. D., and Patricia Bartlett. *Red-eyed Treefrogs and Other Leaf Frogs.* Hauppauge, NY: Barron's Educational Series, Inc., 2000.

Painted-bellied Monkey Frog

Trade Name(s):
Waxy Monkey Frog.

Family & Scientific Name:
Hylidae; *Phyllomedusa sauvagei.*

Identifying Features:
These frogs have a green (occasionally yellowish or brown) back,

Terrarium Type: A dry savanna terrarium is an ideal setup for this species, but a bare terrarium with damp paper towels or unmilled sphagnum moss substrate, a potted plant, diagonal limbs, and a sizable, but shallow, dish of

strongly patterned green and white belly, an opposable thumb and first finger, and are moderate in size.

Similar Species: Other leaf frogs in the pet trade lack the strongly patterned belly.

Range & Origin: Seasonally dry areas of interior southern South America. A few continue to be wild collected for the pet trade, but most are now captive-bred.

Adult Size: 2–3 inches.

Life Span: 3–10 years.

Terrarium Size: From one to several individuals thrive in a 20-gallon terrarium. If a greater number are to be kept, it is best to go to a 40–50-gallon tank.

clean water will also suffice.

Social Structure: These frogs are communal.

Diet: Feed these a variety of insects. Vitamin-mineral (D_3-calcium) supplements should be given to fast growing babies twice weekly and to adults about once a week.

Potential Problems: This has proven a hardy and easily kept treefrog.

References:
Bartlett, R. D., and Patricia Bartlett. *Red-eyed Treefrogs and Other Leaf Frogs.* Hauppauge, NY: Barron's Educational Series, Inc., 2000.

Giant Monkey Frog

Trade Name(s): Same. Also Bicolored Monkey Frog.

Family & Scientific Name: Hylidae; *Phyllomedusa bicolor.*

Identifying Features: This frog is identified by large size; opposable thumb and first finger; green (to brown) back; white belly often delineated by thin black line; whitish fingers and toes; green toepads, and black rings on lower sides, groin, and rear of thighs.

Similar Species: None currently in the pet trade.

Range & Origin: Northern South America. Although the pet trade remains largely dependent on wild collected specimens, a few herpetoculturists are now breeding this species.

Adult Size: 3–4½ inches.

Life Span: 10+ years.

Terrarium Size: From one to three or four individuals thrive in a 20–29-gallon terrarium. If a greater number are to be kept, go to a larger tank.

Terrarium Type: A rain forest terrarium is an ideal setup for this species, but a bare terrarium with damp paper towels or unmilled sphagnum moss substrate, a potted plant, diagonal limbs, and a sizable, but shallow dish of clean water will also suffice.

Social Structure: These frogs are communal.

Diet: Feed these a variety of insects. Vitamin-mineral (D_3-calcium) supplements should be given to fast growing babies twice weekly and to adults about once a week.

Potential Problems: This frog is very cold sensitive. Keep terrarium temperature between 78 and 88°F. Bruises and scrapes should be treated with daily applications of a dilute aqueous solution of sulfa drug. Provided it is kept humid, but not overly wet or too cold, this is a very hardy and easily kept treefrog.

References:

Bartlett, R. D., and Patricia Bartlett. *Redeyed Treefrogs and Other Leaf Frogs.* Hauppauge, NY: Barron's Educational Series, Inc., 2000.

Yellow and Black Poison Frog

Trade Name(s): Same. Also Bumblebee Poison Frog.

Family & Scientific Name: Dendrobatidae; *Dendrobates leucomelas.*

Identifying Features: These are tiny in size, have arboreal tendencies and sport vivid black and yellow bands.

Similar Species: None.

Range & Origin: Northeastern South America. Most pet trade specimens are bred in captivity.

Adult Size: 1¼ inches.

Life Span: 7–15+ years.

Terrarium Size: From one to three or four individuals thrive in a heavily planted 15-gallon terrarium. If a greater number are to be kept, go to a larger tank.

Terrarium Type: A rain forest terrarium planted with vining foliage plants is ideal for this species. Alternatively, provide a substrate of unmilled sphagnum, into which small plants in their pots are sunk, a diagonal limb or two of fair dimensions, and a shallow dish of clean water.

Social Structure: These frogs are communal.

Diet: Feed these frogs a variety of tiny insects: fruit flies, termites, aphids, pinhead crickets, and any other small non-noxious insects. Flour beetle larvae (found in old cereal and old dog biscuits) are a good food source for all dendrobatids. These frogs have a comparatively prodigious appetite. Feed them daily. Vitamin-mineral (D_3-calcium) supplements should be given to fast growing babies twice weekly and to adults about once a week.

Potential Problems: Provided the terrarium is kept warm and humid and ample food is provided, this is a very hardy and easily kept frog.

References:
Bartlett, R. D., and Patricia Bartlett. *Frogs, Toads, and Treefrogs.* Hauppauge, NY: Barron's Educational Series, Inc., 1996.

Green and Black Poison Frog

Trade Name(s): Same.

Family & Scientific Name: Dendrobatidae; *Dendrobates auratus.*

Identifying Features: This frog is identified by tiny size, arboreal tendencies, and vivid black and green (occasionally blue) spots and bars.

Similar Species: None.

Range & Origin: Southern Central America and Hawaii. Most pet trade specimens are now bred in captivity

Adult Size: 1½ inches.

Life Span: 7–15 years.

Terrarium Size: From one to three or four individuals thrive in a heavily planted 15-gallon terrarium. If a greater number are to be kept, use a larger tank.

Terrarium Type: A rain forest terrarium planted with vining foliage plants and containing other visual barriers is ideal for this species. Alternatively, provide a substrate of unmilled sphagnum, into which small plants in their pots are sunk, a diagonal limb or two of fair dimensions, and a shallow dish of clean water.

Social Structure: These frogs are communal.

Diet: Feed these frogs a variety of tiny insects: fruit flies, termites, aphids, pinhead crickets, and any other small non-noxious insects. These frogs have a comparatively prodigious appetite. Feed them heavily. Vitamin-mineral (D_3-calcium) supplements should be given to fast growing babies twice weekly and to adults about once a week.

Potential Problems: Provided the terrarium is kept warm and humid and ample food is provided, this is a very hardy and easily kept frog. It was one of the first species to be captive-bred in large numbers.

References:

Bartlett, R. D., and Patricia Bartlett. *Frogs, Toads, and Treefrogs.* Hauppauge, NY: Barron's Educational Series, Inc., 1996.

Dyeing Poison Frog

Trade Name(s): Same.

Family & Scientific Name: Dendrobatidae; *Dendrobates tinctorius.*

Identifying Features: This frog exists in many morphs. The black body may be patterned with white, yellow, orange, green, or blue. Either the light or the dark color may predominate. This is a large, angular, poison frog, and always sits in a hunch-backed position.

Similar Species: The blue poison frog is more predominantly blue.

Range & Origin: Central eastern South America. Most pet trade specimens are now bred in captivity

Adult Size: To 2½ inches.

Life Span: 7–15 years.

Terrarium Size: From one to three or four individuals thrive in a heavily planted 15-gallon terrarium. If a greater number are to be kept, go to a larger tank.

Terrarium Type: A rain forest terrarium planted with vining foliage plants and containing other visual barriers is ideal for this species. Alternatively, provide a substrate of unmilled sphagnum, into which small plants in their pots are sunk, a diagonal limb or two of fair dimensions, and a shallow dish of clean water.

Social Structure: These frogs are communal.

Diet: Feed these frogs a variety of tiny insects: fruit flies, termites, aphids, pinhead crickets, and any other small non-noxious insects. These frogs have a comparatively prodigious appetite. Feed them heavily. Vitamin-mineral (D_3-calcium) supplements should be given to fast growing babies twice weekly and to adults about once a week.

Potential Problems: Provided the terrarium is kept warm and humid and ample food is provided, this is a very hardy and easily kept frog.

References:

Bartlett, R. D., and Patricia Bartlett. *Frogs, Toads, and Treefrogs.* Hauppauge, NY: Barron's Educational Series, Inc., 1996.

Imitator Poison Frog

Trade Name(s): Same.

Family & Scientific Name: Dendrobatidae; *Dendrobates imitator.*

Identifying Features: This is a tiny and variable frog that can imitate other species in color and pattern. Currently, the phase most readily available has a yellow dorsum with elongated black spots anteriorly and blue-green sides bearing small black spots.

Similar Species: None currently in the pet trade.

Range & Origin: Northwestern South America. Most pet trade specimens are now bred in captivity.

Adult Size: ¾–1 inch.

Life Span: Unknown, but probably from two to six years.

Terrarium Size: From one to three or four individuals thrive in a heavily planted 10-gallon terrarium. If a greater number are to be kept, go to a larger tank.

Terrarium Type: A rain forest terrarium planted with vining foliage plants and containing other visual barriers is ideal for this species. Alternatively, provide a substrate of unmilled sphagnum, into which small plants in their pots are sunk, a diagonal limb or two of fair dimensions, and a shallow dish of clean water.

Social Structure: These frogs are communal.

Diet: Feed these frogs a variety of tiny insects: fruit flies, termites, aphids, pinhead crickets, and any other small non-noxious insects. These frogs have a comparatively prodigious appetite. Feed them heavily. Vitamin-mineral (D_3-calcium) supplements should be given to fast growing babies twice weekly and to adults about once a week.

Potential Problems: Provided the terrarium is kept warm and humid and ample food is provided, this is a very hardy and easily kept frog. It was one of the first species to be captive-bred in large numbers.

References:

Bartlett, R. D., and Patricia Bartlett. *Frogs, Toads, and Treefrogs.* Hauppauge, NY: Barron's Educational Series, Inc., 1996.

Blue Poison Frog

Trade Name(s): Same. Also Azure Poison Frog.

Family & Scientific Name: Dendrobatidae; *Dendrobates azureus.*

Identifying Features: Large size, angular shape, predominantly blue coloration.

Similar Species: None.

Range & Origin: Suriname. Most pet trade specimens are now bred in captivity.

Adult Size: 2+ inches.

Life Span: 2–8 years.

Terrarium Size: From one to three or four individuals thrive in a heavily planted 20-gallon, long terrarium. If a greater number are to be kept, go to a larger tank.

Terrarium Type: A rain forest terrarium planted with vining foliage plants and containing other visual barriers is ideal for this species. Alternatively, provide a substrate of unmilled sphagnum, into which small plants in their pots are sunk, a diagonal limb or two of fair dimensions, and a shallow dish of clean water.

Social Structure: These frogs are communal.

Diet: Feed these frogs a variety of tiny insects: fruit flies, termites, aphids, pinhead crickets, and any other small nonnoxious insects. For such a tiny frog, these are big eaters. Feed them heavily. Vitamin-mineral (D_3-calcium) supplements should be given to fast growing babies twice weekly and to adults about once a week.

Potential Problems: Provided the terrarium is kept warm and humid and ample food is provided, this is a very hardy and easily kept frog. It is just in the last few years that this frog has been successfully captive-bred.

References:

Bartlett, R. D., and Patricia Bartlett. *Frogs, Toads, and Treefrogs.* Hauppauge, NY: Barron's Educational Series, Inc., 1996.

Bicolor Poison Frog

Trade Name(s): Same.

Family & Scientific Name: Dendrobatidae; *Phyllobates bicolor.*

Identifying Features: Small size, olive yellow to olive green body and black rear limbs identify this frog.

Similar Species: The terrible poison frog (*P. terribilis*) usually lacks black legs.

Range & Origin: Ecuador. Some wild collected specimens continue to enter the pet trade, but most available specimens are now captive-bred.

Adult Size: 1½ inches.

Life Span: 6+ years.

Terrarium Size: From one to three or four individuals thrive in a heavily planted 15-gallon terrarium. If a greater number are to be kept, go to a larger tank.

Terrarium Type: A rain forest terrarium planted with vining foliage plants and containing other visual barriers is ideal for this species. Alternatively, provide a substrate of unmilled sphagnum, into which small plants in their pots are sunk, a diagonal limb or two of fair dimensions, and a shallow dish of clean water.

Social Structure: These frogs are communal.

Diet: Feed these frogs a variety of tiny insects: fruit flies, termites, aphids, pinhead crickets, and any other small non-noxious insects. These frogs need to eat heavily. Vitamin-mineral (D_3-calcium) supplements should be given to fast growing babies twice weekly and to adults about once a week.

Potential Problems: Provided the terrarium is kept warm and humid and ample food is provided, this is a very hardy and easily kept frog. Wild collected specimens may have virulent skin secretions; captive-bred examples will not.

References:

Bartlett, R. D., and Patricia Bartlett. *Frogs, Toads, and Treefrogs.* Hauppauge, NY: Barron's Educational Series, Inc., 1996.

Newts, Salamanders, and Caecilians

I n hobbyist popularity, the salamanders (newts are a family of salamanders) and caecilians lag far behind any other herpetological grouping. In fact, because they are
aquatic, several species, most notably the waterdogs, the various races of red-spot-
ted newts, and the aquatic caecilians are more popular with aquarists than with reptile
and amphibian hobbyists.

Although the salamanders are very different from the caecilians, since so few of
either are regularly available, we have elected to discuss both groupings here.

Although they may hail from latitudes as far south as Texas and Spain, the few salamanders that are available in the hobby actually prefer cool temperatures (68–74°F
[20–23°C]) and are perfectly capable of withstanding temperatures several degrees
cooler. On the other hand, the single available caecilian is a denizen of the neotropics
and thrives at temperatures between 74–80°F (23–32°C).

The waterdog is a larval tiger salamander, and when captive usually rapidly
assumes its adult form. Be certain to peruse both species acounts when considering
one. On the other hand, the axolotl, a larva of a Mexican tiger salamander relative, will
retain its prominently gilled appearance throughout its life. All aquatic species will utilize
plants, rocks, and driftwood for cover. Most adult salamanders are secretive burrowers.

Except for the fire salamander and the aquatic caecilian, the creatures discussed in
this short chapter are egg layers. None are commonly bred in captivity.

Like the tailless amphibians, the salamanders and caecilians have a permeable skin
that rapidly absorbs any impurities with which the animals come in contact. Absolute
terrarium/aquarium cleanliness is mandatory. Wash your hands before and after handling—or better yet, move these creatures (when necessary) with a clean fish net—but
take care that they don't clamber or wriggle out and fall.

Aquatic salamanders and caecilians often accept prepared fishfoods, finding their
food by scent. Terrestrial forms are usually drawn to their prey by motion and prefer
worms and insects as dietary items.

Japanese Fire-bellied Newt

Trade Name(s):
Same.

Family & Scientific Name:
Salamandridae;
Cynops pyrrhogaster.

Identifying Features:
These newts are identified by the brown dorsum and variegated dark and bright red belly. Breed-

ing males develop a purplish sheen and a filament on the tailtip.

Similar Species: Oriental fire-bellied newts are smaller and their bellies are more intensely orange. The Hong Kong fire-bellied newt is larger and more angular.

Range & Origin: Japan and surrounding islands. Many of the specimens available in the pet trade are captive-bred and hatched, but the industry is still largely dependent on wild collected imports.

Adult Size: 4–5 inches.

Life Span:
15–25 years.

Terrarium Size:
From one to several can be kept in a filtered 10-gallon (or larger aquarium).

Terrarium Type:
Either a semi-aquatic terrarium or a gently, but efficiently filtered aquarium (with or without gravel substrate) with plant life, will suffice for this newt.

Social Structure: These newts are communal.

Diet: Worms, pelleted fish foods, and pieces of lean raw meat are all eagerly accepted.

Potential Problems: This is one of the hardiest of amphibians. Few problems should be expected if caging is kept clean.

References:
Indiviglio, Frank. *Newts and Salamanders.* Hauppauge, NY: Barron's Educational Series, Inc., 1997.

Red-spotted Newt

Trade Name(s): Same. Also Spotted Newt.

Family & Scientific Name: Salamandridae; *Notophthalmus v. viridescens.*

Identifying Features: This newt is identified by the olive green dorsum with a row of black-edged

crimson spots on each side. The yellow belly is peppered with tiny black spots. The red eft stage is bright to dull orange-red.

Similar Species: There are several other subspecies, some with red stripes and some lacking all brilliant spots.

Range & Origin: Eastern North America. Those offered in the pet trade are collected from the wild.

Adult Size: 3–4½ inches.

Life Span: 4–20 years.

Terrarium Size: From one to several can be kept in a 10-gallon (or larger aquarium).

Terrarium Type: Either a semi-aquatic terrarium or a gently, but efficiently filtered aquarium (with or without gravel substrate) with plant life, will suffice for this newt. The red eft stage is terrestrial.

Social Structure: These newts are communal.

Diet: Worms, pelleted fish foods, and pieces of lean raw meat are all eagerly accepted by aquatic forms. The red efts accept live foods only.

Potential Problems: This is one of the hardiest of amphibians. Few problems should be expected.

References:

Indiviglio, Frank. *Newts and Salamanders.* Hauppauge, NY: Barron's Educational Series, Inc., 1997.

Mandarin Newt

Trade Name(s):
Same. Also
Emperor Newt.

Family & Scientific Name:
Salamandridae;
Tylototriton
shanjing;
formerly *T.*
verrucosum.

Identifying Features: A slate-gray with bright orange head, tail, and limbs, an orange spot over the distal end of each rib, and an orange vertebral stripe help identify these newts.

Similar Species: None.

Range & Origin: China. Those offered in the pet trade are collected from the wild.

Adult Size: 4½–5½ inches.

Life Span: 10+ years.

Terrarium Size: From one to several can be kept in a 10–15-gallon aquarium.

Terrarium Type: A cool semi-aquatic terrarium seems best for this newt.

Social Structure: These newts are communal.

Diet: Worms, pelleted fish foods, and pieces of lean raw meat are all eagerly accepted.

Potential Problems: If kept cool, this is a hardy amphibian.

References:
Indiviglio, Frank. *Newts and Salamanders.* Hauppauge, NY: Barron's Educational Series, Inc., 1997.

Fire Salamander

Trade Name(s): Same.

Family & Scientific Name: Salamandridae; *Salamandra salamandra.*

Identifying Features: There are a dozen or more sub-species of this beautiful sala-mandra. Most are black with spots or stripes of vivid yellow. One race has a brown body with an orangish head. The toxin-producing parotoid glands are very well developed.

Similar Species: None.

Range & Origin: Eurasia. Although some of those offered in the pet trade are collected from the wild, many are now captive-bred.

Adult Size: 4½–6 inches.

Life Span: 10–20 years.

Terrarium Size: From one to several can be kept in a 15-gallon (or larger aquarium).

Terrarium Type: A cool semi-aquatic terrarium is best for this primarily terres-trial salamander.

Social Structure: These sala-manders are communal.

Diet: Worms and pieces of lean raw meat moved on a straw are all eagerly accepted.

Potential Problems: This is one of the hardiest of amphibians. Few problems should be expected.

References:

Indiviglio, Frank. *Newts and Salamanders.* Hauppauge, NY: Barron's Educational Series, Inc., 1997.

Waterdog

Trade Name(s): Same.

Family & Scientific Name: Ambystomatidae; *Ambystoma tigrinum* ssp.

Identifying Features: A long, usually flat (when seen in profile) snout, an olive-gray coloration, and three pairs of bushy gills are typical. The limbs are well developed. Waterdogs are the larval stage of any of the subspecies of tiger salamanders.

Similar Species: The Mexican axolotl has a rounded snout when seen in profile and is common in several color phases. Mudpuppies (*Necturus* sp.) are also sold under the trade name of waterdog.

Range & Origin: North America. Most of those seen in the pet trade are the larvae of the Arizona or blotched tiger salamanders, and are collected from the wild.

Adult Size: 6–9½ inches.

Life Span: Variable as a larva, but after metamorphosis a lifespan of 20+ years is possible.

Terrarium Size: From one to several specimens can be maintained in a 15–29-gallon tank.

Terrarium Type: Gentle but efficient filtration is best for these big salamanders. An aquarium, either with or without a smooth gravel substrate and aquatic plants, is suitable. Gravel should be too large to ingest during feeding. As the gills lessen in size, indicating pending metamorphosis, the water level should be reduced to only two or three inches in depth. Once the gills have become nonfunctioning nubbins, the salamander can be housed in a woodland or a damp savanna terrarium.

Social Structure: Usually communal, but when food is present, these animals don't distinguish between food and the limbs and tails of cagemates. Bitten-off limbs will regenerate.

Diet: Worms, freshly killed minnows, some pelleted fish foods, and pieces of lean meat are all eaten by these ravenous salamanders.

Potential Problems: Usually no problems are encountered, but injuries can be incurred when feeding salamanders kept in colonies.

References:

Indiviglio, Frank. *Newts and Salamanders.* Hauppauge, NY: Barron's Educational Series, Inc., 1997.

Axolotl

Trade Name(s):
Same.
Family & Scien-tific Name:
Ambystomati-dae; *Ambystoma mexicanum.*
Identifying Features: This is a large aquatic sala-mander with a convex snout when viewed in profile. It has

three pairs of large bushy gills, well devel-oped legs, a prominent tailfin, and is seen in albino, leucistic, mottled, and normal morphs.

Similar Species: Larval tiger salamanders (waterdogs) have a flattened snout when seen in profile and are gray-green in color.

Range & Origin: Mexico. All pet trade spec-imens are captive-bred.

Adult Size: 7–9 inches.

Life Span: 10–20 years.

Terrarium Size: From one to several speci-mens can be maintained in a 15–29-gallon tank.

Terrarium Type: Gentle but efficient filtra-tion is best for these big salamanders. This species does not normally metamorphose.

An aquarium, either with or without a smooth gravel substrate and aquatic plants, is suitable. Gravel should be too large to ingest during feeding.

Social Struc-ture: Usually communal, but when food is present, these animals don't distinguish between food and the limbs and tails of cagemates. Bitten-off limbs will regenerate.

Diet: Worms, freshly killed minnows, wax-worms, crickets and some pelleted fish foods are accepted. Limit the quantities of lean meat offered.

Potential Problems: Usually no problems are encountered, but injuries can be incurred when feeding salamanders kept in colonies. Leftover food can sour the water. Feed prudently.

References:

Indiviglio, Frank. *Newts and Salamanders.* Hauppauge, NY: Barron's Educational Series, Inc., 1997.

Tiger Salamanders (all races)

Trade Name(s): Same.

Family & Scientific Name: Ambystomatidae; *Ambystoma tigrinum* ssp.

Identifying Features: These salamanders are identified by large size, big head, black to gray ground color with either darker or yellowish blotches, bars, or irregular spots, and well-developed legs.

Similar Species: Other mole salamanders have a frosted look, round, light spots, or white to silver dorsal bars.

Range & Origin: North America. Most available in the pet trade are wild collected.

Adult Size: 7–10 inches.

Life Span: To 20 years.

Terrarium Size: From one to several specimens can be maintained in a 15–29-gallon tank.

Terrarium Type: This salamander can be housed in a woodland or a damp savanna terrarium, or a simple tank containing several inches of damp, unmilled, sphagnum moss as a substrate. The tank should be covered.

Social Structure: If kept communally, when feeding, the limbs and tails of cagemates may be injured or bitten off.

Diet: Worms, freshly killed minnows, waxworms, crickets and some pelleted fish foods are accepted. Limit the quantities of lean meat offered.

Potential Problems: Usually no problems are encountered, but injuries can be incurred by feeding salamanders kept in colonies.

References:

Indiviglio, Frank. *Newts and Salamanders.* Hauppauge, NY: Barron's Educational Series, Inc., 1997.

Spotted Salamander

Trade Name(s): Same.

Family & Scientific Name: Ambystomatidae; *Ambystoma maculatum.*

Identifying Features: These salamanders are identified by dark (usually black) dorsal color with two (sometimes irregular) rows of yellow spots.

Similar Species: The spots of eastern tiger salamanders are irregular in shape and position.

Range & Origin: Eastern North America. Pet trade specimens are collected from the wild.

Adult Size: 5½–6½ inches.

Life Span: 5–10 years.

Terrarium Size: From one to several specimens can be maintained in a 15–29-gallon tank.

Terrarium Type: This salamander species can be housed in a woodland or a damp savanna terrarium. A simple terrarium containing several inches of damp, unmilled, sphagnum moss is also satisfactory. The moss should be thoroughly rinsed at regular intervals.

Social Structure: When kept communally, the animals may chomp down on the limbs and tails of cagemates during feeding.

Diet: Worms, insects, waxworms, crickets and some pelleted fish foods are accepted. Limit the quantities of lean meat and minnows.

Potential Problems: Usually no problems are encountered, but injuries can be incurred by feeding salamanders kept in colonies.

References:

Indiviglio, Frank. *Newts and Salamanders.* Hauppauge, NY: Barron's Educational Series, Inc., 1997.

Aquatic Caecilian

Trade Name(s): Same. Also Rubber Eel, Sicilian (sic) Eel.

Family & Scientific Name: Typhlonectidae; *Typhlonectes compressicauda.*

Identifying Features: Distinguishing characteristics include dark

gray both above and below; eyes visible but covered by skin; conical snout; no legs; a great number of vertical costal grooves along each side of the body.

Similar Species: There are several congeneric caecilian species that are virtually impossible to identify once removed from habitat.

Range & Origin: Northern South America. The pet trade is dependent on specimens collected from the wild. A very few are now being captive-bred.

Adult Size: 12–18 inches; occasionally to two feet.

Life Span: 2–5+ years.

Terrarium Size: From one to several specimens may be kept in a 10–20-gallon aquarium.

Terrarium Type: Gently but efficiently filtered aquarium with or without smooth gravel substrate and live plants. Tank must be very tightly covered; these are escape artists.

Social Structure: These are not communal.

Diet: Worms, pieces of lean meat, pelleted fish foods, freshly killed small (male guppy-sized) fish are all eagerly eaten.

Potential Problems: Providing water quality is maintained, this is a hardy and long-lived amphibian.

References:

Bartlett, R. D., and Patricia Bartlett. *Terrarium and Cage Construction and Care.* Hauppauge, NY: Barron's Educational Series, Inc., 1999.

Part III
Invertebrates

Arthropods

rthropods, those members of the invertebrates that boast of jointed legs, are perhaps the most interesting of all animals in the pet trade. They possess bodies consisting of jointed segments, an exoskelton that they simply cast off when it becomes too small, and will consume and grow fat on leaf detritus, rotten wood, insects, and leaves. They can adapt to environmental extremes (including some very sophisticated human-invented poisons) and reproduce prodigiously. Fortunately, only a small percentage of the young survive, or we'd be hip deep in an assortment of tarantulas, centipedes, cockroaches, and other clicking, hissing and antenna-waving creatures.

For the pet market, "arthropods" means tarantulas, a few centipedes or millipedes, a dozen or so species of scorpions, walking sticks and mantids, and maybe three or four kinds of cockroaches. The owners want an unusual pet, one that isn't too demanding of space, time, or upkeep costs, yet is still interesting enough and long-lived enough to merit setting up a cage and procuring a steady food supply. Although they live well in a small cage, remember that these creatures wander about in the wild, so provide as large a cage as possible for them.

But there's a practical side to some of these arthropods. That is, to serve as food themselves, not for the owners, thank goodness, but for the owner's other pets. Hissing roaches are a nourishing and practical food item for some of the larger (meaning very big) lizards like monitors. Although many states do not permit both sexes of hissing roaches to cross state lines, the male roaches can be shipped *almost* everywhere. You may not be able to set up your own colony, but you can buy the males in quantity.

Just like the reptile and amphibian market, the numbers and varieties of arthropods available today are amazing. Special interest groups for essentially every class of arthropods have appeared like cat hairs on a dark jacket—they're everywhere.

Those agencies that deal with agriculture are very seriously interested in arthropods. No country needs new agricultural pests. Permitting processes have been set up to control what moves in and out of the United States. Only permitting one sex to enter doesn't always solve the problem. Some come in pregnant. A few of the stick insects are parthenogenic, and reproduce quite happily on their own. No one really enjoys dealing with a bureaucracy or bothering with a permit, but the consequences are too far-reaching to allow otherwise.

Mexican Red-kneed Tarantula

Trade Name(s): Same.

Family & Scientific Name: Theraphosidae; *Brachypelma smithi.*

Identifying Features: This is a stocky-bodied dark brown tarantula. It has distinct reddish orange patches on the legs. The patella, the second leg joint away from the body, is often entirely red-orange. The cephalo thorax is dark.

Similar Species: The Mexican red-legged tarantula has a dark triangle on its reddish cephalothorax.

Range & Origin: Mexico, particularly the southern regions.

Adult Size: Adults may measure up to 4 inches across the legs; the tiny captive hatched babies are just a half-inch across.

Life Span: Few people realize how long-lived tarantulas are, particularly the red-legged. They take 5–7 years to reach maturity. Males may live up to 9 years; females up to 24 years.

Terrarium Size: A 2-gallon Pal Pen is large enough for an adult tarantula, but these wanderers could use more space.

Terrarium Type: Red-knees will burrow if given the chance. Offer a savanna to woodland tank with a sand substrate. A small dish of water may be used, but plan on misting twice weekly.

Social Structure: House individually.

Diet: Crickets, moths, silkworm caterpillars, and once in a while, a pink mouse may be offered.

Potential Problems: The red-legged bears itching or urticating hairs on its abdomen, and when it's irritated, it will rub the hairs off with its hind legs and shower you with the shed hair. Simply rinse the hairs off—if you try to brush them off, you're likely to embed them in your skin and begin itching. Do not *ever* put yourself in a position to have these hairs lodge in your eye.

References:

Marshall, Sam. *Tarantulas and Other Arachnids.* Hauppauge, NY: Barron's Educational Series, Inc., 1991.

de Vosjoli, Philippe. *Arachnomania.* Lakeside CA: Advanced Vivarium Systems, 1991.

Mexican Red-legged Tarantula

Trade Name(s): Same.

Family & Scientific Name: Theraphosidae; *Brachypelma emilia.*

Identifying Features: This is a dark brown, stocky tarantula with reddish orange patches on distal half of each leg. The cephalothorax is reddish with a dark triangle.

Similar Species: The Mexican red-kneed tarantula has a dark cephalo thorax.

Range & Origin: Mexico, particularly the southern and western regions.

Adult Size: Adults may measure up to 3½ inches across the legs; the tiny captive hatched babies are just a half-inch across.

Life Span: *Brachypelma* live longer than the family dog! Males may live up to 9 years; females more than 20 years.

Terrarium Size: A 2-gallon Pal Pen is large enough for an adult tarantula.

Terrarium Type: Red-legs come from slightly drier areas than the red-knees. Offer them a dry savanna tank with a sand substrate. A small dish of water may be used, but plan on misting twice weekly.

Social Structure: House individually.

Diet: Crickets, moths, silkworm caterpillars, and once in a while, a pink mouse may be offered.

Potential Problems: The red-legged bears itching or urticating hairs on its abdomen, and when it's irritated it will rub the hairs off with its hind legs and shower you with the shed hair. Simply rinse the hairs off—if you try to brush them off, you're likely to embed them in your skin and begin itching. Do not *ever* put yourself in a position to have these hairs lodge in your eye.

References:

Marshall, Sam. *Tarantulas and Other Arachnids.* Hauppauge, NY: Barron's Educational Series, Inc., 1991.

de Vosjoli, Philippe. *Arachnomania.* Lakeside CA: Advanced Vivarium Systems, 1991.

Cobalt Blue Tarantula

Trade Name(s): Same.

Family & Scientific Name: Theraphosidae; *Haplopelma lividum.*

Identifying Features: This beautiful tarantula has distinct cobalt/electric blue highlights to the hair on its legs. The coloration is hard to photograph but very easy to see with the naked eye. The cephalothorax is in pale brown and the abdomen, gray. These are fast-moving and unfriendly tarantulas that do not tame well.

Similar Species: None.

Range & Origin: Thailand; a few are captive-bred.

Adult Size: To 4 inches across.

Life Span: A male cobalt blue in good health should live at least 10 years; the females, at least 15 years.

Terrarium Size: A 2-gallon Pal Pen makes a good home for a single cobalt blue tarantula.

Terrarium Type: These are burrowing tarantulas that need moist sand/sphagnum/peat moss to construct their burrow. Add a few pieces of corkbark for additional hiding areas. A small dish of water will be needed, but mist three times a week to ensure that they drink.

Social Structure: Not communal.

Diet: Insects, such as crickets, mealworms, moths, and butterflies are accepted.

Potential Problems: Like Yosemite Sam, all you'll hear from this spider is "Back off!" The cobalt is a very typical Old World tarantula that may be kept, but not handled. They offer to bite at every opportunity.

References:

Marshall, Sam. *Tarantulas and Other Arachnids.* Hauppauge, NY: Barron's Educational Series, Inc., 1991.

Schultz, Stanley, and Marguerite Schultz. *The Tarantula Keeper's Guide.* Hauppauge, NY: Barron's Educational Series, Inc., 1998.

Pink-toed Tarantula

Trade Name(s): South American Pink-toed Tarantula.

Family & Scientific Name: Theraphosidae; the species usually available is *Avicularia avicularia.* Other members of the genus are also pink-toed, and are occasionally available.

Identifying Features: This dark brown spider has pink toe-tips almost as it were wearing pink slippers. Its docile nature and small size makes it seem like a dainty tarantula.

Similar Species: The several species of pink-toed tarantulas are almost impossible to differentiate. All require the same care.

Range & Origin: Members of the genus are found from Peru to Puerto Rico; *A. avicularia* is found in northeast South America.

Adult Size: To 3 inches across.

Life Span: Some *Avicularia* mature within 18 months; although data are lacking on the lifespans of many kinds of *avicularia*, males of most tarantula species die 6–18 months after maturity is reached.

Terrarium Size: If keep singly, a 2-gallon Pal Pen is large enough, providing you provide climbing/hiding surfaces. If like sizes are available, they can be kept communally in a 20-gallon or larger terrarium.

Terrarium Type: These are arboreal spiders, and need vertical pieces of bark or sections of giant bamboo for climbing and hiding. Substrate can be leaves, nonaromatic mulch, or bark chips. They need to be kept in a humid environment, like a humid woodland or a rain forest terrarium.

Social Structure: Pink-toes can be kept communally if all the spiders are about the same size. Separate when they get to about 2 inches across.

Diet: Insects such as crickets, mealworms, and moths are accepted.

Potential Problems: Pink-toes may sometimes have trouble shedding; some causes for this problem include a tank that is too dry. These good-natured tarantulas have urticating hairs that they rarely find cause to fling.

References:

Marshall, Sam. *Tarantulas and Other Arachnids.* Hauppauge, NY: Barron's Educational Series, Inc., 1991.

Schultz, Stanley, and Marguerite Schultz. *The Tarantula Keeper's Guide.* Hauppauge, NY: Barron's Educational Series, Inc., 1998.

de Vosjoli, Philippe. *Arachnomania.* Lakeside CA: Advanced Vivarium Systems, 1991.

Tiger-rumped Tarantula

Trade Name(s): Same. Also called the Tricolored Tree Spider.

Family & Scientific Name: *Avicularia pulchra.*

Identifying Features: This slender-legged spider has an orange to tan cephalothorax

and five orange to tan bands across its dark abdomen.

Similar Species: Other tarantulas may have banded/striped cephalo thoraxes, but the boldly striped abdomen is diagnostic for the tiger-rump.

Range & Origin: Members of the genus are found from Peru to Puerto Rico.

Adult Size: To 3 inches across.

Life Span: Some *Avicularia* mature within 18 months; although data are lacking on the lifespans of many kinds of avicularia, males of most tarantula species die 6–18 months after maturity is reached.

Terrarium Size: If kept singly, a 2-gallon Pal Pen is large enough, providing you supply climbing/hiding surfaces.

Social Structure: If like sizes are available,

tiger-rumps can be kept communally in a 20-gallon or larger terrarium. When they near two inches across, separate them.

Terrarium Type: These are arboreal spiders, and need vertical pieces of bark or sections of giant bamboo for climbing and hiding. Substrate can be leaves, nonaromatic mulch, or bark chips. They need to be kept in a semihumid environment.

Diet: Insects, such as crickets, mealworms and moths are accepted. Small treefrogs may be eaten.

Potential Problems: All *Avicularia* have urticating hairs that they rarely find cause to fling.

References:

Marshall, Sam. *Tarantulas and Other Arachnids.* Hauppauge, NY: Barron's Educational Series, Inc., 1991.

Schultz, Stanley, and Marguerite Schultz. *The Tarantula Keeper's Guide.* Hauppauge, NY: Barron's Educational Series, Inc., 1998.

Birdeating Tarantula

Trade Name(s):
Same. Also called the Brazilian Goliath Tarantula.

Family & Scientific Name: Theraphosidae; *Theraphosa blondi.*

Identifying Features: This is a large, aggressive, dark brown tarantula.

It is one of the few tarantulas that can produce a noise when irritated—it rubs its legs and its pedipalps together to produce a hissing sound. This is also one of the largest of the tarantulas, with an 11-inch leg span not uncommon.

Similar Species: The goliath pinkfoot tarantulas are like the goliath birdeaters but they have a smaller body with proportionally longer legs.

Range & Origin: This spider is found in the northeastern quadrant of South America, in Venezuela, Guyana, Suriname, French Guyana, and northeast Brazil.

Adult Size: To 12 inches across.

Life Span: The goliath reaches sexual maturity in about three years.

Terrarium Size: A 20-gallon terrarium suffices for an adult *blondi;* be certain to provide enough substrate for burrowing.

Terrarium Type: Woodland, with enough substrate to permit burrowing.

Social Structure: These aggressive spiders are best kept singly

Diet: Insects and small animals such as pinkie mice, small treefrogs, lizards and nightcrawlers are accepted.

Potential Problems: This is a large, aggressive tarantula. Give it a large terrarium and move it only with a cup.

References:
Schultz, Stanley, and Marguerite Schultz. *The Tarantula Keeper's Guide.* Hauppauge, NY: Barron's Educational Series, Inc., 1998.

King Baboon Tarantula

Trade Name(s): Same.

Family & Scientific Name: Theraphosidae; *Citharischius crawshayi.*

Identifying Features: This is the second largest tarantula in Africa. They are stout-bodied and covered with fine, dense

hair that make them look velvet-like. This species can be aggressive, coming toward a perceived enemy with upraised fangs and striulating.

Similar Species: The large size and aggressive behavior of the king baboon make it a distinctive species.

Range & Origin: Africa.

Adult Size: To 8 inches across the legs.

Life Span: Unknown, but the babies are very slow growing. This suggests a long-lived spider.

Terrarium Size: A 10-gallon terrarium is large enough for this species.

Terrarium Type: Offer a plain tank with a substrate of moist vermiculite for burrowing, or a savanna/desert tank with a small container of moistened sphagnum.

Social Structure: Keep singly.

Diet: Offer insects, including crickets, mealworms and silkworm caterpillars. An occasional pinkie mouse (prekilled) may be accepted.

Potential Problems: This is not a tarantula to be handled. It is aggressive and willing to bite; do not offer it the opportunity.

References:

Marshall, Sam. *Tarantulas and Other Arachnids.* Hauppauge, NY: Barron's Educational Series, Inc., 1991.

Schultz, Stanley, and Marguerite Schultz. *The Tarantula Keeper's Guide.* Hauppauge, NY: Barron's Educational Series, Inc., 1998.

Costa Rican Zebra Tarantula

Trade Name(s): Same. Also called the Striped Knee or Bamboo Tarantula.

Family & Scientific Name: Theraphosidae; *Aphonopelma seemanni.*

Identifying Features: Distinctive features are lines on the legs (the patella and tibiae) that contrast strongly with the background. Several color morphs exist, from black to chestnut, all with lighter leg markings. This is a high-strung tarantula, and may become very nervous if you attempt to handle it.

Similar Species: The strongly defined white markings running the length of the legs are diagnostic; no other species has these.

Range & Origin: Costa Rica and other Central American countries.

Adult Size: About 4 inches across the legs.

Life Span: Males mature in about three years and die about 6–18 months later. Females may live 10 years or more.

Terrarium Size: A 2-gallon pal pen is large enough for a single specimen.

Terrarium Type: Provide a savanna-like terrarium with soil moist enough to allow for a vertical burrow.

Social Structure: Best kept individually.

Diet: Insects, including crickets, moths, and mealworms are accepted.

Potential Problems: These are hardy tarantulas in captivity, despite their relatively short life span.

References:

Marshall, Sam. *Tarantulas and Other Arachnids.* Hauppauge, NY: Barron's Educational Series, Inc., 1991.

Schultz, Stanley, and Marguerite Schultz. *The Tarantula Keeper's Guide.* Hauppauge, NY: Barron's Educational Series, Inc., 1998.

Millipedes (all types)

Trade Name(s): The arbitrary nature of trade names is reflected in the names given to arthropods in the pet market. The country of origin may be indicated in the trade or common name, such as the Kenya Flat Millipede.

Family & Scientific Name: Class Diplopoda; most in the pet market are from the families Platyrhacidae and Chelodesmidae. Genera may be *Chicobolus, Archispirostrepus*, or any of about a dozen others.

Identifying Features: These are characterized by a long body of interlocking joints; two pairs of legs per segment, and short antennae.

Similar Species: Centipedes have a single pair of legs per segment and long antennae.

Adult Size: 1½–6 inches, depending on species.

Life Span: Unknown in captivity, but probably 1–3 years.

Terrarium Size: A 5-gallon Pal Pen is large enough for any millipede up to 6 inches in length.

Terrarium Type: Although a few are from dry woodland or savanna, most are from tropical areas and need a moist substrate. All live in dark, enclosed places, rarely venturing forth except at night. Offer rotten logs, bark pieces or stones as hiding places. Add a small water dish and mist the cage lightly 2–3 times a week.

Social Structure: These mild-mannered diplodians live well in groups.

Diet: Consists of decomposing wood and leaves, and chopped fruit. (Replace fruit daily.)

Potential Problems: Some can defend themselves by secreting noxious or caustic substances from pores on their segment. Some secretions can cause blisters on human skin if not washed off.

References:

Mattison, Chris. *A Practical Guide to Exotic Pets.* Philadelphia, PA: Running Press, 1994.

Centipedes (all types)

Trade Name(s): Usually reflects area of origin, such as Texas Tiger Centipede.

Family & Scientific Name: Class Chilopoda; those in the pet trade may be *Scolopendra* or *Stigamia*.

Identifying Features: Distinguishing characteristics include a long, slender, multisegmented body, with one pair of legs per segment, and fairly long antennae. The body is usually slightly flattened to facilitate getting under things. Centipedes like to stay in dark places and they like close hiding areas. Fangs on first body segment contain a mild venom; the bite can be painful.

Similar Species: Millipedes have two pairs of legs per segment and short antennae.

Range & Origin: Worldwide in temperate and tropical areas.

Adult Size: 2–5 inches; some tropical forms are larger. (Von Humboldt in 1852 described an 18-inch specimen!)

Life Span: Not much is known about the life span, but probably 3–5 years.

Terrarium Size: A 2-gallon plastic Pal Pen is large enough for most centipedes likely to be kept as pets.

Terrarium Type: A woodland terrarium provides the needed moisture. Use a nonaromatic bark or mulch substrate; add bark pieces for hiding areas. Centipedes find tubes that are just slightly larger than their body width, comfortable hiding places. A small dish of water is important. Keep the substrate barely damp.

Social Structure: Keep singly; centipedes can be cannibalistic.

Diet: Provide earthworms, crickets, and an occasional pinkie mouse.

Potential Problems: The bite of a centipede can be painful, although not fatal.

References:
Imes, Rick. *The Practical Entomologist.* New York: Simon and Schuster, 1992.

Scorpions (all types)

Trade Name(s): Like the centipedes and millipedes, scorpions usually are named for their area of origin.

Family & Scientific Name: Order Scorpionida, multiple families; two genera in the pet trade are *Pandinus*, the emperor scorpions, and *Androctonus*, the desert scorpions.

Identifying Features: Scorpions are identified by eight legs, plus a pair of claws on pinchers that are used to convey food to the mouth. The tail is curled up over the back and is topped with a stinger. Depending on the type, the venom may or may not be dangerous. Only 25 or so of the 1500+ species have a venom dangerous to human beings. Light-shy in behavior; these are essentially nocturnal creatures.

Similar Species: Nothing else looks like a scorpion.

Range & Origin: Both Old and New World, in temperate to tropical areas.

Adult Size: 1–6 inches, depending on the species.

Life Span: The larger emperor scorpions live 5–8 years; smaller scorpions, like the Florida bark scorpions, live 6 years.

Terrarium Size: A 2-gallon Pal Pen is large enough for any scorpion.

Terrarium Type: Most scorpions are desert/scrubland arachnids. They are adept at burrowing or crawling under shrubs and bushes. Provide a savannah to woodland style terrarium, with a nonaromatic mulch substrate and pieces of bark for hiding areas. A small dish of water serves as drinking water and a humidity source.

Social Structure: Hobbyists tend to keep the lesser venomous scorpions communally, and the more venomous species singly.

Diet: Include crickets and mealworms. Most species drink from a small water container; mist forest species gently with water two or three times a week.

Potential Problems: Some of the scorpions have dangerously potent venom in their stinger. Handle all scorpions by grasping the tail or telson with padded tongs and lifting the scorpion by its tail for placement in another container.

References:
de Vosjoli, Philippe. *Arachnomania.* Lakeside, CA: Advanced Vivarium Systems, 1991.

Mattison, Chris. *A Practical Guide to Exotic Pets.* Philadelphia, PA: Running Press, 1994.

Praying Mantis and Flower Mantis

Trade Name(s): Usually named for the area of origin.

Family & Scientific Name: Family Mantidae; genus name may be *Sphodromantis*, *Hierodula*, or any of about a dozen others.

Identifying Features: Man-

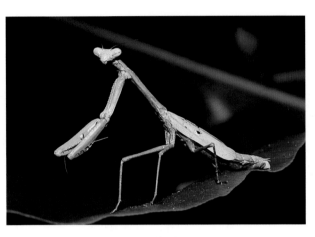

tids are arboreal insects that look something like an elongated grasshopper, without the enlarged hind legs. The forelegs are modified into grasping limbs with toothed edges for holding prey. The eyes are bulbous and set on opposite sides of the triangular head, with the mouth at the apex.

Similar Species: Both katydid and grasshoppers have enlarged hind legs for jumping.

Range & Origin: Tropical and subtropical parts of the world.

Adult Size: Depending on the type, body length is ½–6 inches.

Life Span: Life span is poorly known, but probably 3–5 years.

Terrarium Size: Even adult mantids can be kept in 2-gallon Pal Pens.

Terrarium Type: Woodland with climbing branches. Use any nonaromatic bark or mulch for substrate; add sticks for the mantid to climb. A small water dish may be used; mist three times a week to ensure your mantids drink water.

Social Structure: Mantids are cannibalistic, particularly when newly hatched or when mating has just been completed. Keep singly.

Diet: All mantids are insectivorous, and can eat prey almost as large as they are. Feed crickets, moths, flies and other insects.

Potential Problems: Problems generally result when more than one mantid is kept to a cage; the smaller gets eaten.

References:

Mattison, Chris. *A Practical Guide to Exotic Pets.* Philadelphia, PA: Running Press, 1994.

Walking Sticks

Trade Name(s): Also called Stick Insects. Usually named for area of origin, such as Indian Stick Insects. May simply be called Phasmids.

Family & Scientific Name: Family Phasmidae. Several genera are imported or occur in the U.S.; two common genera in the pet marketplace are *Phyllium* and *Dares.*

Identifying Features: Walking sticks look like not-very-animated sticks. Some are flattened and adorned with spinose processes on the body and legs. (Picking one up is a challenge.) Colors are camouflage colors of browns and greens. Many shed their legs as a defense mechanism.

Similar Species: Mantids have grasping forelegs that can pinch.

Range & Origin: Worldwide in temperate areas. Those from the tropics tend to be more ornate than those from temperate areas.

Adult Size: Body length can vary from 3–12 inches.

Life Span: Depending on species, 1–4 years.

Terrarium Size: In caging, a vertical format is more important than size. A tube of rolled household screening set in a one pound coffee can, and topped with the lid from the coffee can, is large enough for a pair of these creatures.

Terrarium Type: Woodland. Be sure to spray the caging every day, not only to increase the humidity in the cage, but also to provide drinking water for the insects.

Social Structure: These vegetarians live well in groups.

Diet: Experiment, and offer a variety of leafy branches. Put a small jar of water in the cage and stick the cut ends of the branches down into the jar. Change when the leaves begin to wilt. Try privet, oak, plum, raspberry, blueberry, and Osage orange.

Potential Problems: Molting seems to be a difficult time for stick insects. Place a dampened dish of sphagnum moss in the cage to increase the humidity in that part of the cage. Some tropical forms are hermaphroditic, and their import into the U.S. is forbidden.

References:
Mattison, Chris. *A Practical Guide to Exotic Pets.* Philadelphia, PA: Running Press, 1994.

Madagascar Hissing Cockroaches

Trade Name(s): Hissing Roaches.

Family & Scientific Name: Blaberidae; *Grompha-dorhina madagascariensis.*

Identifying Features: Large size; shiny surface to the thorax and abdomen;

hisses loudly when touched, and dark brown/mahogany coloration. Males have two bumps on the thorax (females have none).

Similar Species: Other roaches do not have the shiny appearance of the hissing roaches.

Range & Origin: Madagascar, but are captive-bred in large quantities in some states as animal food and as pets.

Adult Size: To 3 inches.

Life Span: To 2 years.

Terrarium Size: A 1-gallon jar with holes poked through the lid provides enough space for a single specimen. A 2-gallon Pal Pen provides enough space for a group (they like to live close to each other) and is easier to access.

Terrarium Type: Hissing roaches are remarkably adaptive. They evolved in a warm climate, and live well in a plain terrarium with substrate of newspaper or nonaromatic mulch and cardboard tubes, or sheets of cardboard for hideboxes.

Social Structure: Extremely communal.

Diet: Consists of almost anything. Offer fresh fruit, moistened kibble dog food, and/or pelleted rabbit food. Water can be in a shallow container, filled with cotton balls or pebbles so the young won't drown. (If you have a pregnant female, there will be plenty of young.) Change moist food and water daily.

Potential Problems: The young are escape artists, so make certain there are no small openings they can crawl through.

References:

Mattison, Chris. *A Practical Guide to Exotic Pets.* Philadelphia, PA: Running Press, 1994.

Bibliography

Bartlett, R. D. *A Field Guide to Florida Reptiles and Amphibians.* Houston: Gulf, 1998.

____. *A Field Guide to Texas Reptiles and Amphibians.* Houston: Gulf, 1999.

____, and Alan Tennant. *Snakes of North America, Western Region.* Houston: Gulf, 2000.

Bennett, D. *Monitor Lizards: Natural History, Biology, and Husbandry.* Frankfurt, Ger.: Edition Chimaira, 1998.

Branch, Bill. *A Field Guide to the Snakes and Other Reptiles of Southern Africa.* Sanibel, FL: Ralph Curtis Pub., 1988.

Burghardt, G. M., and A. S. Rand (Eds.) *Iguanas of the World: Their Behavior, Ecology and Conservation.* Park Ridge, NJ: Noyes Pub., 1982.

Campbell, Jonathan A. *Amphibians and Reptiles of Northern Guatemala, the Yucatan, and Belize.* Norman, OK: University of Oklahoma Press, 1998.

Cogger, Harold A. *Reptiles and Amphibians of Australia.* Sanibel, FL: Ralph Curtis, 2000.

Conant, Roger, and Joseph T. Collins: *Reptiles and Amphibians, Eastern/Central North America.* Boston: Houghton Mifflin, 1998.

Donosos-Barros, Roberto. *Reptiles de Chile.* Santiago: Universidad de Chile, 1964.

Ernst, Carl H., and Roger W. Barbour. *Turtles of the World.* Washington, DC: Smithsonian Inst. Press, 1989.

Frye, Fredric L. *A Practical Guide for Feeding Captive Reptiles.* Melbourne, FL: Kreiger, 1991.

Glaw, F., and M. Vences. *A Field Guide to the Amphibians and Reptiles of Madagascar.* Leverkusen: Moos Druck, 1994.

Halliday, Tim, and Kraig Adler. *The Encyclopedia of Reptiles and Amphibians.* New York: Facts on File. 1986.

Kornaker, Paul M. *Checklist and Key to the Snakes of Venezuela.* Rheinbach, Ger.: PaKo-Verlag, 1999.

Levell, John P. *A Field Guide to Reptiles and the Law.* Excelsior, MN: Serpent's Tale Books, 1995.

Manthey, Ulrich, and Norbert Schuster. *Agamid Lizards.* Neptune City: TFH, 1996.

Marshall, Samuel D. *Tarantulas and Other Arachnids.* Hauppauge, NY: Barron's Educational Series, Inc., 1996.

Martin, James. *Masters of Disguise, A Natural History of Chameleons.* New York: Facts on File, 1992.

Bibliography

McKeown, Sean. *The General Care and Maintenance of Day Geckos.* Lakeside, CA: Advanced Vivarium Systems, 1993.

____. *A Field Guide to Reptiles and Amphibians in the Hawaiian Islands.* Los Osos, CA: Diamond Head Pub., 1996.

Obst, Fritz Jurgen, et al. *The Completely Illustrated Atlas of Reptiles and Amphibians for the Terrarium.* Neptune City: TFH, 1988.

Peters, James A. *Dictionary of Herpetology.* New York: Hafner, 1964.

Preston-Mafham, Ken. *Madagascar, A Natural History.* New York: Facts on File, 1991.

Rossman, Douglas A., Neil B. Ford, and Richard A. Seigel. *The Garter Snakes, Evolution and Ecology.* Norman, OK: University of Oklahoma Press, 1996.

Schleich, H. Herman, Werner Kastle, and Klaus Kabisch. *Amphibians and Reptiles of North Africa.* Koenigstein, Ger.: Koeltz Scientific Publishers, 1996.

Schwartz, Albert, and Robert W. Henderson. *Amphibians and Reptiles of the West Indies.* Gainesville, FL: University of Florida Press, 1991.

Smith, Hobart M. *Handbook of Lizards.* Ithaca: Comstock, 1946.

Sprackland, Robert George. *Giant Lizards.* Neptune City: TFH, 1992.

Starace, Fausto. *Guide des Serpents et Amphisbenes de Guyane.* Guadaloupe: Ibis Rouge, 1998.

Stebbins, Robert C. *A Field Guide to Western Reptiles and Amphibians.* Boston: Houghton Mifflin, 1985.

Walls, Jerry G. *Poison Frogs—Jewels of the Rainforest.* Neptune City: TFH, 1994.

Zhao, Ermi, and Kraig Adler. *Herpetology of China.* Lawrence, KS: SSAR, 1993.

Zimmerman, Elke. *Breeding Terrarium Animals.* Neptune City: TFH, 1983.

Index

Index

Index

Index

Index